Java™ Persistence
with JPA.

Daoqi Yang, Ph.D.

Outskirts Press, Inc.
Denver, Colorado

This book is dedicated to my son: Forrest C. Yang

Preface

Java persistence refers to the process of saving data to and retrieving data from a database. JDBC (Java Database Connectivity) has been the most popular method for Java persistence since it was released in 1997. Its strength is a set of standard API (Application Programming Interface) for executing SQL (Structured Query Language) statements and database stored procedures using Java. When using JDBC, a developer typically first writes and debugs SQL statements in some database client tool. Once these SQL statements work, he would write Java code to execute such SQL statements and construct Java objects based on the values or result sets returned from the SQL statements. In this process, the developer needs to be proficient in SQL programming and JDBC programming, both of which are of procedural programming style, and the OO (Object Oriented) features of Java such as inheritance and polymorphism cannot be directly taken advantage of. Also, for performing every database transaction and query, the developer needs to be very knowledgeable about the database table structures and relationships.

JPA (Java Persistence API) was introduced in 2006. Its goal is to simplify software development in Java persistence and provide the Java community with a single, standard, and object-oriented persistence API. JPA 1.0 is originally part of Enterprise JavaBeans (EJB) 3.0. Although it belongs to Java Enterprise Edition (Java EE) 5.0, it can be used in Java Standard Edition (Java SE) 5.0 or later. Starting from the 2009 release of JPA 2.0, it is separated from EJB and is now a standalone Java EE 6.0 standard.

When using JPA, developers map Java classes and their fields to database tables and columns, and write Java code to manipulate these Java classes, then the underlining JPA implementation generates JDBC code and SQL statements to persist Java objects into database tables. Once the mapping from Java classes to database tables is done correctly, performing database transactions and queries will just be manipulation of Java objects, and further knowledge on the database such as table structures, column types, and relationships is not needed. In this way, developers can write Java classes and manipulate Java objects fully utilizing object oriented features of Java, but do not have to write and debug SQL statements. The Java code should be portable across different databases, which makes switching from one database to another much easier. JPA provides many easy-to-use features such as optimistic locking, pessimistic locking, lazy-loading, object caching, bean validation, and listeners for transactional events, which would be daunting tasks for a typical developer to implement when using JDBC. Software development productivity can be instantly improved and maintenance cost can be reduced as well. Also, a JPA implementation is capable of automatically generating code optimized for your database system and possibly outperforms your otherwise hand-written JDBC and SQL code.

The process of mapping object oriented entities of classes and their fields to relational database tables and columns is called OR mapping (Object Relational Mapping). Built on the successes of popular tools such as TopLink, Hibernate, and JDO (Java Data Objects), the Java Persistence API is the only OR mapping standard for Java persistence. Also, EclipseLink (JPA version of TopLink), Hibernate, and Apache OpenJPA provide open source implementations of JPA standards (together with their own extensions as well). Being an open Java standard with strong industry support and open source implementations, JPA is becoming developers' paradise for doing Java persistence.

This book intends to provide easy, concise, and complete coverage of JPA 2.0 to Java developers and architects. The goal is that it may serve as an introductory text for Java developers who do not know anything about JPA, and a reference book for experienced JPA developers. Concepts are first illustrated through examples and then explained in detail. It also contains a special chapter on JPA design patterns and performance tuning. The prerequisite is basic familiarity of Java and SQL programming. Certain knowledge of EJB and Java EE is needed only for some parts of the book when JPA is applied in the context of Java EE.

For all coding examples, EclipseLink JPA implementation and Apache Derby database are used in Java SE and Java EE environments, and JBoss application server is used in the context of EJB and JSF (JavaServer Faces). Most of the example code is developed in the Eclipse IDE. Some relevant references to Hibernate and OpenJPA are also provided. All of these tools and libraries are open source and available freely. Chapter 9 on Resources gives instructions on how to download and configure each of them.

The source code and errata for this book may be downloaded at the author's website: http://YangDaoqi.info. The reader is welcome to provide comments to the author at d_q_yang@yahoo.com.

Finally, the author would like to express his sincere thanks to the following individuals for reviewing the book and providing valuable suggestions: Frank Arico, Shankar Krishnamoorthy, Steven Nie, and Katie Wang.

1 Introduction

This chapter provides an overview of JPA (Java Persistence API) with two examples. The first example is a standalone Java program that can be run in any Java SE 5.0 or later environment, while the second example is based on a stateless session bean that must be run in an EJB 3.0 or later container. The reader is not expected to understand every detail of the chapter, but to get the big picture on how JPA works and its main functionalities. Detailed explanations will come in later chapters.

1.1 Overview

When performing database transactions in Java, Java objects are saved into a database as table rows. On the other hand, when retrieving data from a database, table rows are returned and converted to Java objects. The Java objects and table rows are two representations of the same piece of data. However, there are main differences between these two representations. Database tables, rows, and columns are relational (in a relational database system) and have database types (without behaviors), while Java objects can be object oriented (encapsulation, inheritance, polymorphism, relationship, and composition) and have Java types and behaviors (methods). Such differences are generally called *impedance mismatch*. Software engineering requires innovative thinking and adroit technical skills. It is time and effort consuming for a developer to be proficient in the OO (object oriented) programming paradigm for Java objects and procedural programming paradigm for database systems. JPA aims to relieve developers from the mundane tasks of SQL programming and JDBC programming. When using JPA, Java classes and their fields are mapped to database tables and columns. Once such a mapping is made, the developer can just concentrate on OO programming in Java on the mapped Java objects, which is what many developers are good at and can apply their creative thinking in.

Persisting Java objects into a relational database using JPA consists of two main tasks. The first task is OR mapping (Object Relational Mapping). In this step, Java classes (called *entities* in JPA) and their fields/properties are mapped to relational database tables and columns, and the relationships (one-to-one, one-to-many, etc) between the entities are mapped to primary key and foreign key columns in database tables.

The second task is to manipulate (create, read, update, and delete) the Java entities so that the underlying JPA implementation will translate the Java operations into database operations. Thus operations on Java objects are persisted into database tables, with JPA generating JDBC calls and executing SQL statements behind the scene.

With such OR mapping, Java objects and database rows become two different but equivalent representations of the same piece of data, and operations on Java objects are then equivalent to database operations. This is the philosophy and end goal of JPA. The developer deals with Java objects and JPA does the magic by translating Java code into database operations.

For example, suppose there is a Java class called `Vehicle` with fields `vin` (Vehicle Identification Number), `make`, `model`, `year`, and `version`, and there is a database table named `VEHICLE` with columns `VIN`, `MAKE`, `MODEL`, `MODEL_YEAR`, and `VERSION`. The DDL (Data Definition Language) for creating such as a table in Derby database (see Section 9.4) reads:

```
CREATE TABLE VEHICLE
(
  VIN          VARCHAR(17)   PRIMARY KEY,
  MAKE         VARCHAR(40),
  MODEL        VARCHAR(40),
  MODEL_YEAR   INTEGER,
  VERSION      INTEGER
);
```

Using JPA annotations, we can map the Java class `Vehicle` to the table `VEHICLE` in the way as described in Listing 1-1.

Listing 1-1 Vehicle.java: Definition of a JPA entity class.

```
package jpatest;

import javax.persistence.Entity;
import javax.persistence.Table;
import javax.persistence.Id;
import javax.persistence.Column;
import javax.persistence.Version;

@Entity
@Table(name = "VEHICLE", schema = "JPATEST")
```

```java
public class Vehicle {
  @Id
  @Column(name = "VIN")
  protected String vin;

  @Column(name = "MAKE")
  protected String make;

  @Column(name = "MODEL")
  protected String model;

  @Column(name = "MODEL_YEAR")
  protected int year;

  @Version
  protected int version;

  public Vehicle() {          // default constructor is required.
    super();
  }

  public Vehicle(String vin) {
    super();
    this.vin = vin;
  }

  public Vehicle(String vin, String make, String model, int year) {
    super();
    this.vin = vin;
    this.make = make;
    this.model = model;
    this.year = year;
  }

  public String getVin() {
    return this.vin;
  }

  public String getMake() {
    return this.make;
  }

  public void setMake(String make) {
    this.make = make;
  }
```

```java
  public String getModel() {
    return this.model;
  }

  public void setModel(String model) {
    this.model = model;
  }

  public int getYear() {
    return this.year;
  }

  public void setYear(int modelYear) {
    this.year = modelYear;
  }

  public int getVersion() {
    return version;
  }

  public void setVersion(int version) {
    this.version = version;
  }
}
```

All standard JPA annotation types are in the package `javax.persistence`. If a Java class is to be persisted to a database table, it may be annotated with `@Entity`, which corresponds to the JPA class `javax.persistence.Entity` and must be imported to the class using the import statement. Alternatively, the mapping can be defined in some XML files; see Section 1.5. An entity must not be a final class. When it is not an abstract class, it must have a public or protected no-argument constructor (either user-defined or the default). JPA may choose to extend such a class behind the scene and construct instances of the class using the no-argument constructor.

The annotation

```java
@Table(name = "VEHICLE", schema = "JPATEST")
```

specifies that this Java class is to be mapped to the table with name VEHICLE in schema JPATEST. In this book, we adopt the convention of using all capital letters for database object names, unless otherwise stated as in Section 6.2.1 for delimited database identifiers.

The `@Id` annotation indicates that the `vin` field uniquely identifies the entity, which corresponds to the primary key column `VIN`, as the `@Column` annotation indicates (the `name` element specifies the name of the column):

```
@Id
@Column(name = "VIN")
protected String vin;
```

When the column name is the same as the field name, the annotation `@Column` may be omitted. Database object names in annotations are case-insensitive if the database is case-insensitive. In this case, the annotation `@Column(name="VIN")` can actually be omitted. Here the mapping is put directly on the declaration of the Java field `vin`. Alternatively, the mapping can be done on the getter method (also called *property*, according to JavaBeans convention): `getVin()`. In this chapter, the field-based access mapping approach is taken.

The next three fields: `make`, `model`, and `year` are mapped directly to the columns `MAKE`, `MODEL`, and `MODEL_YEAR`:

```
@Column(name = "MAKE")
protected String make;

protected String model;

@Column(name = "MODEL_YEAR")
protected int year;
```

Notice that the annotation for the field `model` is omitted since it maps to the database column with the same name (case-insensitive when the database is case-insensitive). The last annotation

```
@Version
protected int version;
```

indicates that it is a version field for optimistic locking. By default, it maps the Java field `version` to database column `VERSION`. When a new instance of `Vehicle` is inserted into a database row, JPA automatically fills in a value (typically 0 or 1) to the version field in the Java entity and to the VERSION column. When it is updated, the value is automatically incremented by 1. When a user retrieves an object of Vehicle, the value of the VERSION column is also retrieved. If the user makes some changes to the Vehicle object (or simply delete the object) and attempts to commit the change to the database, but in the meantime another user has updated or deleted this same database row before the commit, JPA will throw an OptimisticLockException. This resolves the so-called *stale data* issue, through a simple annotation (of course, JPA does the magic behind the scene).

Once a Java class is mapped to a database table (or tables), JPA manages the CRUD (create, retrieve, update, delete) operations of the entity through a Java interface called EntityManager. Below is some sample code to create and save a new Vehicle object into the database, update the model year to 2011, and then remove the newly inserted/updated row from the database.

```
Vehicle v = new Vehicle("6B7HF16Y7SS244324", "Ford", "Flex", 2010);
em.persist(v);      // insert the new record into database
v.setYear(2011);    // update the value of the record
em.remove(v);       // finally delete the record from database
```

Here *em* is an instance of javax.persistence.EntityManager, which refers to some database instance, specified in a configuration file (see next section). The assumption for the code above to work is that a transaction must have been started before the persist operation and the transaction must have been committed at the end. There are different ways of obtaining a transaction. Details are shown in the next two sections. Notice that when the Java code em.persist(v) is executed, an SQL insert statement is generated and executed by JPA behind the scene so that the data in object v is inserted into a row in the database table VEHICLE. Similarly, for the Java code v.setYear(2011), an update SQL is generated and executed, and for em.remove(v), a delete SQL statement is executed. If there is another entity called Part and it is mapped to have a many-to-one relationship with Vehicle, then when accessing Part through Vehicle, JPA will generate SQL statements joining their corresponding tables. When there are complex relationships between entities, it would be hard and time-consuming for a developer to hand-write and debug SQL statements. Instead, we can trust JPA for doing the hard work for us.

From the code above, we can see that once the hard work of mapping Java classes to database tables is done, data persistence is just to write Java code to manipulate Java objects. The tedious and error-prone JDBC code for executing SQL statements is no longer needed. Since the developer deals with Java classes, OO (object oriented) features can be fully utilized. In fact, JPA entities are POJOs (plain old Java objects), in that they do not need to inherit from any framework super classes or interfaces. Thus OO features (such as inheritance and polymorphism) can be fully supported on JPA entities, in contrast to pre-EJB 3.0 entity beans. For example, we may have two other entity classes: `LightTruck` and `Minivan`, both inheriting from `Vehicle` and being mapped to some database tables. In this inheritance hierarchy, `Vehicle` is the super class and `LightTruck` and `Minivan` are derived classes.

1.2 A Standalone Java Example

In this section, some CRUD operations are performed on the `VEHICLE` table in a standalone Java environment (Java SE 5.0 or later). The OR mapping is based on the one from the previous section without any change. JPA requires an XML file called `persistence.xml`, where a database instance must be configured. JPA introduces a concept called *persistence unit,* which is a logical grouping of entities and a database configuration. In our example, the `persistence.xml` file can be defined as in Listing 1-2.

Listing 1-2 persistence.xml: Definition of a persistence unit with resource-local data source.

```
<?xml version="1.0" encoding="UTF-8"?>

<persistence version="2.0"
  xmlns="http://java.sun.com/xml/ns/persistence"
  xmlns:xsi="http://www.w3.org/2001/XMLSchema-instance"
  xsi:schemaLocation="http://java.sun.com/xml/ns/persistence
      http://java.sun.com/xml/ns/persistence/persistence_2_0.xsd">

  <persistence-unit name="jpaTestPU"
                    transaction-type="RESOURCE_LOCAL">
    <provider>org.eclipse.persistence.jpa.PersistenceProvider
    </provider>
    <class>jpatest.Vehicle</class>
```

```
      <properties>
        <property name="javax.persistence.jdbc.url"
                  value="jdbc:derby://localhost:1527/jpatest" />
        <property name="javax.persistence.jdbc.user"
                  value="jpatest" />
        <property name="javax.persistence.jdbc.password"
                  value="jpatest" />
        <property name="javax.persistence.jdbc.driver"
                  value="org.apache.derby.jdbc.ClientDriver" />
        <property name="eclipselink.logging.level" value="FINEST" />
        <property name="eclipselink.target-database" value="Derby" />
      </properties>
    </persistence-unit>
</persistence>
```

The name of the persistence unit is called *jpaTestPU* and the transaction type is RESOURCE_LOCAL, which means that transaction will be managed by the entity manager (on the top of the underlying JDBC connection), not by JTA (Java Transaction API). The file persistence.xml must be in the META-INF directory on the class path, or in a jar file. The other valid value for transaction-type is JTA, in which a JTA data source must be provided for a given persistence unit. JTA data sources typically require a Java EE container and are considered in the next section.

In each persistence unit, a persistence provider must be specified, unless in a Java EE container where a default provider may be used. In this case, the provider tag

```
<provider>org.eclipse.persistence.jpa.PersistenceProvider</provider>
```

indicates that the JPA provider is EclipseLink, whose implementation library eclipselink.jar must be downloaded and put on the class path. The standard JPA API file javax.persistence_<version>.jar, which is included in any Java EE 5.0 or later application server, must also be put on the class path in Java SE environments (this file is named differently in different JPA implementations. See Sections 9.8 and 9.9 for Hibernate and OpenJPA, respectively). See EclipseLink in Section 9.3 for download and installation information.

A class tag such as

```
<class>jpatest.Vehicle</class>
```

lists an entity class, which can repeat as many times as the number of entities. The properties tag specifies standard and vendor-specific properties. In this case, it contains mainly the configuration of a database instance, which is Derby. Similarly, the Derby JDBC driver jar file `derbyclient.jar` must be on the class path also. See Derby Database in Section 9.4 on how to download and manage the database.

With all these configurations, we can now show a sample program that does some CRUD operations on the `VEHICLE` table as depicted in Listing 1-3.

Listing 1-3 VehicleTest.java: Standalone Java test program.

```java
package jpatest;

import java.util.List;
import javax.persistence.EntityManager;
import javax.persistence.EntityManagerFactory;
import javax.persistence.Persistence;
import javax.persistence.TypedQuery;

public class VehicleTest {
  EntityManagerFactory emf = null;

  public VehicleTest() {
    // There is one entity manager factory per persistence unit
    emf = Persistence.createEntityManagerFactory("jpaTestPU");
  }

  public void createVehicle(Vehicle v) {
    // create a new entity manager from entity manager factory
    EntityManager em = emf.createEntityManager();

    try {
      em.getTransaction().begin();      // start transaction
      em.persist(v);                     // insert v into database
      em.getTransaction().commit();      // commit transaction
    } catch (Throwable t) {
      t.printStackTrace();
      em.getTransaction().rollback();   // rollback transaction
    } finally {
      em.close();                        // close entity manager
    }
}
```

Java Persistence with JPA

```java
}

public List<Vehicle> retrieveVehicles(String make) {
  EntityManager em = emf.createEntityManager();
  List<Vehicle> result = null;
  try {
    // create a JPA query on the Java entity Vehicle with a
    // parameter. The 1st argument is the query string, and the 2nd
    // argument indicates the type of the query result.
    TypedQuery<Vehicle> query = em.createQuery(
      "SELECT v FROM Vehicle v WHERE v.make = ?1", Vehicle.class);
    query.setParameter(1, make);

    // get a list of vehicles from database for the given make
    result = query.getResultList();
  } finally {
    em.close();
  }

  return result;
}

public Vehicle updateVehicle(Vehicle v) {
  EntityManager em = emf.createEntityManager();
  Vehicle v2 = null;
  try {
    em.getTransaction().begin();        // start transaction
    v2 = em.merge(v);                    // merge v into managed state
    v2.setYear(2011);                    // update value again
    em.getTransaction().commit();        // commit transaction
  } catch (Throwable t) {
    t.printStackTrace();
    em.getTransaction().rollback();      // rollback transaction
  } finally {
    em.close();                          // close entity manager
  }
  return v2;                             // return the updated object
}

public void deleteVehicle(Vehicle v) {
  EntityManager em = emf.createEntityManager();
  try {
    em.getTransaction().begin();        // start transaction
    em.remove(em.merge(v));              // delete v from database
    em.getTransaction().commit();        // commit transaction
  } catch (Throwable t) {
```

10

```
      t.printStackTrace();
      em.getTransaction().rollback(); // rollback transaction
    } finally {
      em.close();                     // close entity manager
    }
  }


public void close() {
  if (emf != null & emf.isOpen()) {
    emf.close();                      // close entity manager factory
  }
}


public static void main(String[] args) {
  try {
    VehicleTest vehTest = new VehicleTest();
    String vinPrimaryKey = "6B7HF16Y7SS244324";
    Vehicle v = new Vehicle(vinPrimaryKey, "Ford", "Flex", 2010);

    // insert the new Vehicle object into database. JPA assigns a
    // value (typically 0 or 1) to the version field
    vehTest.createVehicle(v);

    // do update, then version should be incremented by 1
    v.setMake("Mercury");
    Vehicle v2 = vehTest.updateVehicle(v);
    Assert v2.getVersion()==v.getVersion()+1:"Update version error";

    // retrieve all vehicles with make "Mercury"
    List<Vehicle> vehicles = vehTest.retrieveVehicles("Mercury");
    for (Vehicle h : vehicles) {
      System.out.println("vehicle retrieved: " + h.getVin());
    }

    // delete newly inserted/updated vehicle. Must pass in v2 as a
    // parameter instead of v. Otherwise, OptimisticLockException
    // would be thrown
    vehTest.deleteVehicle(v2);

    // clean up resource
    vehTest.close();
  } catch (Throwable t) {
    t.printStackTrace();
  }
}
```

}

Notice that there is a one-to-one correspondence between a persistence unit and an entity manager factory. Given the name of a persistence unit, the following code creates the entity manager factory:

```
emf = Persistence.createEntityManagerFactory("jpaTestPU");
```

To avoid hard-coded password in `persistence.xml`, we may pass database information such as user name and password to the `createEntityManagerFactory` method above as a second parameter. See Listing 3-6 in Section 3.3.2.

The entity manager factory may be used to create entity manager instances before CRUD operations are performed on entities managed in this persistence unit. Unlike the entity manager factory which is thread-safe, an entity manager is not thread-safe and is typically created before performing transactions or queries, and closed after the transactions or queries are finished, as shown in Listing 1-3. The method call `em.getTransaction()` returns an `javax.persistence.EntityTransaction` object associated with a resource-local entity manager. When the transaction type for a persistence unit is configured to be `RESOURCE_LOCAL`, this is the only way of getting a transaction.

The method `createVehicle` looks straightforward. It takes an instance of the `Vehicle` class, creates an entity manger, gets the transaction from the entity manger, and calls the `persist` method of the entity manger to save the `Vehicle` object into a database row in table `VEHICLE`, if the transaction commits successfully. Notice that a transaction is required for such an operation.

In method `retrieveVehicles`, a transaction is not needed to perform a query, although queries can be performed inside a transaction, possibly together with some other CRUD operations. Notice the SQL-like query:

```
"SELECT v FROM Vehicle v WHERE v.make = ?1"
```

It acts directly upon Java entities and their attributes, instead of database tables and columns, and is written in JPA Query Language (JPQL for short; see Chapter 1). It takes one parameter indicated by "?1" (similar to the syntax in JDBC prepared statements) for the `make` field of class `Vehicle`. JPA generates an SQL select statement and returns the results as a list of `Vehicle` objects. When there are derived entities such as

12

`LightTruck` and `Minivan`, this returned list also contains objects of the derived classes if the OR mapping has been done correctly. This is called a *polymorphic query*. Note that the developer does not need to convert a result set into a list of objects of a desired type as in JDBC programming. JPA does the conversion for us behind the scene.

In the `updateVehicle` method, a `Vehicle` object *v*, typically containing new changes, is passed in as a parameter. It must be merged into the so-called *persistence context* by the following method call:

```
v2 = em.merge(v);
```

A *persistence context* is a set of managed entity instances whose states and lifecycle are managed by an entity manager associated with the persistence context. In this case, the persistence context starts when the entity manager is created using `EntityManagerFactory` and ends after the `close` method of the entity manager is called. If an object is managed by a persistence context, it is called to be in *managed state*. If an object was in managed state, but now goes out of the scope of the persistence context (when the `em.close()` method is called in this case), it is called to be in *detached state*. In the call `v2 = em.merge(v)`, the input object *v* is assumed to be in detached state, and the returned object *v2* becomes in managed state. The changes on an object in managed state will be tracked by JPA and saved automatically into the database before or when the transaction enlisted with the persistence context commits. When `em.close()` is called inside the method `updateVehicle`, the object *v2* goes out of the scope of the persistence context and becomes in detached state.

Similarly, the input object *v* to the method `deleteVehicle(v)` must be merged into managed state before the `em.remove()` method can be called on it to remove it from the database. When an instance *v* of an entity class is created using the *new* operator, it is not in managed state. The method call `em.persist(v)` makes it in managed state, and its value is inserted into the database when the transaction commits. This is what happened to the `createVehicle(v)` method, explained in terms of persistence context.

Looking at all the methods in this class, a common pattern is to close the entity manager resource in a *finally* block:

```
try {
  // create entity manager and perform transactions or queries
} finally {
```

```
    em.close();        // close entity manager in finally block
}
```

This is a recommended best practice for an application-managed (not Java EE container-managed) entity manager like this. That is, create a new instance of the entity manager inside a method call and close it before the method call is finished.

On the other hand, the entity manager factory can be cached at the application level and only needs to be closed at the end of the program.

In the following, we provide two ways to run the sample program above. One way is to use the DOS command line (using Unix or Linux command line is similar) and the other way is to use the Eclipse Java EE IDE (Integrated Development Environment).

DOS Command Line. In Windows, the files may be organized as:

C:\jpa\java\DOS\	(top level folder)
jpatest\	(subfolder for Java files)
Vehicle.java	
VehicleTest.java	
lib\	(subfolder for libraries)
eclipselink.jar	(downloaded from EclipseLink)
javax.persistence_2.0.0.jar	(downloaded from EclipseLink)
derbyclient.jar	(downloaded from Apache Derby)
META-INF\	(subfolder for configuration files)
persistence.xml	
run.bat	(DOS batch file to run the program)

Note that the XML configuration file `persistence.xml` must be put in the *META-INF* folder, together with possibly other OR mapping files. Compilation and execution of the program is managed by the DOS batch file in Listing 1-4:

Listing 1-4 run.bat: DOS batch file to compile and run the sample program.

```
set CLASSPATH=.;lib/javax.persistence_2.0.0.jar;lib/eclipselink.jar;
```

```
set CLASSPATH=%CLASSPATH%;lib/derbyclient.jar

javac jpatest/Vehicle.java jpatest/VehicleTest.java

java -ea jpatest/VehicleTest
```

When the program runs, SQL statements generated by JPA are logged to the console, with the logging level configured in persistence.xml file; see Listing 1-2. The assumption here is that the table VEHICLE has been created and the Derby database server has been started. See Section 9.3 on how to download EclipseLink JPA jar files, and see Derby Database in Section 9.4 on how to create a database and how to start the database server.

Eclipse IDE. Start the IDE (see Eclipse in Section 9.5 for installation) and create a JPA project by choosing menu *File → New → Other → JPA → JPA Project*. Enter a name for the project such as *jpatest*. Then a subfolder *src/META-INF* is automatically created, together with two blank XML files persistence.xml and orm.xml. Choose not to use the JPA jar files in the Eclipse IDE, since these jar files may not be up-to-date. Instead, manually download the desired version of the JPA jar files and add them to the project (see below). Copy the content of the persistence unit definition from Listing 1-2 to the persistence.xml file, and leave the file orm.xml unchanged for now (alternatively, OR mapping can be defined in XML here, instead of using annotations. See Section 1.5). Refer to Figure 1-1.

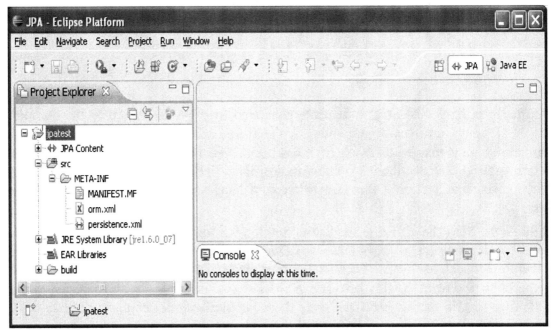

Figure 1-1 *Creation of JPA project jpatest in Eclipse IDE.*

Right click on the folder *src* and choose *New* → *Class* to create two Java files: `Vehicle.java` and `VehicleTest.java` with Java package *jpatest*. Similarly, copy the contents of Listing 1-1 and Listing 1-3 into these two Java files, respectively.

Right click on project *jpatest*, then choose menu *Properties* → *Java Build Path*. Click on tab *Libraries*, then click on button *Add External JARs*. Add the jar file for Derby JDBC driver (`derbyclient.jar`), EclipseLink JPA implementation jar file (`eclipselink.jar`) and the JPA standard API jar file (`javax.persistence_2.0.0.jar`), as Figure 1-2 shows.

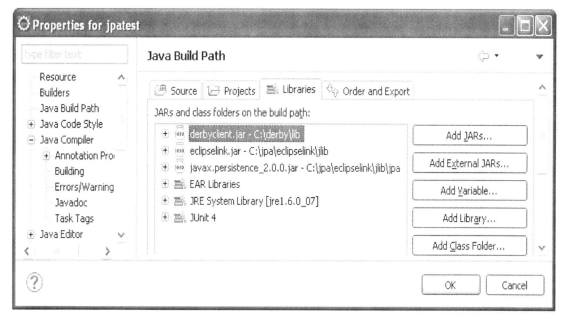

Figure 1-2 Add external jars to project jpatest.

Now the project structure and configuration looks like the one in Figure 1-3.

To run it, start the database server and then right click on VehicleTest.java in *Project Explorer* view and choose menu *Run As → Java Application.* The output messages then fly by in the *Console* pane.

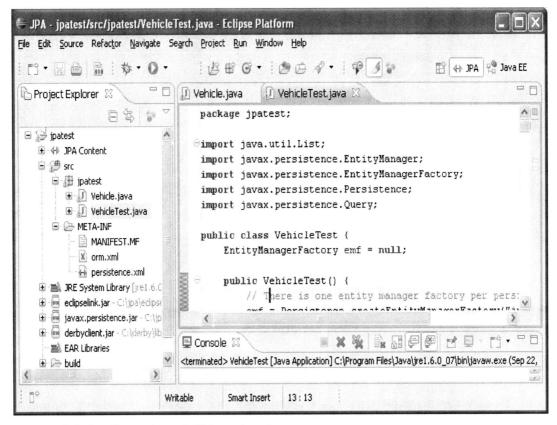

Figure 1-3 Configuration of JPA project jpatest.

1.3 An EJB Example

In this section, a stateless session bean is used for performing CRUD operations on the VEHICLE table. Transactions will be managed by an EJB 3.0 or later container, for which a JTA data source is required. The persistence.xml file defines a persistence unit *jpaTestJtaPU* as shown in Listing 1-5.

Listing 1-5 persistence.xml: Definition of a persistence unit with JTA data source.

```
<?xml version="1.0" encoding="UTF-8"?>
```

```
<persistence version="2.0"
  xmlns="http://java.sun.com/xml/ns/persistence"
  xmlns:xsi="http://www.w3.org/2001/XMLSchema-instance"
  xsi:schemaLocation="http://java.sun.com/xml/ns/persistence
      http://java.sun.com/xml/ns/persistence/persistence_2_0.xsd">

  <persistence-unit name="jpaTestJtaPU" transaction-type="JTA">
    <provider>org.eclipse.persistence.jpa.PersistenceProvider
    </provider>
    <jta-data-source>java:/jpaTestJtaDS</jta-data-source>
    <mapping-file>META-INF/orm.xml</mapping-file>
    <class>jpatest.Vehicle</class>

    <properties>
      <property name="eclipselink.logging.level" value="FINEST" />
      <property name="eclipselink.target-server" value="JBoss" />
      <property name="eclipselink.target-database" value="Derby" />
    </properties>
  </persistence-unit>
</persistence>
```

Notice the transaction type is JTA for the persistence unit *jpaTestJtaPU* and the tag

```
<jta-data-source>java:/jpaTestJtaDS</jta-data-source>
```

specifies a JTA data source which must have been configured in the application server. See JBoss in Section 9.6 on how to configure a data source.

The stateless session bean and its local business interface can be defined as in Listing 1-6 and Listing 1-7. Note that in EJB 3.1 or later, the business interface definition in Listing 1-6 is not required.

> Listing 1-6 VehicleSLLocal.java: Local business interface for stateless session bean.

```
package jpatest.ejb;

import java.util.List;
import javax.ejb.Local;
import jpatest.Vehicle;

@Local
```

```
public interface VehicleSLLocal {
  public void createVehicle(Vehicle v);
  public List<Vehicle> retrieveVehicles(String make);
  public Vehicle updateVehicle(Vehicle v);
  public void deleteVehicle(Vehicle v);
}
```

Listing 1-7 VehicleSL.java: Stateless session bean implementation.

```
package jpatest.ejb;

import java.util.List;
import javax.ejb.Stateless;
import javax.persistence.EntityManager;
import javax.persistence.PersistenceContext;
import javax.persistence.TypedQuery;

@Stateless
public class VehicleSL implements VehicleSLLocal {
  @PersistenceContext(unitName = "jpaTestJtaPU")
  EntityManager em;

  public VehicleSL() {
  }

  public void createVehicle(Vehicle v) {
    em.persist(v);                    // insert v into database
  }

  public List<Vehicle> retrieveVehicles(String make) {
    TypedQuery<Vehicle> query = em.createQuery(
       "SELECT v FROM Vehicle v WHERE v.make = ?1", Vehicle.class);
    query.setParameter(1, make);
    List<Vehicle> result = query.getResultList();

    return result;
  }

  public Vehicle updateVehicle(Vehicle v) {
    Vehicle v2 = em.merge(v);       // merge v into managed state
    v2.setYear(2011);               // update model year to 2011
    return v2;
  }
```

```
public void deleteVehicle(Vehicle v) {
  em.remove(em.merge(v));    // merge v into managed state & delete
  }
}
```

The EJB 3.0 (or later) annotation `@Local` specifies a local interface and `@Stateless` specifies a stateless session bean. Notice the JPA annotation

```
@PersistenceContext(unitName = "jpaTestJtaPU")
EntityManager em;
```

The `@PersistenceContext` designates a persistence unit name to be *jpaTestJtaPU*, which must have been defined in `persistence.xml` as being of JTA transaction type. The EJB container will manage the lifecycle of the entity manager *em* and transaction. In this case, a persistence context spans the duration of a container-managed JTA transaction. The persistence context starts when the transaction starts, and ends and its managed entities become detached when the transaction ends. The developer is not supposed to call the `close` and `getTransaction` methods on container-managed entity managers. The CRUD operations are dramatically simplified. The create method

```
public void createVehicle(Vehicle v) {
  em.persist(v);        // insert v into database
}
```

has just one line of code, as compared to 11 lines of code in the case of application-managed persistence context in the previous section:

```
public void createVehicle(Vehicle v) {
  // create a new entity manager from entity manager factory
  EntityManager em = emf.createEntityManager();

  try {
    em.getTransaction().begin();    // start transaction
    em.persist(v);                  // insert v into database
    em.getTransaction().commit();   // commit transaction
  } catch (Throwable t) {
    t.printStackTrace();
    em.getTransaction().rollback(); // rollback transaction
  } finally {
    em.close();                     // close entity manager
```

```
        }
}
```

With all the preparation, we are ready to show how the stateless session bean can be invoked from a JSF managed bean in Listing 1-8.

Listing 1-8 TestBean.java: call EJB from JSF managed bean.

```java
package jpatest.web;

import java.util.List;
import javax.ejb.EJB;

import jpatest.Vehicle;
import jpatest.ejb.VehicleSLLocal;

public class TestBean {

  @EJB              // Dependency injection in a container-managed class
  protected VehicleSLLocal vehLocal;

  public String doSubmit() {      // JSF action method on button submit
    try {
      String vinPrimaryKey = "3B7HF16Y7SS244324";
      Vehicle v = new Vehicle(vinPrimaryKey, "Ford", "Flex", 2010);

      // insert the new Vehicle object into database
      vehLocal.createVehicle(v);

      // after update, version should be incremented by 1
      v.setMake("Mercury");
      Vehicle v2 = vehLocal.updateVehicle(v);

      // retrieve all vehicles with make "Mercury"
      List<Vehicle> vehList = vehLocal.retrieveVehicles("Mercury");
      for (Vehicle veh: vehList) {
        System.out.println("retrieved vehicle: " + veh.getMake());
      }

      // delete the newly inserted/updated vehicle
      vehLocal.deleteVehicle(v2);
```

```
    } catch (Exception e) {
      e.printStackTrace();
    }

    return null;
  }
}
```

To configure and run this EJB example using the Eclipse IDE and the JBoss application server, go to Section 9.7.

1.4 Entity Operations

In the previous few sections, we have encountered the entity operations: persist, merge, and remove. We now talk briefly about a few more, which will be covered in depth in later chapters.

The flush operation saves the current modification of all managed entity instances to the database, which must be executed within a transaction. To reduce the number of database calls, the operations persist, merge, and remove may not cause immediate database changes. Instead, they may be batched together (even with some optimization) and saved to the database at flush or commit time. By default, the entity manager does the flush automatically. The flush operation may be invoked by the developer to programmatically force a flush to the database.

The refresh operation refreshes the state of a managed entity instance from the database, overwriting changes made to the entity, if any. The detach operation makes a managed entity instance detached by removing it from the persistence context. A detached object is sometimes sent to a different application tier (eg, the presentation tier) or to a remote interface (eg, through a web service call) for modification and then merged back to a persistence context later using the merge operation, before saving the modification to the database. Note there are many ways that a managed object may become detached, and the detach operation is just there when you need it. The find operation finds an entity instance by the specified class and primary key. If the entity instance is contained in the persistence context, it is returned from there, saving a trip to the database. Similar to performing a query, the find operation may not have to be invoked inside a transaction.

They may be used as in the following code snippet:

```java
public class VehicleTest {

  // other methods are omitted here.

  public Vehicle updateVehicle(Vehicle v) {
    EntityManager em = emf.createEntityManager();
    Vehicle v2 = null;
    try {
      em.getTransaction().begin();

      // merge v into managed state
      v2 = em.merge(v);

      // force a flush of current changes to database
      em.flush();

      // make more changes
      v2.setYear(2011);
      em.getTransaction().commit();
    } catch (Throwable t) {
      t.printStackTrace();
      em.getTransaction().rollback();
    } finally {
      em.close();
    }

    return v2;
  }

  public Vehicle redoChanges(Vehicle v) {
    EntityManager em = emf.createEntityManager();
    Vehicle v2 = null;

    try {
      em.getTransaction().begin();

      // merge v into managed state
      v2 = em.merge(v);

      // undo the changes by overwriting current values
      // by values from database
      em.refresh(v2);

      // make new changes from here
      v2.setYear(2004);
```

```
      v2.setMake("Buick");
      v2.setModel("Rendezvous");
      em.getTransaction().commit();
   } catch (Throwable t) {
      t.printStackTrace();
      em.getTransaction().rollback();
   } finally {
      em.close();
   }
   return v2;
}

public Vehicle findVehicle(String vin) {
   EntityManager em = emf.createEntityManager();
   Vehicle v = null;

   try {
      em.getTransaction().begin();

      // find Vehicle instance by primary key
      v = em.find(Vehicle.class, vin);

      // detach v from persistence context
      em.detach(v);

      // changes on v will not be saved to database, since v is
      // detached unless it is merged later into a persistence
      // context.
      v.setMake("GMC");
      v.setYear(2012);
      em.getTransaction().commit();
   } finally {
      em.close();
   }

   return v;
}
}
```

In Section 1.2, the query of selecting vehicles by a given make is constructed at run-time. Such a query is called a *dynamic query*. In addition, JPA supports *named queries*, which are static queries. Named queries may be precompiled once and re-executed as many times as needed. The annotation @NamedQuery may be used to configure a static query on an entity class like this:

```
@Entity
@Table(name = "VEHICLE", schema = "JPATEST")
@NamedQuery(name="selectVehiclesByMake",
  query="SELECT v FROM Vehicle v WHERE v.make = ?1"
)
public class Vehicle { ... }
```

It defines a named query with name "selectVehiclesByMake". A named Query object can be created using the createNamedQuery method by passing the name of the query to it, and executed in the same way as a dynamic query. The code looks like this:

```
public class VehicleTest {

  public List<Vehicle> retrieveVehicles(String make) {
    EntityManager em = emf.createEntityManager();
    List<Vehicle> resultList = null;

    try {
      // create a named query and set the query parameter
      TypedQuery<Vehicle> query =
        em.createNamedQuery("selectVehiclesByMake", Vehicle.Class);
      query.setParameter(1, make);

      // execute the query to get a list of vehicles from database
      resultList = query.getResultList();
    } finally {
      em.close();
    }

    return resultList;
  }
}
```

Named queries are typically pre-compiled and lead to performance gains.

Since this is an introductory chapter, we may not have explained everything well enough. Otherwise, this book would not need other chapters. The main purpose of this chapter is to provide an overview of JPA and touch upon its important features. To this end, we list a few other features of JPA without going into any details:

- **Pessimistic Locking**. JPA enables one to lock database records pessimistically for concurrency control.

- **Lazy Loading**. Persistent attributes may be configured with lazy-fetching to defer the loading from the database until they are first accessed, to potentially improve efficiency.
- **Shared Cache**. Entity objects may be cached at the application level, so that different users may share the cached objects. Queries and the `find` method can be configured to access the cached objects without going to the database, if possible.
- **Validation**. Validation rules may be specified using annotations so that values of entity attributes (persistent fields or properties) may be validated (such as maximum value and length) before being saved to the database.
- **Listeners.** Callback methods and listeners may be registered on entities so that specified business logic (such as logging and filling in auditing fields) may be executed automatically on certain events (such as insert and update of an entity).
- **Bulk Updates**. It refers to updating/deleting many database rows as one JPA operation. Bulk updates may be performed on many entity instances at a time without fetching the corresponding data from the database into the JVM.
- **Native SQL**. JPA provides a feature-rich query language (JPQL). However, it allows one to go native when it is needed.
- **Criteria Queries**. This is a type-safe way of constructing queries programmatically, which reduces run-time query errors.

1.5 OR Mapping in XML

In previous sections, annotations are used for defining object-relational mapping (OR mapping). For every annotation, JPA also introduces its equivalent XML descriptor. Thus an application has the option to choose either annotations, XML files, or a combination of both, to define its OR mapping.

The default OR mapping file is `orm.xml`, located in the same directory as the `persistence.xml` file; see Figure 1-1 in Section 1.2. An application may choose to use many XML files for modularity. In this case, their names and locations must be defined in the `persistence.xml` file and use a separate `mapping-file` tag for each ORM file (see Listing 1-5).

For the vehicle example, all the annotations defined in early sections may be replaced by the XML mapping file as shown in Listing 1-9.

Listing 1-9 orm.xml: Object-relational mapping in XML descriptors.

```xml
<?xml version="1.0" encoding="UTF-8"?>
<entity-mappings version="2.0"
  xmlns="http://java.sun.com/xml/ns/persistence/orm"
  xmlns:xsi="http://www.w3.org/2001/XMLSchema-instance"
  xsi:schemaLocation="http://java.sun.com/xml/ns/persistence/orm
      http://java.sun.com/xml/ns/persistence/orm/orm_2_0.xsd">

  <persistence-unit-metadata>
    <xml-mapping-metadata-complete/>
    <persistence-unit-defaults>
      <schema>jpatest</schema>    <!-- database schema for tables -->
      <access>FIELD</access>      <!-- map fields, not getters -->
    </persistence-unit-defaults>
  </persistence-unit-metadata>

  <named-query name="selectVehiclesByMake">
    <query>SELECT v FROM Vehicle v WHERE v.make = ?1</query>
    <hint name="javax.persistence.query.timeout" value="1000" />
  </named-query>

  <entity class="jpatest.Vehicle" metadata-complete="true">
    <table name="VEHICLE" />
    <attributes>
      <id name="vin">
        <column name="VIN" length="17" />
      </id>
      <basic name="make" />
      <basic name="model" />
      <basic name="year" optional="true">
        <column name="MODEL_YEAR" />
      </basic>
      <version name="version">
        <column name="VERSION" />
      </version>
    </attributes>
  </entity>
</entity-mappings>
```

The tag persistence-unit-metadata defines the metadata for the entire persistence unit, no matter how many mapping files there are. The tag xml-mapping-metadata-complete specifies that all the mapping information is completely defined inside XML mapping files. In this case JPA will ignore the annotations, if any, defined in entity classes. When this tag is not specified, the OR mapping information may be partially defined in XML files and partially defined in entity classes, with the OR mapping in the XML files overwriting that in the annotations (if defined in both places).

The tag `named-query` defines a named query with a given name. Use a separate `named-query` tag for each named query. The query names must be unique per persistence unit. This query also includes a query hint for query timeout in milliseconds.

The tag `entity` defines an entity class. Use a separate `entity` tag for each entity class. The tag `table` inside the `entity` tag specifies the database table name to which the entity is mapped. The `attributes` tag maps entity attributes: persistent fields or properties (getters) to database columns. In particular, the `id` tag designates the primary key of the entity. The `basic` tag specifies a basic entity attribute (not a relationship attribute). The `column` tag is required when the name of the entity field or property is different from the database column name, such as for the entity attribute `year` (whose corresponding database column is `MODEL_YEAR`). The `version` tag specifies the column for optimistic locking.

More details on XML mapping rules are explained in Chapter 6.

We now have completed our overview of main features of JPA. There is no doubt that you are anxious to learn more about JPA, including the theory, examples, and even tricks. Read the remaining chapters for everything that you want to know. Enjoy!

2 Object Relational Mapping

This chapter talks about how to map object oriented Java classes to relational database tables, which is commonly called OR mapping (Object Relational mapping). The first step to a successful JPA application is to do OR mapping correctly. Thus this chapter plays a critical role in any JPA application. Fortunately, JPA annotations make OR mapping very intuitive and easy to understand (well, for the most part). Also, for every JPA annotation, there is an equivalent XML descriptor. A developer can choose one of the two ways for doing OR mapping, and even has the flexibility of using XML files to override annotations.

The first section presents an object model with objects and relationships, and later sections try to apply standard JPA annotations to these objects. This chapter deals only with fundamental and most-often-used features of OR mapping. Advanced features, such as composite primary keys, element collections, and entity inheritance, are covered in Chapter 4. XML descriptors are explained in Chapter 6.

2.1 Object Model

In this chapter, assume that we are going to build an application for an online book ordering system. Books are classified into different categories and a category may contain many subcategories. Besides regular customers, there are preferred customers who are eligible for some special discount rate and gold customers who have a gold charge card. A customer may place orders on line-items of a book, which will be sent to the customer's address.

Based on the requirements, a software engineer typically first creates a *domain model*, which consists of domain objects and their relationships. Objects in a domain model represent conceptual business objects that can be persisted into a permanent storage. The domain model for this simple online book ordering system may be described using UML notation in Figure 2-1.

The domain objects are `Category`, `Book`, `LineItem`, `Order`, `Address`, `Customer`, `PreferredCustomer`, and `GoldCustomer`. A parent category can have subcategories. `Category` and `Book` have many-to-many relationship, in that a `Category` may contain many `Books` and a `Book` may belong to many instances of `Category`. An `Order` may contain many `LineItems` and thus `Order` has one-to-many relationship to `LineItem`, which has many-to-one relationship to `Book`. A `Customer` may place many `Orders` and thus `Customer` has one-to-many relationship to `Order`. `Customer` has an inheritance hierarchy with two specialized objects: `PreferredCustomer` and `GoldCustomer`. A customer is allowed to have zero or one address in this simplified model, and thus `Customer` has one-to-one relationship to `Address`. Some relationship is unidirectional (such as `LineItem` to `Book` and `Customer` to `Address`) and others are bidirectional (such as `Book` and `Category`, `Customer` and `Order`, and `LineItem` and `Order`).

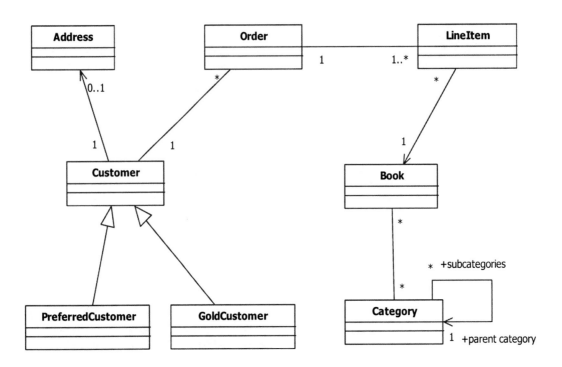

Figure 2-1 Domain model for an online book ordering system.

From the domain model, one can further investigate the problem and analyze the requirements, and come up with something called the *analysis model*. Objects in an analysis model represent logical software objects, which are typically technology agnostic (applicable to Java and C++, for example). The analysis model for our book ordering system can be depicted as in Figure 2-2. Architecturally significant methods may be added to these objects as well, but are omitted here.

Based on the analysis model, a data architect can easily arrive at the *logical data model*, by applying certain database principals such as normalization and data integrity constraints. A bidirectional relationship in the analysis model (such as Customer and Order) can only be conveniently modeled by a unidirectional relationship in the logical data model (Order has a foreign key to Customer but not vice versa). The logical data model is listed in Figure 2-3, which shows the names of database tables and their columns, and primary key and foreign key relationships. In this model, we have used suffix PK for a primary key column, FK for a foreign key column, and FPK for a column that is both a primary key and a foreign key. A logical data model is typically not dependent on a particular database management system. Not shown in this picture are the VERSION column and auditing columns: CREATE_USER, CREATE_TIME, MODIFY_USER, and MODIFY_TIME, to save space.

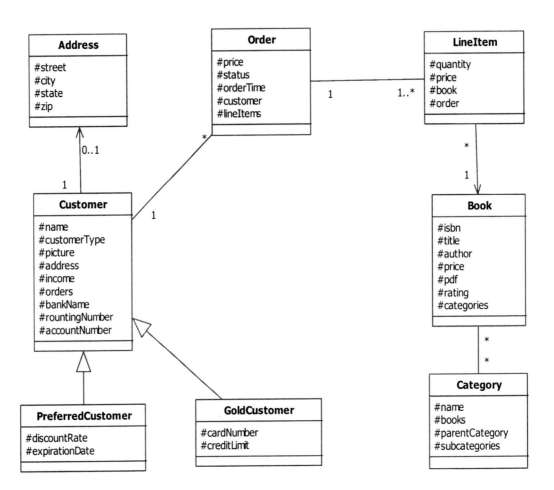

Figure 2-2 Analysis model for online book ordering system.

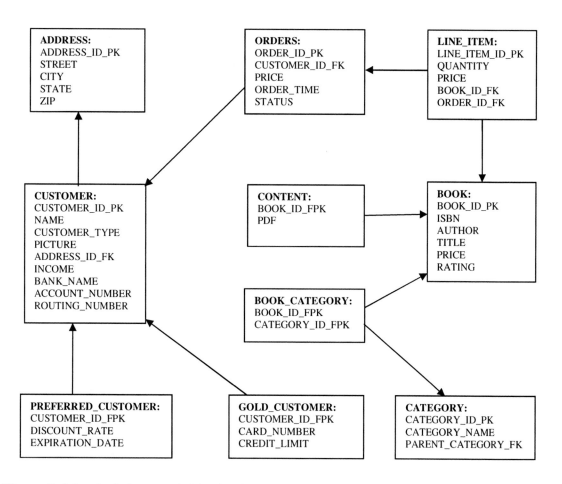

Figure 2-3 Logical data model for book ordering system.

In the logical data model, the table ORDERS has primary key ORDER_ID_PK, and foreign key CUSTOMER_ID_FK, which points to the primary key CUSTOMER_ID_PK in table CUSTOMER. For the CATEGORY table, the foreign key PARENT_CATEGORY_FK points to the primary key CATEGORY_ID_PK in the same table to model the parent-child relationship. The join table (or association table) BOOK_CATEGORY is introduced to model the many-to-many relationship. Also, the table CONTENT is created to store just the large-size PDF contents of BOOKs, which is mainly due to performance consideration (see Section 2.2.11). Note that we have used the table name ORDERS since ORDER is a reserved key word in SQL. Also, each table is designed to have a sequence number as its primary key (except for the join table), which is a convenient approach since JPA provides automatic ways of handling such columns. The tables PREFERRED_CUSTOMER and GOLD_CUSTOMER just have columns specific to them and common data are stored in the root table CUSTOMER. This resembles the class hierarchy in the analysis model quite well, in that the derived classes PreferredCustomer and GoldCustomer inherit fields from the super class Customer. JPA supports two other design strategies for the table hierarchy; see Section 4.3.

From the logical data model, we can get the *physical data model* for a particular database, by taking into consideration on things such as specific data types in the underlying database and naming conventions. We will not show the physical data model in the Derby database here, but refer the reader to download the source code to view the DDL.

Based on the analysis model and physical data model, a developer can create a Java-specific *design model* that represents an implementable solution, which consists of Java objects utilizing Java data types and object oriented features. Finally Java classes are written to implement the design model. In the next few sections, we will try to map these Java classes to our Derby database tables and columns using JPA annotations.

2.2 Entity Mapping

In this section, we talk about JPA annotations that map to a single entity class or part of an entity class. Mappings on entity relationship will be dealt with in the next section.

2.2.1 @Entity

The @Entity annotation should be applied to a Java class that is meant to be persisted to the database. JPA entities are POJOs (plain old Java objects) in that a JPA entity is not required to inherit from any framework super classes or interfaces. However, if a JPA entity will be cached in HTTP session or a stateful session bean, transported to a remote system, or passed by value as a detached object, it must implement the java.io.Serializable interface.

For example, the Address class can be annotated as:

```
package jpatest.entity;

import javax.persistence.Entity;

@Entity
public class Address {
```

```
  // ... fields

  public Address() {        // no-argument constructor
    super();
  }

  // ... other methods
}
```

However, not all Java classes can be annotated with `@Entity`. Below are the guidelines on a JPA entity.

- It must not be a final class, an *enum*, an interface, or an inner class. No persistent attributes (fields or properties) may be final, static, or transient.
- An entity can be an abstract or a concrete class. Non-abstract entities must have either a public or a protected no-argument constructor. Other constructors are optional. It is fine if we do not define any constructor, since the compiler will generate a public no-argument constructor.
- It may be an abstract class if it is not meant to be instantiated directly, but is mapped to a table. In this case, derived entity classes must be defined to persist the data inherited from abstract entities. See Section 4.3.
- It may inherit from a class that is annotated with `@MappedSuperclass`. In this case, persistent attributes from the mapped super class are also persistent in the derived entity. See Section 2.2.13. A mapped super class does not map directly to a database table.
- It may inherit from a class that is annotated by `@Entity`. See Section 4.3.
- It may inherit from a *non-entity class* (any class not annotated with `@Entity` or `@MappedSuperclass`). In this case, all fields or properties inherited from the super class are ignored when the entity is persisted. Similarly, a non-entity class may also inherit from an entity class.
- The state of an entity is available to clients only through the entity's methods: accessor methods (getter/ setter methods) or other business methods.

The `@Entity` annotation takes one optional `name` element, which defaults to the unqualified name of the class. This is typically used to provide an alias for an entity in defining queries. For example, two entities may have the same unqualified name, but should be given different aliases for use in queries (see Chapter 1). The definition of the annotation is:

```
@Target(TYPE) @Retention(RUNTIME)
public @interface Entity {
  String name() default "";
}
```

Annotation is a feature introduced in Java SE 5.0. This definition says that it applies to type declarations (classes) only (not to fields or methods) and it has a run-time retention policy (annotation retained at run-time). It may be used as:

```
@Entity(name = "MyAddress")
@NamedQuery(name="myQuery",
  query="SELECT a FROM MyAddress a WHERE a.zip = ?1"
)
public class Address { ... }
```

2.2.2 @Table

The @Table annotation specifies the primary table to which an entity is mapped. An example is

```
@Entity
@Table(name = "ADDRESS", schema = "JPATEST", catalog = "JPATEST")
public class Address { ... }
```

The name element specifies the name of the table, and schema and catalog specify the names of the schema and the catalog in the database, respectively. All the elements are optional. If the name element is omitted, it defaults to the unqualified name of the entity class. The schema and catalog elements, if omitted, would be the default schema and catalog for the database user. The @Table annotation may be omitted, in which case the default values of its elements apply. The definition of the annotation is:

```
@Target({TYPE}) @Retention(RUNTIME)
public @interface Table {
  String name() default "";       // table name, default to entity name
  String catalog() default "";
  String schema() default "";
  UniqueConstraint[] uniqueConstraints() default {};
}
```

The uniqueConstraints element is typically used only for table generation. Certain JPA providers (such as EclipseLink, Hibernate, and OpenJPA) support the generation of tables from entity definition. This element provides an opportunity to put certain unique constraints on the columns to be generated. For example, the following annotation puts a unique constraint on the ZIP and STREET columns.

```
@Entity
@Table(name="ADDRESS",
  uniqueConstraints=@UniqueConstraint(columnNames={"ZIP", "STREET"})
)
public class Address { ... }
```

For small or proof-of-concept projects, this may be a good feature. You define Java classes and the mapping. Then let your JPA implementation generate the database schema for you. Similarly, certain IDEs or tools generate Java classes with annotations from a database schema. However, the generated database schema or Java code with annotation is typically not of production quality, and you need to improve it manually. Note that the schema or Java code generation is not part of JPA standards and is vendor-specific (such properties may be configured in persistence.xml).

2.2.3 @Column

To map a field or property of an entity to a specific database column, use the @Column annotation. When putting annotation directly on an entity field (which must be private, protected, or package-visible), it is referred to as *field-based access*. When applying annotation on getter methods following the JavaBeans style property access approach, it is referred to as *property-based access* (see the next subsection). The @Column annotation is optional. If omitted, JPA maps the field or property to a column with the same name. That is, an *attribute* (a field for field-based access, or a property for property-based access) of an entity is persistent by default. If we do not want an attribute to be persisted, declare it to be transient or use the @Transient annotation. The following example uses field-based access:

```
@Entity
public class Address {
  @Column(
    name = "STREET", updatable=true, insertable=true, nullable=false
  )
  protected String street;

  protected String city;      // default to map to CITY column
  protected String state;     // default to map to STATE column

  @Column(name = "ZIP", length=5, nullable=false)
```

```
  protected String zip;         // string length at most 5

  @Transient
  protected boolean isResidential;  // field not persisted to database
}
```

The `name` element of `@Column` specifies the column name to which the entity field or property is to be mapped. When omitted, it defaults the column name to be the name of the entity field or property. Database object names specified in the annotations are case-insensitive if the database in use is case-insensitive. The `updatable` element, defaulted to `true`, controls whether or not the column is included in SQL update statements generated by JPA. A value of `false` indicates that this column cannot be updated. Similarly, the `insertable` element, also defaulted to `true`, specifies whether the column is included in generated SQL insert statements; A value of `false` indicates that this column cannot be inserted. Setting both `insertable` and `updatable` elements to `false` for an attribute means that attribute is read-only and any attempt to insert or update it would lead to an error. The `nullable` element specifies if the column can take null as its value. It is worth noting that the `length` element specifies the length of the data and is applicable only to string-valued columns; this element may be used by vendors that support table generation based on mapping metadata (annotation or XML) and can also be used to validate data before saving to the database.

The `@Column` annotation's definition, applicable to only fields and properties as specified in `@Target`, is:

```
@Target({METHOD, FIELD}) @Retention(RUNTIME)
public @interface Column {
   String name() default "";          // column name
   boolean unique() default false;    // Are values unique?
   boolean nullable() default true;   // is this column nullable?
   boolean insertable() default true; // include it in SQL insert?
   boolean updatable() default true;  // include it in SQL update?
   String columnDefinition() default "";
   String table() default "";         // table name
   int length() default 255;          // for string-valued column
   int precision() default 0;         // precision for decimal column
   int scale() default 0;             // scale for decimal column
}
```

Note that `precision` is the number of digits in a decimal number and `scale` is the number of digits to the right of the decimal point. The `table` element enables the developer to specify the name of a secondary table that contains the column, which must be used in conjunction with the @SecondaryTable annotation (see Section 2.2.11 for details). If omitted, it defaults to the name of the primary table. An example is to store the PDF content of Books in a separate table CONTENT, whose primary key BOOK_ID_FPK is also a foreign key to the primary key BOOK_ID_PK of table BOOK; see the data model in Figure 2-3. The columnDefinition element is meant to specify a database specific SQL fragment for the column type that may be used when generating the DDL for the column. This element is only used by vendors that support database generation from mapping metadata (annotation or XML). The following illustrates typical usages of these features (Section 2.2.11).

```
@Entity
@Table(name="BOOK")
@SecondaryTable(name="CONTENT", pkJoinColumns=@PrimaryKeyJoinColumn(
  name="BOOK_ID_FPK", referencedColumnName="BOOK_ID_PK")
)
public class Book {
  @Column(
    table="CONTENT", name="PDF", columnDefinition="BLOB NOT NULL"
  )
  protected byte[] pdf;

  @Column(name="PRICE", precision=12, scale=2)
  protected double price;
}
```

JPA requires that a persistent attribute (field or property) must have one of the following data types:

- Java primitive types, such as int, double, long, short
- Java primitive wrappers, such as java.lang.Integer, java.lang.Double
- String type, such as java.lang.String
- Java API serializable types, such as java.math.BigDecimal, java.util.Date, java.util.Calendar, java.sql.Date, java.sql.Time, and java.sql.Timestamp
- User-defined serializable types: any class that implements java.io.Serializable
- Array types, such as byte[], char[], Byte[], Character[]
- Enumerated types, such as enum OrderStatus {COMPLETE, FILLED, NEW}

- Entity types, and collection of entity types, such as `Set<Book>`, `List<Category>`, `Collection<Address>`, and `Map<Integer, LineItem>`
- Embeddable classes: any classes that are annotated with `@Embeddable` (Section 2.2.12)
- Collection of basic types and embeddable classes

2.2.4 Access Types

In contrast to *field-based access*, where annotations are put directly on entity fields, one can also apply annotations on getter methods following the JavaBeans property access convention. This is referred to as *property-based access*. In this approach, the accessor methods must be either public or protected, and cannot be final. For example, the `Address` entity presented in Section 2.2.3 can be rewritten as:

```
@Entity
public class Address {
  // fields

  @Column(name = "STREET",
    updatable=true, insertable=true, nullable=false
  )
  public String getStreet() {
    return this.street;
  }

  public void setStreet(String street) {
    this.street = street;
  }

  @Column(name = "CITY")
  public String getCity() {
    return this.city;
  }

  public void setCity(String city) {
    this.city = city;
  }

  public String getState() {    // default to map to STATE column
    return this.state;
  }

  public void setState(String state) {
```

```
    this.state = state;
  }

  @Column(name = "ZIP", length=5, nullable=false)
  public String getZip() {      // string length must be <= 5
    return this.zip;
  }

  public void setZip(String zip) {
    this.zip = zip;
  }

  @Transient                    // this property not persisted to database
  public boolean isResidential() {
    // …
  }
}
```

In JPA 1.0, we have to use only one of the two access types for an entire entity class hierarchy. Starting from JPA 2.0, we can explicitly mix field-based access with property-based access for different classes (within a class hierarchy or not), and even for different attributes in an entity using @Access. For example,

```
@Entity
@Access(AccessType.PROPERTY)
public class Address {
  private String street;

  @Access(AccessType.FIELD)
  private String city;          // field-based access for this field only

  private String state;
  private String zip;

  @Column(name = "STREET",
    updatable=true, insertable=true, nullable=false
  )
  public String getStreet() {   // property-based access
    return this.street;
  }

  public void setStreet(String street) {
    this.street = street;
  }
```

```
  public String getState() {      // property-based access from class
    return this.state;            // default to map to STATE column
  }
}
```

The @Access annotation is used to specify an access type to be applied to an entity class, mapped super class, or embeddable class, or to a specific field or property of such a class. It is defined as:

```
@Target({TYPE, METHOD, FIELD}) @Retention(RUNTIME)
public @interface Access {
  AccessType value();
}

public enum javax.persistence.AccessType { FIELD, PROPERTY }
```

Nevertheless, a single access type (field or property access) applies to an entity hierarchy, by default. The default access type of an entity hierarchy is determined by the placement of mapping annotations on the fields or properties of the class hierarchy that do not explicitly specify an access type. When mixing field-based access with property-based access types, it is recommended to explicitly and unambiguously specify the access type using the @Access annotation or XML files. It is an error if our persistence provider cannot determine which access type is being used.

The question now is when to use field-based access vs. property-based access? When using field-based access type, a persistent field of an entity is persisted to the database and its getter and setter methods are not used by JPA. Since fields are typically defined at the beginning of an entity class, this approach does make the entity class look neat and well-organized by putting all annotations together and at the beginning of the entity definition. The downside seems to be that we give up the benefit of encapsulation and data hiding offered through the getter and setter methods. Even when field-based access is used, the getter/setter accessor methods are still recommended to be defined in an entity class.

When using property-based access type, the getter and setter methods are used and the corresponding fields are ignored by JPA. This approach seems to fit OO better. Also, certain business logic may be put in the accessor methods. For example, one may put some validation logic in the setter method to make sure that the value returned by the getter method can be correctly persisted to the database.

However, from now on, all examples in this book are shown using field-based access, unless certain features must be explained using property-based access.

2.2.5 @Lob and @Basic

Binary large objects (BLOB) and character large objects (CLOB) can be stored in many relational database systems. The annotation `@Lob` designates an attribute as CLOB or BLOB. Since large objects often occupy a lot of memory in the JVM, they are typically lazily-loaded using the annotation `@Basic` with fetch type specified to be `LAZY` (which is a hint that they are loaded from database only when they are first accessed). For example,

```
@Entity
public class Book {
  @Lob
  @Basic(fetch=FetchType.LAZY)
  @Column(table="CONTENT", name="PDF")
  protected byte[] pdf;
}

@Entity
public class Customer {
  @Lob
  @Basic(fetch=FetchType.LAZY, optional=false)
  @Column(name="PICTURE", columnDefinition="BLOB NOT NULL")
  protected byte[] picture;
}
```

When we fetch a `Book` object, say *book*, from the database, the values of all other fields of *book* are loaded except for the lazily-loaded `pdf` field. Only when we access the field such as in invoking `book.getPdf()`, will JPA fire another query to fetch the field from the database. However, this is a hint and JPA does not mandate this behavior. A persistence provider is permitted to eagerly load a field/property for which a lazy-loading strategy is specified. In reality, most JPA providers support lazy-loading.

JPA determines whether a `@Lob` annotated attribute is BLOB or CLOB by checking the data type. If the data is of type `char[]`, `Character[]`, `java.sql.CLOB`, or `String`, JPA maps the data as CLOB. Otherwise (for types such as `byte[]`, `Byte[]`, `java.sql.BLOB`, or other `java.io.Serializable`) it is mapped as BLOB.

The annotation `@Lob` does not have any element. However, `@Basic` has two optional elements:

```
@Target({METHOD, FIELD}) @Retention(RUNTIME)
public @interface Basic {
  FetchType fetch() default EAGER;
  boolean optional() default true;
}

public enum FetchType { LAZY, EAGER };
```

The `fetch` element may take two possible values: `FetchType.LAZY` and `FetchType.EAGER`. The latter means that the field or property must be eagerly fetched (at the same time when the entity is loaded, the opposite of lazy loading). The `optional` element is a hint to the persistence provider whether the value of the field/property may be null. When `optional` is specified to be true, the attribute is optional and may take on null value. `@Basic` may be applied to any persistent attribute of basic types that is mapped to a database column, and thus is not applicable to relationship attributes or element collections (see Section 2.3 and Section 4.1.3). Use of `@Basic` is optional. When omitted, the default values of its elements will apply.

Lazy loading is a powerful feature that may improve performance, since loading of such a field (potentially time and memory intensive) can be delayed to when it is first used by the application. However, it requires one more trip to the database when it is loaded. Thus use lazy loading only when it is appropriate.

2.2.6 @Temporal

Temporal data types differ in granularity levels corresponding to `DATE` (storing day, month, and year), `TIME` (storing just time, but not day, month, or year), and `TIMESTAMP` (storing time, day, month, and year). The annotation `@Temporal` must be specified for persistent attributes of type `java.util.Date` and `java.util.Calendar` to indicate such a granularity level. For example,

```
@Entity
@Table(name="PREFERRED_CUSTOMER")
public class PreferredCustomer {
  @Column(name = "EXPIRATION_DATE")
  @Temporal(TemporalType.DATE)
  protected java.util.Date expirationDate;    // only day, month, year
}
```

The @Temporal annotation must take one required value of type TemporalType, which is defined as

```
@Target({METHOD, FIELD}) @Retention(RUNTIME)
public @interface Temporal {
  TemporalType value();
}

public enum TemporalType {
  DATE,           // java.sql.Date
  TIME,           // java.sql.Time
  TIMESTAMP       // java.sql.Timestamp
}
```

If a persistent attribute has type java.sql.Date, java.sql.Time, or java.sql.Timestamp, such a mapping using @Temporal would be redundant and thus is not needed.

2.2.7 @Enumerated

If a persistent attribute has an enumeration type such as

```
public enum OrderStatus{ COMPLETE, FILLED, BILLED, NEW }
```

it can only take on one of the four values listed above, with the first element OrderStatus.COMPLETE having ordinal value of 0, the second element OrderStatus.FILLED having ordinal value of 1, and so on.

JPA provides two options when persisting such values into the database. One option is to persist the ordinal values (such as 0 for OrderStatus.COMPLETE) and the other is to persist the string values (such as "COMPLETE" for OrderStatus.COMPLETE). As we would imagine, persisting as ordinal values is the default behavior. For example,

```
@Entity
@Table(name="ORDERS")
public class Order {
  @Column(name="STATUS")
  @Enumerated(EnumType.ORDINAL)     // ORDINAL is actually the default
  protected OrderStatus status;
}
```

If the field `status` has value `OrderStatus.NEW`, then the value of 3 is persisted to the database. If we were to change the persistent enumeration type to

```
@Column(name="STATUS")
@Enumerated(EnumType.STRING)
protected OrderStatus status;
```

then for the field `status` with value of `OrderStatus.NEW`, the string `"NEW"` would be persisted to the database.

The `@Enumerated` annotation is defined as:

```
@Target({METHOD, FIELD}) @Retention(RUNTIME)
public @interface Enumerated {
  EnumType value() default ORDINAL;
}

public enum EnumType { ORDINAL, STRING }
```

The `@Enumerated` annotation itself is optional. When omitted, the enumerated type for the enumerated persistent field/property is assumed to be `ORDINAL`.

2.2.8 @Version

If any of the entities in an application are accessed concurrently by different users, with at least one of the users (or processes) modifying the data, then there is a chance that stale data may occur. That is, a user may be accessing some entities whose values are not current (being stale) from what is in the database, due to the fact that another user has modified them in the same time. If two or more users are modifying the same data at the same time, data corruption may occur.

People have mainly used two ways to resolve this issue: optimistic locking and pessimistic locking. JPA supports both. In pessimistic locking, an entity is locked so that only one transaction can modify or delete the data at a time (see Section 3.4). This is very secure since no two users can modify/delete the data at the same time. The downside is that it can be very inefficient since other users have to wait until the transaction that obtained the lock is finished. Optimistic locking assumes that contention does not happen very often, and allows different users to modify/delete the same data at the same time. However, if contention happens, it will be detected (typically by checking a version field), and stale data or corrupted data will not be committed to the database. See Section 3.4.1 for more details.

JPA introduces the @Version annotation to enable optimistic locking. All a developer needs to do is to create an extra column in the primary database table for an entity and map it to an attribute annotated with @Version in the entity. For example,

```
@Entity
public class Address {
  @Version
  @Column(name="VERSION")
  protected int version;
}
```

If a user retrieves an Address record from the database with address id 12345 and version 100, sees it displayed on a web page, and then modifies the zip code to be 48331, then JPA would generate an SQL update statement like this:

```
UPDATE ADDRESS SET ZIP = 48331, VERSION = 101
WHERE ADDRESS_ID_PK = 12345 AND VERSION = 100
```

Assume during the time interval after the user retrieved the record and before she committed the changes to the database, another user has modified the same record and the version has been incremented to 101. Then the update for the first user will fail and JPA throws an OptimisticLockException. This is typically how JPA ensures that stale data would not cause problems to data integrity.

The version field/property should be of type long, Long, int, Integer, short, Short, or Timestamp. The developer should not insert/modify this field since JPA manages it directly. Every time a versioned entity is modified, JPA increments the value of the version attribute automatically. JPA also uses this attribute to ensure data integrity when performing the merge operation. When a detached entity instance is merged to a persistent context, JPA checks the version value to ensure that the data in the detached entity has not become stale (otherwise, an optimistic lock exception will be thrown). Numeric versioning is recommended as a numeric value is more precise, portable, and performant than a timestamp value. Some databases even do not store a timestamp's milliseconds or do not store them precisely.

The @Version annotation is also simple to use since it does not contain any elements. Only a single Version property or field should be used per class.

2.2.9 @Id

All persistent entities must be uniquely identifiable by their primary keys in a persistence context managed by an entity manager. Thus the primary key is arguably the most important attribute in an entity. To specify the simple primary key field or property of an entity, use the annotation @Id. For example,

```
@Entity
@Table(name="BOOK")
public class Book {
  @Id
  @Column(name = "BOOK_ID_PK", updatable=false)
  protected int bookId;
}
```

The @Id annotation is also arguably the simplest one to use, as it does not contain any elements. Every entity must have an identity, which corresponds to the simple or composite primary key in the database table. See Sections 4.1.1 and 4.1.2 for composite primary keys. Once an entity instance becomes managed by a persistence context, or detached from it, the application must not change the value of a primary key or the value of a field in a composite primary key.

The primary key (or a field/property of a composite primary key) should have one of the following types:

- any Java primitive type, such as `long, int, short, double, float`
- any primitive wrapper type, such as `Long, Integer, Short, Double, Float`
- `java.math.BigInteger, BigDecimal, java.lang.String`
- `java.util.Date, java.sql.Date`

In general, however, approximate numeric types (e.g., floating point types such as float and Double) should never be used for primary keys. If generated primary keys are used (see the next subsection), only integral types will be portable. If `java.util.Date` is used as a primary key field or property, the temporal type should be specified as `DATE` (see Section 2.2.6).

The primary key must be defined on the root entity or mapped super class of an entity hierarchy, and it must be defined exactly once in the hierarchy. See Sections 2.2.13 and 4.3.

2.2.10   @GeneratedValue

In the data model in Figure 2-3, each table (except for the join table) has an ID column as its primary key, which is meant to be managed by JPA as an automatically generated field. Such a primary key is often referred to as *surrogate key*. Many people prefer to use surrogate keys over *natural keys*. The latter consists of business data (such as birthday and social security number), which is not easy to guarantee uniqueness from the business perspective and cannot be easily updated (the only way to update a primary key is to delete the record and insert a new one). Also, numeric sequence numbers are more efficient for querying, indexing, and managing foreign key relationships, than natural keys.

JPA provides an annotation @GeneratedValue to facilitate auto-generated fields such as surrogate keys, in three different ways: using identity columns, sequence number generators, and table sequence generators.

Identity Columns
Many databases such as DB2, MySQL, SQL Server, and Sybase support identity columns, which can be used to automatically generate primary keys as:

```
@Entity
@Table(name="BOOK")
public class Book {
  @Id
  @GeneratedValue(strategy = GenerationType.IDENTITY)
  @Column(name = "BOOK_ID_PK", updatable=false)
  protected int bookId;
}
```

This assumes that an identity constraint has been created on the BOOK_ID_PK column in the BOOK table. For databases that support it, this is very easy to use. Make sure you do not call Book.setBookId() in your code since JPA manages it automatically for you. However, there are a few issues. Since the ID is not assigned by the database until the record is inserted, the value of the ID may not be available until after commit or after a flush call on the entity manager. Also, identity sequencing does not support sequence preallocation (allocating a chunk of ID values at a time) and it may require a select call to the database to get the ID value for each object that is inserted. This could potentially cause performance problems.

Sequence Number Generators

This technique applies to databases that support sequence number generators such as Oracle. The first step is to create a sequence such as the following one in Oracle:

```
CREATE SEQUENCE BOOK_SEQ START 1 INCREMENT BY 30;
```

Then it can be used to define a JPA sequence generator and an auto-generated field as

```
@Entity
@Table(name="BOOK")
@SequenceGenerator(name = "BOOK_SEQ_GEN", sequenceName ="BOOK_SEQ",
  initialValue = 1, allocationSize = 30
)
public class Book {
  @Id
  @GeneratedValue(strategy=GenerationType.SEQUENCE,
    generator="BOOK_SEQ_GEN"
  )
  @Column(name = "BOOK_ID_PK", updatable=false)
  protected int bookId;
}
```

The `@SequenceGenerator` annotation creates a sequence generator in JPA named `BOOK_SEQ_GEN`, which is used in `@GeneratedValue` for the `generator` element. Notice that `BOOK_SEQ_GEN` relies on the database-defined sequence `BOOK_SEQ`. The `initialValue` element specifies the start value of the sequence and `allocationSize` specifies the amount to increment by when allocating sequence numbers from this sequence. Notice that we have used the same value for `INCREMENT BY` in the definition of the database sequence object and for `allocationSize` in `@SequenceGenerator`, which is recommended and may cause errors when these two values are not specified the same. Its full definition is:

```
@Target({TYPE, METHOD, FIELD}) @Retention(RUNTIME)
public @interface SequenceGenerator {
  String name();                          // generator name in JPA
  String sequenceName() default "";       // database sequence name
  String catalog() default "";       // database catalog for sequence
  String schema() default "";        // database schema for sequence
  int initialValue() default 1;      // start value for the sequence
  int allocationSize() default 50;
}
```

Note this annotation can be defined at class level and used for multiple entities and attributes.

Table Sequence Generators

This technique applies to all databases since it utilizes a database table to support sequence generation. The table has two columns, one storing the sequence name and the other storing the sequence value (which is the last ID value that was assigned). Each sequence object corresponds to a row in the sequence table. Each time a new entity object is inserted into the database, the number in the sequence value column for the entity is incremented and assigned to the new object.

For example, we create the following sequence table in Derby:

```
CREATE TABLE SEQUENCE_GENERATOR_TB
(
  SEQUENCE_NAME  VARCHAR(40) PRIMARY KEY,
  SEQUENCE_VALUE INTEGER
);
```

The column `SEQUENCE_NAME` is meant to store the name of a sequence and column `SEQUENCE_VALUE` to store the current value of the sequence. Then we can create many sequences such as `BOOK_SEQ` and `ADDRESS_SEQ` in the table as:

```
INSERT INTO SEQUENCE_GENERATOR_TB(SEQUENCE_NAME, SEQUENCE_VALUE)
  VALUES ('BOOK_SEQ', 1);

INSERT INTO SEQUENCE_GENERATOR_TB(SEQUENCE_NAME, SEQUENCE_VALUE)
  VALUES ('ADDRESS_SEQ', 1);
```

Each sequence occupies a row in the table. This may be pictorially depicted as in Figure 2-4.

SEQUENCE_GENERATOR_TB table	
SEQUENCE_NAME	SEQUENCE_VALUE
BOOK_SEQ	1
ADDRESS_SEQ	1

Figure 2-4 Table layout for table sequence generators.

With the one-time preparation work (which can be put in the same script as the table creation DDL and loaded once), then we can define JPA table generators and auto-generated fields as:

```
@Entity
@TableGenerator(name = "BOOK_SEQ_GEN", schema="JPATEST",
  table = "SEQUENCE_GENERATOR_TB",
  pkColumnName = "SEQUENCE_NAME",
  valueColumnName = "SEQUENCE_VALUE",
  pkColumnValue = "BOOK_SEQ"
)
public class Book {
  @Id
  @GeneratedValue(
    strategy=GenerationType.TABLE, generator="BOOK_SEQ_GEN"
  )
  @Column(name = "BOOK_ID_PK", updatable=false)
  protected int bookId;
}

@Entity
@TableGenerator(name = "ADDRESS_SEQ_GEN", schema="JPATEST",
  table = "SEQUENCE_GENERATOR_TB", pkColumnName = "SEQUENCE_NAME",
  valueColumnName = "SEQUENCE_VALUE", pkColumnValue = "ADDRESS_SEQ"
)
public class Address {
  @Id
  @GeneratedValue(strategy=GenerationType.TABLE,
    generator="ADDRESS_SEQ_GEN"
  )
  @Column(name = "ADDRESS_ID_PK", updatable=false)
  protected int addressId;
}
```

The following code snippet shows how easily this can be used for the insertion of a `Book` object:

```
Book b = new Book();
b.setIsbn("isbn1");
b.setTitle("Book1 Title");
b.setPrice(20.50);
```

54

```
b.setPdf("samplecontents".getBytes());

em.getTransaction().begin();
em.persist(b);

// auto generated ID is available after the persist operation
int bookId = b.getBookId();
System.out.println("inserted book id is: " + bookId);

em.getTransaction().commit();
```

The @TableGenerator annotation is defined as:

```
@Target({TYPE, METHOD, FIELD}) @Retention(RUNTIME)
public @interface TableGenerator {
  String name();                          // name of table sequence generator
  String table() default "";        // table to store sequences as rows
  String catalog() default "";
  String schema() default "";
  String pkColumnName() default "";     // column for sequence names
  String valueColumnName() default ""; // column for sequence values
  String pkColumnValue() default "";    // value of sequence name
  int initialValue() default 0;
  int allocationSize() default 50;      // default allocation size 50
  UniqueConstraint[] uniqueConstraints() default {};
}
```

Table sequencing is more portable than using database sequence objects and identity columns, because it just uses a regular database table, and can be used on any database.

The downside of table sequencing is that the sequence table may become a concurrency bottleneck. If the sequence IDs are allocated in the same transaction as the insert, the sequence row may be locked for the duration of the transaction. Thus choosing an appropriate allocation size (not too small) and storing an appropriate number of sequences in each sequence table will improve performance. Some JPA implementations even use a separate non-JTA connection to allocate the sequence IDs, and allow the configuration of a non-JTA data source, in addition to a JTA data source, in the case of JTA transactions.

Both sequence generators and table generators can be defined at the class level (or in XML at persistence unit level) and used by multiple entities, fields, or properties. Both of them support preallocation for possibly improving performance.

Default Generator

JPA supports the option for the persistence provider to choose a default strategy as in:

```
@Entity
public class Address {
  @Id
  @GeneratedValue(strategy=GenerationType.AUTO)
  @Column(name = "ADDRESS_ID", updatable=false)
  protected int addressId;
}
```

This is the simplest way to use automatic field generation. Depending on the underlying database characteristics, your JPA implementation provider hopefully chooses the best strategy. However, it may not be the case. Some persistence providers just use table generators since it is supported by all databases. Also, a persistence provider may choose to use identity columns for some databases and preallocation may not be supported.

2.2.11 @SecondaryTable

An entity can be mapped to multiple tables, with one being the primary table and others secondary tables. The annotation @Table is used to map the primary table, @SecondaryTable to map a secondary table, and @SecondaryTables to group all secondary tables together. JPA requires that the primary table and secondary tables share the same primary key, with the primary key of a secondary table mapped to the primary key of the primary table using @PrimaryKeyJoinColumn.

Mapping one entity to multiple tables seems to happen more frequently in legacy databases. However, it is the recommended approach in certain cases. For example, in the data model Figure 2-3, the table BOOK points to table CONTENT for PDF content. Since a book's PDF content can be very large in size, it could slow down queries using the BOOK table if it were stored together in the BOOK table. It is advisable to put the PDF content in a separate table and lazily load the book content only when it is needed. The mapping may look like this:

```
@Entity
@Table(name="BOOK")
@SecondaryTable(name="CONTENT", pkJoinColumns=@PrimaryKeyJoinColumn(
  name="BOOK_ID_FPK", referencedColumnName="BOOK_ID_PK")
)
public class Book {
```

```
@Basic(fetch=FetchType.LAZY)
@Lob
@Column(table="CONTENT", name="PDF")
protected byte[] pdf;
}
```

The annotation

```
@PrimaryKeyJoinColumn(
  name="BOOK_ID_FPK", referencedColumnName="BOOK_ID_PK"
)
```

joins the tables BOOK and CONTENT using their primary keys. The name element specifies the primary key for the source table CONTENT, which is BOOK_ID_FPK. It is a foreign key to the primary key BOOK_ID_PK of the target table BOOK, which populates the referencedColumnName element. Both elements are optional. When omitted, the name element defaults to the primary key of the source table, and the referencedColumnName element defaults to the primary key of the referenced table. In the case above, both tables have simple primary keys. In case of composite primary keys, the syntax for the mapping would use a comma-separated list inside a pair of braces – the same way as array initialization:

```
@SecondaryTable(name="CONTENT", pkJoinColumns={
  @PrimaryKeyJoinColumn(name="BOOK_ID_FPK",
    referencedColumnName="BOOK_ID_PK"),
  @PrimaryKeyJoinColumn(name="BOOK_ID_FPK2",
    referencedColumnName="BOOK_ID_PK2")}
)
```

If there is more than one secondary table, use @SecondaryTables as (again, the same way as array initialization):

```
@SecondaryTables({
  @SecondaryTable(name="table1", pkJoinColumns=...),
  @SecondaryTable(name="table2", pkJoinColumns=...)
})
```

The annotation definitions are:

```
@Target({TYPE}) @Retention(RUNTIME)
public @interface SecondaryTable {
```

```
  String name();                       // name of secondary table
  String catalog() default "";         // catalog of secondary table
  String schema() default "";          // schema of secondary table
  PrimaryKeyJoinColumn[] pkJoinColumns() default {};
  UniqueConstraint[] uniqueConstraints() default {};
}

@Target({TYPE}) @Retention(RUNTIME)
public @interface SecondaryTables {
  SecondaryTable[] value();
}

@Target({TYPE, METHOD, FIELD}) @Retention(RUNTIME)
public @interface PrimaryKeyJoinColumn {
  String name() default "";                    // PK of source table
  String referencedColumnName() default ""; // PK of referenced table
  String columnDefinition() default "";
}
```

The annotation @PrimaryKeyJoinColumn may be used in mapping secondary tables, entity inheritance (Section 4.3), and one-to-one relationship (Section 2.3.1). But the annotation itself is optional. When omitted, the default values of its elements will apply.

2.2.12   @Embeddable and @Embedded

The annotations @Embeddable and @Embedded are to model objects that are merely data holders, which are stored as part of a separate entity. Embeddable classes do not have their own identity and are not directly persisted into a database table. Instead, they are intended to be embedded into entities that have identities and are mapped to database tables. For example, we may group banking information together as an embedded object for the Customer entity as:

```
@Embeddable
public class BankInfo {
  @Column(name = "BANK_NAME_X")
  private String bankName;

  @Column(name = "BANK_ACCOUNT_NUMBER")
  private String accountNumber;

  @Column(name = "BANK_ROUTING_NUMBER")
  private String routingNumber;
```

```
  // getter and setter methods
}
```

The `BankInfo` class is not an entity, since it does not have an identity and is not directly mapped to any table (although its fields can be mapped to certain columns that we do not know to which table they belong at this moment). Its main purpose is to be embedded into an entity, which is mapped to a specific table, as:

```
@Entity
@Table(name = "CUSTOMER")
public class Customer {
  @Embedded
  private BankInfo bank;

  @Id private int customerId;
}
```

It implies that the field `bank.bankName` is mapped to the `BANK_NAME_X` column of the `CUSTOMER` table, by default. In fact, the column mapping of `BankInfo` can be overridden when it is embedded into an enclosing entity. For example,

```
@Entity
@Table(name = "CUSTOMER")
public class Customer {
  @Embedded
  @AttributeOverrides({
    @AttributeOverride(
      name="bankName", column=@Column(name="BANK_NAME")),
    @AttributeOverride(
      name = "accountNumber",
      column = @Column(name ="ACCOUNT_NUMBER")),
    @AttributeOverride(
      name = "routingNumber",
      column = @Column(name = "ROUTING_NUMBER"))
  })
  private BankInfo bank;

  @Id private integer customerId;
}
```

The definitions of `@AttributeOverride` and `@AttributeOverrides` are:

```
@Target({TYPE, METHOD, FIELD}) @Retention(RUNTIME)
public @interface AttributeOverride {
```

```
    String name();
    Column column();
}

@Target({TYPE, METHOD, FIELD}) @Retention(RUNTIME)
public @interface AttributeOverrides {
    AttributeOverride[] value();
}
```

The `name` element specifies the name of a persistent attribute (field or property) to override, and the `column` element specifies the column in the table corresponding to the containing class. Thus the code above means that the persistent field `bank.bankName` is overridden to map to BANK_NAME column in the CUSTOMER table. Similar explanation holds for other fields. See Section 2.2.13 for an example with `@AttributeOverride` applied at a class level.

An embeddable class may contain other embeddable classes or relationships to other entities. It may also contain a collection of a basic type or other embeddable class. To access fields/properties of nested embeddable objects, a dot (".") notation syntax must be used; see Section 2.3.4 for an example.

2.2.13   @MappedSuperclass

If there are common persistent attributes among different classes, those attributes can certainly be put into a super class, annotated with `@MappedSuperclass`, which can be inherited by different derived classes. The mapped super class may have its own identity, but must not map to a database table directly (otherwise it will be a standalone entity and `@Entity` should be used). It is similar to `@Embeddable`, which supports composition. But `@MappedSuperclass` supports inheritance. For example, all our entities have the version and auditing fields, which can certainly be put into a super class and inherited by every entity:

```
import java.io.Serializable;
import java.sql.Timestamp;
import java.util.Date;
import javax.persistence.Column;
import javax.persistence.MappedSuperclass;
import javax.persistence.Temporal;
import javax.persistence.TemporalType;
import javax.persistence.Version;

@MappedSuperclass
```

```
public class BaseEntity implements Serializable {
  @Version protected int version;

  @Column(name="CREATE_USER")
  protected String createUser;

  @Column(name="CREATE_TIME")
  @Temporal(TemporalType.TIMESTAMP)
  protected Date createTime;

  @Column(name="UPDATE_USER")
  protected String updateUser;

  @Column(name="UPDATE_TIME")
  @Temporal(TemporalType.TIMESTAMP)
  protected Date updateTime;

  // getters and setters
}
```

A mapped super class or entity may inherit the persistent attributes of the mapped super class as:

```
@MappedSuperclass
public class User extends BaseEntity { ... }

@Entity
public class Customer extends User { ... }
```

A derived entity such as `Book` can override the mapping on the inherited attributes as:

```
@Entity
@Table(name="BOOK")
@AttributeOverrides({
  @AttributeOverride(name = "createUser",
    column = @Column(name = "BOOK_CREATE_USER")),
  @AttributeOverride(name = "createTime",
    column = @Column(name = "BOOK_CREATE_TIME")),
  @AttributeOverride(name = "updateUser",
    column = @Column(name = "BOOK_UPDATE_USER")),
  @AttributeOverride(name = "updateTime",
    column = @Column(name = "BOOK_UPDATE_TIME"))
})
public class Book extends BaseEntity { ... }
```

The persistent attribute `createUser` is overridden to map to column `BOOK_CREATE_USER` in the `BOOK` table. The definition of the annotation `@AttributeOverride` is given in Section 2.2.12.

2.3 Relationship Mapping

Entities are most often inter-connected with relationships in the form of one-to-one, one-to-many, many-to-one, or many-to-many. They are typically mapped to multiple tables that are joined together with foreign keys and possibly association tables. This section talks about how to map entity relationships to database tables.

2.3.1 @OneToOne

A one-to-one relationship is most often modeled in the database by a foreign key. For example, entity `Customer` has a one-to-one relationship to entity `Address`. On the database side, table `CUSTOMER` has a foreign key pointing to the primary key of table `ADDRESS`. The annotations `@OneToOne` and `@JoinColumn` are used to map such a scenario:

```
@Entity
@Table(name = "CUSTOMER")
public class Customer extends User {
  @OneToOne(cascade=CascadeType.PERSIST)
  @JoinColumn(
    name = "ADDRESS_ID_FK", referencedColumnName="ADDRESS_ID_PK"
  )
  protected Address address;
}
```

The annotation `@OneToOne` indicates a one-to-one relationship from `Customer` to `Address`. Its cascade policy element has value: `CascadeType.PERSIST`, which means when a `Customer` object is persisted, its associated `Address` object is persisted as well and there is no need to invoke the `persist()` method on the associated `Address` object explicitly. For example,

```
Customer c = new Customer();
Address a = new Address();
c.setAddress(a);
em.persist(c);  // no need to call em.persist(a) due to cascade policy
```

Other cascade policies are: `CascadeType.MERGE` (the `merge` operation propagates to associated objects), `CascadeType.REMOVE`, and `CascadeType.REFRESH`, `CascadeType.DETACH`, and `CascadeType.ALL` (all of above operations propagate to associated objects).

The `@JoinColumn` annotation specifies how the two related tables are joined. The `name` element specifies the name of the foreign key column, while the `referencedColumnName` element indicates the column name referenced by the foreign key column, which may be omitted when it is the primary key column of the referenced table. When the `name` element is omitted, it defaults to the concatenation of the following: name of the relationship field/property of the referencing entity or embeddable; "_"; name of the referenced primary key column. In the case above, it would default to `ADDRESS_ADDRESS_ID_PK`. For a valid one-to-one relationship, a unique constraint must be imposed on the foreign key column. The `@JoinColumn` annotation is optional. When it is omitted, its default values apply.

For a bidirectional relationship, JPA defines the owning side and the inverse side. The *owning side* refers to the side that is responsible for updating the relationship in the database, while the *inverse side* is the opposite side. A unidirectional relationship has only an owning side. In the `Customer` and `Address` relationship, if we model it as bidirectional, the `Customer` side is the owning side since it is responsible for updating the foreign key `ADDRESS_ID_FK` and the `Address` side is the inverse side. JPA requires that mapping be defined on the owning side and the inverse side simply refers to it by using the `mappedBy` element of the `@OneToOne` annotation. On the inverse side, the code looks like this:

```
@Entity
public class Address extends BaseEntity {
  @OneToOne(mappedBy="address")
  protected Customer customer;          // inverse side of relationship
}
```

The `mappedBy` element refers to the field/property of the relationship on the owning side. Notice that JPA supports *polymorphic association* in that the `customer` field of `Address` may be of type `GoldCustomer`, `PreferredCustomer`, or even a regular `Customer`. Its real type is determined at run-time. This is similar to *polymorphic queries* (see Section 5.3.5).

All the elements of the annotation `@OneToOne` and their default values are given below.

```
@Target({METHOD, FIELD}) @Retention(RUNTIME)
public @interface OneToOne {
  Class targetEntity() default void.class;
  CascadeType[] cascade() default {};    // cascade policy
  FetchType fetch() default EAGER;    // lazy- or eager-loading?
  boolean optional() default true;    // association field required?
  String mappedBy() default "";       // inverse side of relationship
  boolean orphanRemoval() default false; // remove orphaned objects?
}
```

The `targetEntity` element defines the entity class that is the target of the association. It is not normally necessary to specify it explicitly since it can usually be inferred from the type of the referenced object. It is more often used in one-to-many and many-to-many relationships. The `orphanRemoval` element is intended for child entities that are privately "owned" by their parent entity, which means that the child entities cannot exist without their parent. If `orphanRemoval` is true, then an orphaned entity object will be removed at the time of the `flush` or `commit` operation. A child entity object becomes orphaned when it is removed from the relationship with its parent object (e.g., by setting the relationship to null or by deleting the parent object). For example,

```
@Entity
public class Customer {
  @OneToOne(orphanRemoval=true, targetEntity=Address.class)
  @JoinColumn(
    name = "ADDRESS_ID_FK", referencedColumnName="ADDRESS_ID_PK"
  )
  protected Address address;
}
```

In this case, when an `Address` object in managed state is removed from its related parent `Customer` object, it will become orphaned and the `remove` operation of the entity manager will be applied to it by JPA at `flush` time. Also, if the `Customer` parent object is removed, the `address` child object is automatically deleted. Thus specifying a `CascadeType.REMOVE` policy on the `address` relationship attribute would be redundant.

If the entity being orphaned is a detached, new, or removed entity, the semantics of `orphanRemoval` do not apply. Portable applications must not depend upon a specific order of removal in an object hierarchy, and must not reassign an orphaned object to another relationship or attempt to persist it.

The definition of the `@JoinColumn` annotation is:

```
@Target({METHOD, FIELD}) @Retention(RUNTIME)
public @interface JoinColumn {
  String name() default "";                      // foreign key column
  String referencedColumnName() default ""; // referenced column
  boolean unique() default false;       // values in column unique?
  boolean nullable() default true;      // values in column nullable?
  boolean insertable() default true;    // foreign key insertable?
  boolean updatable() default true;     // foreign key updatable?
  String columnDefinition() default "";// SQL for FK column type
  String table() default "";            // table containing FK column
}
```

The `name` and `referencedColumnName` elements and their defaults are explained early in this subsection. All remaining elements refer to the column indicated by the `name` element and have the same semantics as `@Column` (see Section 2.2.3). In particular, the `table` element refers to the name of the table that contains the column identified by the `name` element. Such table may be the join table or the table for the target entity in a unidirectional one-to-many mapping (see the next subsection). When the annotation `@JoinColumn` itself is omitted, the default values of its elements apply and the corresponding foreign key column names have to follow the defaulted naming convention.

If there is more than one join column, the annotation `@JoinColums` must be used, which specifies an array of `@JoinColumn` elements. For example,

```
@OneToOne(cascade={CascadeType.PERSIST,CascadeType.REMOVE})
@JoinColumns({
  @JoinColumn(name="STREET_FK", referencedColumnName="STREET_PK"),
  @JoinColumn(name="ZIP_FK", referencedColumnName="ZIP_PK")
})
protected Address2 address2;
```

When using a foreign key mapping strategy, if the foreign key is also the primary key (that is, the two tables share the same primary key values), the relationship mapping can be simplified using the annotation `@PrimaryKeyJoinColumn`. For example, the tables BOOK and CONTENT share the same primary key values. If we were to model this as a one-to-one relationship verses the way in Section 2.2.11, we would introduce an entity `Content` and do the following mapping:

```
@Entity
public class Book {
  @OneToOne(mappedBy="book", fetch=FetchType.LAZY)
  protected Content content;
}

@Entity
public class Content {
  @Id
  @Column(name = "BOOK_ID_FPK")
  protected int bookId;

  @OneToOne
  @PrimaryKeyJoinColumn(
    name = "BOOK_ID_FPK", referencedColumnName = "BOOK_ID_PK"
  )
  protected Book book;

  @Lob
  @Column(name = "PDF")
  protected byte[] pdf;
}
```

The definition of `@PrimaryKeyJoinColumn` is given in Section 2.2.11. If it is a composite primary key (see Section 4.1.1 and Section 4.1.2), use `@PrimaryKeyJoinColumns`. For example,

```
@OneToOne
@PrimaryKeyJoinColumns({
  @PrimaryKeyJoinColumn(
    name="STREET_FK",referencedColumnName="STREET_PK"),
  @PrimaryKeyJoinColumn(
    name="ZIP_FK", referencedColumnName="ZIP_PK")
})
protected Address2 address;
```

Another way (which is very rare) of mapping a one-to-one relationship is to use a join table (association table) to store the primary keys of the two related tables. Each row of the join table relates a primary key of the source entity to a primary key of the target entity. A unique constraint should be imposed on the two primary key columns in the join table to ensure a valid one-to-one mapping. Its mapping is similar to the case of many-to-many relationship and the annotation @JoinTable is used; see Section 2.3.3 for details.

2.3.2 @ManyToOne and @OneToMany

In a bidirectional one-to-many relationship, the *many* side is typically responsible for updating the relationship. For example, for Customer and Order, the *many* side (Order side) stores the foreign key pointing to the primary key of Customer. When a relationship changes, this foreign key has to be updated in the ORDERS table. Thus the Order side is the owning side and the Customer side is the inverse side. Similarly, in the many-to-one relationship between LineItem and Order, the LineItem side is the owning side and the Order side is the inverse side. Mappings must be done on the owning side and the mappedBy element should be used on the inverse side as:

```
@Entity
@Table(name="ORDERS")
public class Order extends BaseEntity {
  @ManyToOne(optional=false)          // an order must have a customer
  @JoinColumn(
    name="CUSTOMER_ID_FK", referencedColumnName="CUSTOMER_ID_PK"
  )
  protected Customer customer;        // owning side of relationship
}

@Entity
public class Customer extends User {
  @OneToMany(mappedBy = "customer", orphanRemoval=true)
  protected Set<Order> orders;        // inverse side of relationship
}
```

Similarly, the mapping for the LineItem to Order many-to-one relationship can be done as:

```
@Entity
@Table(name="LINE_ITEM")
public class LineItem extends BaseEntity {
  @ManyToOne
  @JoinColumn(name="ORDER_ID_FK", referencedColumnName="ORDER_ID_PK")
  protected Order order;                  // owning side of the relationship
}

@Entity
@Table(name="ORDERS")
```

```
public class Order extends BaseEntity {
  @OneToMany(mappedBy="order",
    cascade={CascadeType.PERSIST, CascadeType.REMOVE}
  )
  protected List<LineItem> lineItems;  // inverse side of relationship
}
```

The definitions of these two annotations are:

```
@Target({METHOD, FIELD}) @Retention(RUNTIME)
public @interface ManyToOne {
  Class targetEntity() default void.class;
  CascadeType[] cascade() default {};   // cascade policy
  FetchType fetch() default EAGER;      // lazy or eager-loading?
  boolean optional() default true;      // required field or not?
}

@Target({METHOD, FIELD}) @Retention(RUNTIME)
public @interface OneToMany {
  Class targetEntity() default void.class; // type of target entity
  CascadeType[] cascade() default {};
  FetchType fetch() default LAZY;          // default is LAZY here
  String mappedBy() default "";            // only on inverse side
  boolean orphanRemoval() default false;   // remove orphaned object?
}
```

When Java generics is not used, the targetEntity element on the *one* side of a one-to-many relationship is essential to specify the type of the target entity:

```
@Entity
public class Customer extends User {
  @OneToMany(mappedBy="customer",
    orphanRemoval=true, targetEntity=Order.class
  )
  protected Set orders;    // set objects specified by target entity
}
```

In this case, the association field is of type Set. The targetEntity element specifies that it is a set of Order objects. Note that orphanRemoval element is set to true, which means that if an order of a customer is removed from the relationship (either by removal from the collection or by setting the relationship to null), the remove operation of the entity manager will be applied to the orphaned order object.

When the type of a relationship collection attribute is `java.util.Map`, the map value must be the associated entity and the map key may be a basic type, embeddable class, or an entity (Section 4.2.1). Also, the `cascade` element and the `orphanRemoval` element apply to the map value. The `CascadeType.REMOVE` applies to only one-to-one and one-to-many relationship attributes. Using it on many-to-one and many-to-many relationships is not portable.

An interesting one-to-many relationship is the one for parent category and child categories, both sides being in the same entity and in the same table:

```
@Entity
public class Category extends BaseEntity {
  @ManyToOne
  @JoinColumn(
    name="PARENT_CATEGORY_FK", referencedColumnName="CATEGORY_ID_PK"
  )
  protected Category parentCategory;

  @OneToMany(mappedBy="parentCategory")
  protected Collection<Category> childCategories;
}
```

JPA 2.0 adds support on unidirectional one-to-many relationship on the *one* side using a foreign key mapping. For example, if we decide to model `Customer` and `Order` as unidirectional with the same table structure, we would define the mapping on the *one* (`Customer`) side as:

```
@Entity
public class Customer extends User {
  @OneToMany(orphanRemoval=true)
  @JoinColumn(
    name="CUSTOMER_ID_FK", referencedColumnName="CUSTOMER_ID_PK"
  )
  protected Set<Order> orders;
}

@Entity
@Table(name="ORDERS")
public class Order extends BaseEntity {
  // customer is not defined here for the unidirectional mapping
}
```

In some cases, a join table (association table) is used to store the primary keys of the two related tables in a one-to-many or many-to-one relationship. Each row of the join table relates a primary key of the source entity to a primary key of the target entity. Its mapping is similar to the case of many-to-many relationship and the annotation `@JoinTable` is used; see Section 2.3.3 for details. It should be noted that, with the JPA 2.0 new feature, the join table mapping strategy is typically no longer needed for unidirectional one-to-many relationship, due to its complexity and possible performance problems (joins would be needed between the primary table and the association table).

However, there is a small downside to this JPA 2.0 new feature. In the example above, the `Order` entity has no reference back to `Customer`. Thus the foreign key column `CUSTOMER_ID_FK` in table `ORDERS` cannot be controlled by the `Order` entity. If there is some update to an `Order` instance and this order has to be changed to belong to another `Customer`, two database accesses would be needed to update this one row in the `ORDERS` table: once for updating the columns corresponding to `Order` and another for updating the foreign key column through the corresponding `Customer`. This would be accomplished in one database access in a bidirectional relationship.

In this subsection, we have encountered collection-valued persistent attributes, such as the `orders` field of `Customer`. In JPA, a collection-valued persistent attribute must be defined using one of the interface types: `Collection`, `List`, `Set`, or `Map` in package `java.util`. The implementation classes of these types may be used to initialize fields or properties before an entity instance is made persistent. Once the entity instance becomes managed or detached, subsequent access must be through the interface types.

2.3.3 @ManyToMany

For a many-to-may relationship such as `Book` and `Category`, a join table (association table) such as `BOOK_CATEGORY` in Figure 2-3 is created to store the relationship (foreign keys pointing to both tables). Both entities are symmetrical in this relationship, and any side may be picked as the owning side and the other side will be the inverse side. For the `Book` and `Category` many-to-many relationship, let us pick `Book` as the owning side and `Category` as the inverse side. Then the mapping can be done like this:

```
@Entity
@Table(name="BOOK")
public class Book extends BaseEntity {
  @ManyToMany
  @JoinTable(name = "BOOK_CATEGORY",
```

```
    joinColumns=@JoinColumn(
      name="BOOK_ID_FPK", referencedColumnName="BOOK_ID_PK"),
    inverseJoinColumns=@JoinColumn(
      name="CATEGORY_ID_FPK",
      referencedColumnName = "CATEGORY_ID_PK")
  )
  protected Set<Category> categories;
}

@Entity
public class Category extends BaseEntity {
  @ManyToMany(mappedBy="categories")
  protected Set<Book> books;
}
```

The name element of @JoinTable specifies the name of the join table. It contains only two columns BOOK_ID_FPK and CATEGORY_ID_FPK that form the composite primary key for the join table and are foreign keys to primary keys of tables BOOK and CATEGORY. If the name element is omitted, it defaults to the concatenation of the name of the primary table on the owning side; "_"; and the name of the primary table on the inverse side. The joinColumns element specifies the relationship to table BOOK on the owning side and the inverseJoinColumns element describes the relationship to table CATEGORY on the inverse side. The default foreign key columns in the join table are: the concatenation of the name of the relationship attribute; "_"; and the name of the primary key column in the table, to which this relationship attribute corresponds. In the example above, the defaulted foreign key columns would be: BOOKS_BOOK_ID_PK and CATEGORIES_CATEGORY_ID_PK. In the case of a unidirectional relationship, the missing relationship attribute name has to be replaced by its corresponding entity name. If the relationship attribute books were to be removed from the Category entity, the corresponding defaulted foreign key column name would be BOOK_BOOK_ID_PK instead of BOOKS_BOOK_ID_PK.

When the annotation @JoinTable is omitted, all the default values of its elements apply. The annotation @JoinTable is defined as:

```
@Target({METHOD, FIELD}) @Retention(RUNTIME)
public @interface JoinTable {
  String name() default "";                 // name of the join table
  String catalog() default "";              // catalog of join table
  String schema() default "";               // schema of join table
  JoinColumn[] joinColumns() default {};        // for owning side
```

```
  JoinColumn[] inverseJoinColumns() default {};  // for inverse side
  UniqueConstraint[] uniqueConstraints() default {};
}
```

All the elements of the @ManyToMany annotation are:

```
@Target({METHOD, FIELD}) @Retention(RUNTIME)
public @interface ManyToMany {
  Class targetEntity() default void.class;
  CascadeType[] cascade() default {};
  FetchType fetch() default LAZY;
  String mappedBy() default "";
}
```

The mappedBy element can only be applied to the inverse side of a bidirectional relationship. It makes use of the mapping defined on the owning side and thus avoids redundancy.

Mapping a unidirectional many-to-many relationship is trivial in that it only defines the mapping on the owning side and the inverse side does not exist.

2.3.4 @AssociationOveride

The @AssociationOverride annotation is used to override a relationship mapping defined in a mapped super class or an embeddable class. For example, suppose we have a mapped super class User, where a one-to-one relationship is defined to Address, and we want to override this relationship in a derived class Customer. Then the code would look like this:

```
@MappedSuperclass
public class User extends BaseEntity {
  protected String name;

  @Lob
  @Basic(fetch=FetchType.LAZY, optional=false)
  protected byte[] picture;

  @OneToOne(cascade=CascadeType.PERSIST)
  @JoinColumn(name = "ADDRESS_ID", referencedColumnName="ADDRESS_ID")
  protected Address address;

  @Access(AccessType.PROPERTY)
  @Lob
```

```
@Basic(fetch=FetchType.LAZY, optional=false)
@Column(name="PICTURE", columnDefinition="BLOB NOT NULL")
public byte[] getPicture() {
  return this.picture;
}

// ...
}


@Entity
@Table(name = "CUSTOMER")
@AssociationOverride(name="address", joinColumns=@JoinColumn(
  name = "ADDRESS_ID_FK", referencedColumnName="ADDRESS_ID_PK"))
public class Customer extends User {... }
```

The `name` element of `@AssociationOverride` specifies the name of the relationship filed/property whose mapping is being overridden. To override mappings at multiple levels of embedded objects, a dot (".") notation syntax must be used in the name element to indicate an attribute within an embedded attribute. For example, to override an association defined in embedded class `Country`, which is embedded in `Address`, we may do:

```
@AssociationOverride(name = "address.country",
  joinColumns=@JoinColumn(name = "COUNTRY_ID_FK")
)
```

If the relationship is mapped using a foreign key, the `joinColumns` element of `@AssociationOverride` must be used. If the relationship mapping uses a join table, the `joinTable` element must be specified to override the mapping of the join table and/or its join columns. The definition is:

```
@Target({TYPE, METHOD, FIELD}) @Retention(RUNTIME)
public @interface AssociationOverride {
  String name();
  JoinColumn[] joinColumns() default {};
  JoinTable joinTable() default @JoinTable;
}
```

When there is more than one association to override, use `@AssociationOverrides` as:

```
@AssociationOverrides({
  @AssociationOverride(name = "address", joinColumns =...),
  @AssociationOverride(name = "phone", joinTable =...)
```

```
})
```

2.3.5 @OrderBy and @OrderColumn

For one-to-many and many-to-many associations, there may be a list of associated entity instances to be returned. The annotation `@OrderBy` may be used to specify an order for the list of associated entity instances at the point when the association is retrieved from the database. It can also be used for element collections of a basic type and an embeddable class (Section 4.1.3).

For example, for a `Category` there may be many `Books`, and we may specify the books to be sorted by `title` in ascending order and `price` in descending order, as:

```java
@Entity
public class Category extends BaseEntity {
  @ManyToMany(mappedBy="categories")
  @OrderBy("title ASC, price DESC")
  protected List<Book> books;
}
```

Generally, specify the order as a list of comma-delimited fields/properties and use `ASC` for ascending order and `DESC` for descending order (default is `ASC`). When there are embedded classes (or multiple levels of them), a dot (".") notation syntax may be used. If no fields or properties are specified, `@OrderBy` assumes ordering by the primary key of the associated entity.

The annotation `@OrderColumn` specifies a column that is used to maintain the persistent order of a list upon retrieval and in the database. JPA is responsible for updating the ordering upon flushing to the database to reflect any insertion, deletion, or reordering affecting the list. Imagine how much overhead it is to maintain such an ordered list of elements in memory and in the database. In order for this to be done efficiently, JPA requires that the order column be of integral type. This annotation may be specified on a one-to-many or many-to-many relationship or on an element collection (Section 4.1.3). The `@OrderBy` annotation need not be used when `@OrderColumn` is specified. Notice that `@OrderBy` does the ordering in memory only, not in the database, while `@OrderColumn` does both. For example, the orders for a customer may be sorted by its order ID upon retrieval and in the database, and the categories for a book may be sorted by its category ID as:

```
@Entity
public class Customer extends BaseEntity {
  @OneToMany(mappedBy = "customer", orphanRemoval=true)
  @OrderColumn(name="ORDER_ID_PK")
  protected List<Order> orders;
}


@Entity
public class Book extends BaseEntity {
  @ManyToMany
  @JoinTable(name = "BOOK_CATEGORY",
    joinColumns=@JoinColumn(
      name="BOOK_ID_FPK", referencedColumnName="BOOK_ID_PK"),
    inverseJoinColumns=@JoinColumn(
      name="CATEGORY_ID_FPK", referencedColumnName = "CATEGORY_ID_PK")
  )
  @OrderColumn(name="CATEGORY_ID_PK")
  protected List<Category> categories;
}
```

The `name` element of `@OrderColumn` specifies the name of the ordering column. If omitted, it defaults to the concatenation of the following: name of the referencing field/property; "_"; "ORDER".

JPA maintains a contiguous (non-sparse) ordering of the values of the order column when updating the association or element collection. The ordering column value for the first element of the list is 0. The annotation for `@OrderColumn` is:

```
@Target({METHOD, FIELD}) @Retention(RUNTIME)
public @interface OrderColumn {
  String name() default "";           // name of the order column
  boolean nullable() default true;    // is this column nullable?
  boolean insertable() default true;  // included in insert SQL?
  boolean updatable() default true;   // included in update SQL?
  String columnDefinition() default "";
}
```

2.4 Sample Mapping

In this section, we show the complete annotation mapping for the sample entities: `Order`, `LineItem`, `Book`, and `Category`. For brevity, we use field-based access and show just the annotations on the fields. All getter, setter, and other methods are omitted. The entities `Address`, `Customer`, `PreferredCustomer`, and `GoldCustomer` are shown in Section 4.4.

Listing 2-1 BaseEntity.java: Mapped super class for all entities in book ordering system.

```java
@MappedSuperclass
public class BaseEntity implements Serializable {

  @Version
  protected int version;

  @Column(name="CREATE_USER")
  protected String createUser;

  @Column(name="CREATE_TIME")
  @Temporal(TemporalType.TIMESTAMP)
  protected Date createTime;

  @Column(name="UPDATE_USER")
  protected String updateUser;

  @Column(name="UPDATE_TIME")
  @Temporal(TemporalType.TIMESTAMP)
  protected Date updateTime;
}
```

Listing 2-2 Order.java: The Order entity.

```java
@Entity
@Table(name="ORDERS")
public class Order extends BaseEntity {
  @Id
  @TableGenerator(name = "ORDER_SEQ_GEN",
    table = "SEQUENCE_GENERATOR_TB",
    pkColumnName = "SEQUENCE_NAME",
    valueColumnName = "SEQUENCE_VALUE",
    pkColumnValue = "ORDERS_SEQ"
  )
  @GeneratedValue(
```

```
    strategy = GenerationType.TABLE, generator = "ORDER_SEQ_GEN"
  )
  @Column(name="ORDER_ID_PK", updatable=false)
  protected int orderId;

  protected double price;

  @Column(name="ORDER_TIME")
  protected Timestamp orderTime;

  @Column(name="STATUS")
  @Enumerated(EnumType.ORDINAL)
  protected OrderStatus status;

  @ManyToOne(optional=false)
  @JoinColumn(
    name="CUSTOMER_ID_FK", referencedColumnName="CUSTOMER_ID_PK"
  )
  protected  Customer customer;        // owning side of the relationship

  @OneToMany(mappedBy="order",
    cascade={CascadeType.PERSIST, CascadeType.REMOVE}
  )
  protected  List<LineItem> lineItems;
}
```

Listing 2-3 LineItem.java: The LineItem entity.

```
@Entity
@Table(name="LINE_ITEM")
public class LineItem extends BaseEntity {
  @Id
  @TableGenerator(name = "LM_SEQ_GEN",
    table = "SEQUENCE_GENERATOR_TB",
    pkColumnName = "SEQUENCE_NAME",
    valueColumnName = "SEQUENCE_VALUE",
    pkColumnValue = "LINE_ITEM_SEQ"
  )
  @GeneratedValue(
    strategy = GenerationType.TABLE,  generator = "LM_SEQ_GEN"
  )
  @Column(name="LINE_ITEM_ID_PK", updatable=false)
  protected int lineItemId;
```

```java
    protected int quantity;

    protected double price;

    @ManyToOne
    @JoinColumn(name="BOOK_ID_FK", referencedColumnName="BOOK_ID_PK")
    protected Book book;

    @ManyToOne
    @JoinColumn(name="ORDER_ID_FK", referencedColumnName="ORDER_ID_PK")
    protected Order order;              // owning side of the relationship
}
```

Listing 2-4 Book.java: The Book entity.

```java
@Entity
@Table(name = "BOOK")
@SecondaryTable(name = "CONTENT", pkJoinColumns =
@PrimaryKeyJoinColumn(
  name = "BOOK_ID_FPK", referencedColumnName = "BOOK_ID_PK")
)
@AttributeOverrides({
  @AttributeOverride(
    name = "createUser", column = @Column(name = "BOOK_CREATE_USER")),
  @AttributeOverride(
    name = "createTime", column = @Column(name = "BOOK_CREATE_TIME")),
  @AttributeOverride(
    name = "updateUser", column = @Column(name = "BOOK_UPDATE_USER")),
  @AttributeOverride(
    name = "updateTime", column = @Column(name = "BOOK_UPDATE_TIME"))
})
@TableGenerator(name = "BOOK_SEQ_GEN",
  table = "SEQUENCE_GENERATOR_TB",
  pkColumnName = "SEQUENCE_NAME", valueColumnName = "SEQUENCE_VALUE",
  pkColumnValue = "BOOK_SEQ"
)
public class Book extends BaseEntity {
  @Id
  @GeneratedValue(
    strategy = GenerationType.TABLE, generator = "BOOK_SEQ_GEN"
  )
  @Column(name = "BOOK_ID_PK", updatable = false)
```

```java
    protected int bookId;

    protected String isbn;
    protected String author;
    protected String title;
    protected int rating;

    @Column(name = "PRICE", precision = 12, scale = 2)
    protected double price;

    @OneToMany(mappedBy = "book", cascade = CascadeType.ALL)
    protected Set<LineItem> lineItems;

    @ManyToMany
    @JoinTable(name = "BOOK_CATEGORY",
      joinColumns = @JoinColumn(
        name = "BOOK_ID_FPK",
        referencedColumnName = "BOOK_ID_PK"),
      inverseJoinColumns = @JoinColumn(
        name = "CATEGORY_ID_FPK",
        referencedColumnName = "CATEGORY_ID_PK")
    )
    protected Set<Category> categories;

    @Basic(fetch = FetchType.LAZY)
    @Lob
    @Column(table = "CONTENT", name = "PDF",
      columnDefinition = "BLOB NOT NULL"
    )
    protected byte[] pdf;
}
```

Listing 2-5 Category.java: The Category entity.

```java
@Entity
@TableGenerator(name = "CATEG_SEQ_GEN", schema="JPATEST",
  table = "SEQUENCE_GENERATOR_TB", pkColumnName = "SEQUENCE_NAME",
  valueColumnName = "SEQUENCE_VALUE", pkColumnValue = "CATEGORY_SEQ"
)
public class Category extends BaseEntity {
  @Id
  @GeneratedValue(
```

```
      strategy = GenerationType.TABLE, generator = "CATEG_SEQ_GEN"
  )
  @Column(name="CATEGORY_ID_PK", updatable=false)
  protected int categoryId;

  @Column(name="CATEGORY_NAME")
  protected String categoryName;

  @ManyToOne
  @JoinColumn(
    name="PARENT_CATEGORY_FK", referencedColumnName="CATEGORY_ID_PK"
  )
  protected Category parentCategory;

  @OneToMany(mappedBy="parentCategory")
  protected Set<Category> childCategories;

  @ManyToMany(mappedBy="categories")
  @OrderBy("title ASC, price DESC")
  protected List<Book> books;
}
```

3 Persistence Management

Once the mapping from Java entity classes to database tables is complete, a developer may manipulate Java objects and JPA translates Java operations into database operations. In this chapter, we talk about how to perform Java operations through the standard API that is provided by JPA. In a sense, this is the core of JPA. All the hard work of OR mapping on entities would render useless without being manipulated by the persistence API.

The most important interface in JPA is `javax.persistence.EntityManager`. It is covered in the first section. Then the semantics of persistence operations and entity lifecycle is covered in the second section, the persistence context is explained in the third section, locking and concurrency in the fourth section, and entity listeners and callback methods in the fifth section. Finally, bean validation and caching are covered in the last two sections. The `Query` API and Java Persistence Query Language (JPQL) are left for Chapter 1.

3.1 The EntityManager Interface

The `EntityManager` interface defines methods for managing entity instances and their lifecycle. It is used to create, update, and remove persistent entity instances, to find persistent entities by primary key, and to query over persistent entities. An `EntityManager` instance is always associated with a persistence context (see Section 3.3). However, we cannot interact with a persistence context directly, but rather through an `EntityManager` associated with it.

As we have mentioned earlier that Java entity objects and database records are two different but equivalent representations of the same piece of data. The `EntityManager` serves as the ambassador between the OO and relational worlds. When you request that an entity object be persisted, the `EntityManager` translates the entity instance into a new database record. When you update a managed entity instance, it tracks down the relational data that corresponds to the entity instance and updates it in the database. When you remove a managed entity instance, it deletes the corresponding database record. Similarly, when you try to find an entity by primary key or query over the entities, it finds the relational database record or result set and translates it into an entity object or a list of entity objects.

Table 3.1 lists all the methods defined in the `EntityManager` interface together with some high level description. The purpose here is to give an overview on what the interface provides and they are covered in more detail in later sections and chapters. See the full Javadoc of the interface and its methods at the link provided in Section 9.1.

Table 3.1 The `javax.persistence.EntityManager` interface and its methods.

Method Signature	High Level Description
`public void persist(` `   Object entity);`	Make an entity instance managed, and persist it to database when or before transaction commits.
`public <T> T merge(T entity);`	Merge a detached entity instance to the current persistence context and return the managed instance. Changes on managed entities are saved to database at flush or commit time.
`public void remove(` `   Object entity);`	Remove a managed entity instance from the persistence context and delete it from database when or before transaction commits.
`public void detach(` `   Object entity);`	Make a managed entity instance detached by removing it from the persistence context.

`public void lock(`
`   Object entity,`
`   LockModeType lockMode);`
 	
`public void lock(`
`   Object entity,`
`   LockModeType lockMode,`
`   Map<String, Object>`
`   properties);`
	Lock a managed entity instance with a specified lock mode type: `OPTIMISTIC`, `OPTIMISTIC_FORCE_INCREMENT`, `READ`, `WRITE`, `PESSIMISTIC_READ`, `PESSIMISTIC_WRITE`, `PESSIMISTIC_FORCE_INCREMENT`, `NONE`, and specified properties.
	
	One standard property key is: `javax.persistence.lock.timeout`. Specify a positive integer in milliseconds or 0 for a no-wait call.

`public LockModeType` `   getLockMode(Object entity);`	Return the lock mode type for the specified entity instance or `LockModeType.NONE` if it is not locked.
`public void refresh(` `   Object entity);`	Refresh the state of a managed entity instance from database, overwriting changes made to

| ```
public void refresh(
  Object entity,
  Map<String, Object>
  properties);

public void refresh(
  Object entity,
  LockModeType lockMode);

public void refresh(
  Object entity,
  LockModeType lockMode,
  Map<String, Object>
  properties);
``` | the entity, if any.<br><br>The second version allows certain properties (eg, cache store mode) to be specified during the refresh. The third version refreshes the state and locks it with given lock mode. The fourth version refreshes it and locks it with given lock mode, and specified properties. |
| ```
public void flush();
``` | Synchronize the persistence context to the underlying database (save current state of all managed instances to database, if different from database). It requires an active transaction. |
| ```
public void setFlushMode(
  FlushModeType flushMode);

public FlushModeType
  getFlushMode();
``` | Set and get the persistence context's current flush mode type: COMMIT or AUTO. The former means that the entity manager synchronizes to database at transaction commit time, and the latter means that it is done automatically (at or possibly before commit time). The default is AUTO. |
| ```
public <T> T find(
  Class<T> entityClass,
  Object primaryKey);

public <T> T find(
  Class<T> entityClass,
  Object primaryKey,
  Map<String, Object>
  properties);

public <T> T find(
  Class<T> entityClass,
  Object primaryKey,
  LockModeType lockMode);

public <T> T find(
``` | Find an entity instance by the specified class and (simple or composite) primary key. It returns null if the entity does not exist in the database. If the entity instance is contained in the persistence context, it is returned from there. Otherwise, it may try to find the entity in the second-level cache, if enabled and configured properly.<br><br>The second version allows some standard or vendor-specific properties/hints (eg, cache mode). The third version finds the entity instance, and locks it with the specified lock |

`Class<T> entityClass,`
`Object primaryKey,`
`LockModeType lockMode,`
`Map<String, Object>`
`properties);`
	mode. The fourth version finds the entity instance and locks it, with given lock mode and specified properties/hints.

`public <T> T getReference(`
`Class<T> entityClass,`
`Object primaryKey);`
	Get a reference to an entity instance, whose state may be lazily fetched. The application should not expect that the instance state is available upon detachment, unless it was accessed by the application while the entity manager was open.

`public boolean contains(` `Object entity);`	Check to see if the instance is a managed entity instance belonging to the current persistence context.
`public void clear();`	Clear the persistence context, causing all managed entities to become detached. Changes made to entities that have not been flushed to database will not be persisted.

`public void setProperty(`
`String propertyName,`
`Object value);`
 	
`public Map<String, Object>`
`getProperties();`
	Set an entity manager property, such as cache mode. If a vendor-specific property is not recognized, it is silently ignored.
	
	The second method gets all the properties and their values that are in effect with the entity manager.

`public Query`
`createNamedQuery(`
`String queryName);`
 	
`public <T> TypedQuery<T>`
`createNamedQuery(`
`String queryName,`
`Class<T> resultClass);`
 	
`public Query createQuery(`
`String jpqlString);`
 	
`public <T> TypedQuery<T>`
`createQuery(`
`String jpqlString,`
`Class<T> resultClass);`
	The first two methods create an instance of `Query` or `TypedQuery` for executing a pre-configured named query in JPQL or in native SQL. The second method takes a type parameter for the type of the query result.
	
	The third and fourth methods takes a JPQL statement as a string (possibly generated dynamically). The fourth method also takes a type parameter for the type of the query result. The fifth method is for executing a criteria query (Chapter 7).

`public<T> TypedQuery<T>`
`   createQuery(`
`   CriteriaQuery<T>`
`   criteriaQuery);`	

`public Query`
`   createNativeQuery(`
`   String sqlString);`
 	
`public Query`
`   createNativeQuery(`
`   String sqlString,`
`   Class resultClass);`
 	
`public Query`
`   createNativeQuery(`
`   String sqlString,`
`   String resultSetMapping);`
	Create an instance of `Query` for executing a native SQL (select/insert/update/delete) statement for a given native SQL query string.
	
	The second method specifies the entity type of the resulting instances, while the third specifies a result set mapping for the returned entity instances.

`public void` `   joinTransaction();`	Join an active JTA transaction. This method should be called on a JTA application-managed `EntityManager` that was created outside the current JTA transaction to associate it with the transaction.
`public <T> T unwrap(` `   Class<T> cls);`	Return an object of the specified type to allow access to the provider-specific API, for a given `EntityManager` implementation.
`public Object getDelegate();`	Return the underlying provider object for the `EntityManager`, if available. The `unwrap` method is preferred over this one for new applications.

`public void close();`
 	
`public boolean isOpen();`
	Close an application-managed `EntityManager`. If this method is called when the `EntityManager` is associated with an active transaction, the persistence context remains managed until the transaction completes.
	
	The `isOpen()` method returns *false* if the entity manager is closed and *true* otherwise.

`public EntityTransaction` `   getTransaction();`	Return the resource-level (non-JTA) transaction object. The `EntityTransaction`

	instance may be used serially to begin and commit multiple transactions.
`public EntityManagerFactory getEntityManagerFactory();`	Return the entity manager factory for the entity manager.
`public CriteriaBuilder getCriteriaBuilder();`	Return an instance of `CriteriaBuilder` for the creation of `CriteriaQuery` objects (Chapter 7).
`public Metamodel getMetamodel();`	Return an instance of `Metamodel` interface for access to the `Metamodel` of the persistence unit (Chapter 7).

The `persist, merge, remove,` and `refresh` methods must be invoked within a transaction context when an entity manager with a transaction-scoped persistence context (see Section 3.3) is used. If there is no transaction context, the `TransactionRequiredException` is thrown.

The `lock` methods with a lock mode other than `LockModeType.NONE` and the `flush` method must be invoked within a transaction context. If there is no transaction context, the `TransactionRequiredException` is thrown.

The `find` method (provided it is invoked without a lock or invoked with `LockModeType.NONE`), the `Query` and `TypedQuery` interfaces (except for its methods involving database update/delete), and the `getReference` method are not required to be invoked within a transaction context. In this case, if an entity manager with transaction-scoped persistence context is in use, the returned entities will be detached; if an entity manager with an extended persistence context is used, they will be managed. See Section 3.3.

The `Query, TypedQuery,` and `EntityTransaction` objects obtained from an entity manager are valid while that entity manager is open.

If the argument to the `createQuery` method is not a valid Java Persistence query string or a valid `CriteriaQuery` object, the `IllegalArgumentException` may be thrown or the query execution will fail. If a native query is not a valid query for the database in use or if the result set specification is incompatible with the result of the query, the query execution will fail and a `PersistenceException` (which may have wrapped the underlying database exception) will be thrown when the query is executed.

Runtime exceptions thrown by the methods of the `EntityManager` interface other than the `LockTimeoutException` will cause the current transaction to be marked for rollback.

The methods `close`, `isOpen`, `joinTransaction`, and `getTransaction` are used to manage application-managed entity managers and their lifecycle. The method `joinTransaction` is used to join a JTA transaction, while `getTransaction` is used to get a resource-local transaction. See Section 3.3.2.

3.2 Entity Lifecycle

Although JPA entities are POJOs (plain old Java object), they have a well-defined lifecycle maintained by an `EntityManager`. An entity instance may be characterized as being *new, managed, detached*, or *removed*.

- A *new* entity instance has no persistent identity, and is not yet associated with a persistence context. When we create an entity object using the new operator, it is in the *new* state.

- A *managed* entity instance is an instance with a persistent identity that is currently associated with a persistence context. The `EntityManager` periodically checks the state of managed entity instances. Any changes on these instances and their relationships are automatically synchronized to the underlying database upon transaction commit or as a result of the `flush` operation, although a persistence provider is permitted to do the synchronization at other times when a transaction is active.

- A *detached* entity instance is an instance with a persistent identity that is no longer associated with a persistence context.

- A *removed* entity instance is an instance with a persistent identity, still associated with a persistence context, that will be removed from the database upon transaction commit or as a result of the `flush` operation.

The following subsections describe the effect of lifecycle operations on entities. The cascade policy (see Section 2.3.1) may be used to propagate the effect of an operation to associated entities. The cascade functionality is most typically used in parent-child relationships.

3.2.1 Persist an Entity Instance

An entity instance is created by the *new* constructor. At this moment, it is not yet managed and is said to be in the *new* state. A new entity instance becomes managed by invoking the `persist` method on it or by cascading the `persist` operation.

Let *v* be an entity instance and *em* be an `EntityManager` instance associated with a persistence context, then the effect of applying the `persist` operation on the entity instance by invoking `em.persist(v)` is as follows.

- If *v* is a new entity instance, it becomes managed.

- If *v* is a managed entity instance, it is ignored by the `persist` operation.

- If *v* is a removed entity instance, it becomes managed again.

- If *v* is a detached object, the `EntityExistsException` or another `PersistenceException` may be thrown when the `persist` operation is invoked, or at flush or commit time.

- If *v* is a managed entity instance, or becomes managed as a result of the `persist` operation, then the `persist` operation is cascaded to entities referenced by it through a relationship specified with `CascadeType.PERSIST` or `CascadeType.ALL`.

The following code snippet in Listing 3-1 illustrates how the `persist` operation is invoked on new entity instances and its cascading effect.

Listing 3-1 The persist operation on the `Order` entity, which has relationship to `LineItem` with cascade policy of `CascadeType.PERSIST`. A named query is also defined for later use.

```
@Stateless
public class OrderSL implements OrderSLLocal {
```

```
public void createBookAndOrder(double price) {
   Order order = new Order();          // order is in new state
   order.setOrderTime(new Timestamp( new Date().getTime()));
   order.setPrice(price);

   Book book = new Book();             // book is in new state
   book.setIsbn("12345");

   LineItem li = new LineItem();    // li is in new state
   li.setPrice(10.00);
   li.setQuantity(10);
   li.setBook(book);                   // set relationship to book
   li.setOrder(order);                 // set relationship to order

   Set<LineItem> lineItems = new HashSet<LineItem>();
   lineItems.add(li);
   order.setLineItems(lineItems);

   em.persist(book);                   // book is in managed state

   // This causes LineItem li to be persisted due to cascade policy.
   // Otherwise, we would need to call em.persist(li) separately.
   em.persist(order);                  // order and li are now managed

   // At or before the return of this EJB method, the newly managed
   // entities: book, order, li will be inserted to database if
   // transaction commits successfully. In any case, after the method
   // returns, all three managed entity instances will become
   // detached.
   }
}

@Entity
@Table(name="ORDERS")
@NamedQuery(name="queryOrders",
   query="SELECT o FROM Order o WHERE o.orderTime < ?1"
)
public class Order extends BaseEntity {
   @OneToMany(
      mappedBy="order",
      cascade={CascadeType.PERSIST, CascadeType.REMOVE}
   )
   protected  Set<LineItem> lineItems;
}
```

3.2.2 Remove an Entity Instance

A *managed* entity instance becomes *removed* by invoking the `remove` method on it or by cascading the `remove` operation.

Let *v* be an entity instance and *em* be an `EntityManager` instance associated with a persistence context, then the effect of applying the `remove` operation on the entity instance by invoking `em.remove(v)` is as follows.

- If *v* is a new entity instance, it is ignored by the `remove` operation. However, the `remove` operation is cascaded to entities referenced by it through a relationship specified with `CascadeType.REMOVE` or `CascadeType.ALL`.

- If *v* is a managed entity, the `remove` operation causes it to become removed. Also, the `remove` operation is cascaded to entities referenced by it through a relationship specified with `CascadeType.REMOVE` or `CascadeType.ALL`.

- If *v* is a detached entity, an `IllegalArgumentException` will be thrown by the `remove` operation, or the transaction commit will fail.

- If *v* is a removed entity, it is ignored by the `remove` operation.

- A removed entity will be deleted from the database at or before transaction commit or as a result of the `flush` operation.

3.2.3 Refresh an Entity Instance

The state of a managed entity instance is refreshed from the database by invoking the `refresh` method on it or by cascading the `refresh` operation.

Let *v* be an entity instance and *em* be an `EntityManager` instance associated with a persistence context, then the effect of applying the `refresh` operation on the entity instance by invoking `em.refresh(v)` is as follows.

- If *v* is a managed entity, its state is refreshed from the database, overwriting changes made to the entity, if any. The `refresh` operation is cascaded to entities referenced by it through a relationship specified with `CascadeType.REFRESH` or `CascadeType.ALL`.

- If *v* is a new, detached, or removed entity, the `IllegalArgumentException` is thrown.

3.2.4 Detach an Entity Instance

An entity instance is detached from the persistence context by invoking the `detach` method on it or cascading the `detach` operation. Changes made to a detached entity will not be synchronized to the database. Applications must invoke the `flush` method prior to the `detach` method in order to force new changes to be synchronized to the database.

Let *v* be an entity instance and *em* be an `EntityManager` instance associated with a persistence context, then the effect of applying the `detach` operation on the entity instance by invoking `em.detach(v)` is as follows.

- If *v* is a managed entity, the `detach` operation causes it to become detached. The `detach` operation is cascaded to entities referenced by it through a relationship specified with `CascadeType.DETACH` or `CascadeType.ALL`. Entities which previously referenced it prior to the detachment will continue to reference it.

- If *v* is a new or detached entity, it is ignored by the `detach` operation.

- If *v* is a removed entity, the `detach` operation is cascaded to entities referenced by it through a relationship specified with `CascadeType.DETACH` or `CascadeType.ALL`.

There are many ways to cause entity detachment. A detached entity may result

- from transaction commit if a transaction-scoped entity manager is used;
- from transaction rollback (see Section 3.3);
- from detaching the entity explicitly by invoking the `detach` method on it;
- from clearing the persistence context;
- from closing an entity manager; or
- from serializing an entity or otherwise passing it by value (eg, through a remote interface).

A detached entity instance continues to live outside the persistence context in which it was persisted or retrieved, and its state is no longer synchronized with the database. Its available state includes any persistent field/property that is not marked `fetch=LAZY`, or was accessed by the application prior to detachment.

If the persistent field/property of a detached entity instance is an association, its available state may only be safely accessed if the associated instance is available. Such available associated instances include:

- Any entity instance retrieved using the `find` operation.
- Any entity instances retrieved using a query or explicitly requested in a `FETCH JOIN` clause (see Section 5.3.2).
- Any entity instance for which an instance variable holding non-primary-key persistent state was accessed by the application.
- Any entity instance that was reached from another available entity instance.

Thus, if we want to access the state of a detached entity for certain attributes that are configured with lazy loading, we need to force loading of such attributes before the entity is detached. For example, suppose the `customer` and `lineItems` attributes of `Order` are marked with lazy fetching, we may want to invoke the `getName` method (it must be a non-primary key) on `customer` and `size` method on `lineItems` to force the loading of these attributes:

```
@Stateless
public class OrderSL implements OrderSLLocal {

  public Order getOrder(int orderID) {
    Order order = em.find(Order.class, orderID);
    Customer cust = order.getCustomer();
    if (cust != null) {
      // call non-primary-key attribute to force loading
      cust.getName();
    }

    List<LineItem> lineItems = order.getLineItems();
    if (lineItems != null) {
      // call size() is OK for collection-valued attributes
      lineItems.size();
    }

    return order;
```

```
    }
}
```

In an N-tier architecture, detached entities in the persistence tier may be passed to the service tier or the presentation tier. They are typically modified there and returned to the persistence tier. Then they are merged into a persistence context and the changes are saved to the database.

3.2.5 Merge Detached Entity State

The `merge` operation allows for the propagation of state from detached entities onto persistent entities managed by the `EntityManager`.

Let *v* be an entity instance and *em* be an `EntityManager` instance associated with a persistence context, then the effect of applying the `merge` operation on the entity instance by invoking `em.merge(v)` is as follows.

- If *v* is a detached entity, its state is copied onto a pre-existing managed entity instance of the same identity or a new managed copy of it is created.

- If *v* is a new entity instance, a new managed entity instance is created and the state is *copied* into the new managed entity instance.

- If *v* is a removed entity instance, an `IllegalArgumentException` will be thrown by the merge operation, or the transaction commit will fail.

- If *v* is a managed entity, it is ignored by the `merge` operation. However, the `merge` operation is cascaded to entities referenced by it through a relationship specified with `CascadeType.MERGE` or `CascadeType.ALL`.

- If an entity instance is merged into a persistence context, all entities referenced by it through a relationship specified with `CascadeType.MERGE` or `CascadeType.ALL` are merged accordingly.

JPA does not `merge` fields/properties marked `LAZY` that have not been fetched. If you want to merge them, try to access these attributes prior to detachment. Also, make sure that relationships of an entity are merged properly. Any `Version` column used by the entity is checked by JPA during the `merge` operation, or at `flush` or `commit` time. See Section 3.4.1.

3.3 Persistence Context

The concept of persistence context is mentioned in Section 1.2. In this section, we explain in more depth. A *persistence context* is a set of managed entity instances in which for any persistent entity identity there is a unique entity instance. These entity instances and their lifecycle are managed by an entity manager associated with the persistence context.

There are *transaction-scoped persistence context* that is scoped to a single transaction, and *extended persistence context* that may span multiple transactions and non-transactional invocations of the `EntityManager`. The managed entities of a transaction-scoped persistence context become detached when the transaction commits. An `EntityManager` with an extended persistence context maintains its references to the entity objects after a transaction has committed. These entity objects remain managed by the `EntityManager`, and may be updated as managed objects between transactions. Updates on these managed entities outside a transaction will be queued and saved to the database when a transaction is available. Various examples of transaction-scoped and extended persistence contexts are given in this section.

A *container-managed entity manger* is the one whose lifecycle is managed by the Java EE container. Its corresponding persistence context is automatically propagated with the current JTA transaction across `EntityManager` references for the given persistence unit. An *application-managed entity manager* is the one whose lifecycle is managed by the application and the corresponding persistence context is not propagated; Instead, each instance of creating an entity manager causes a new isolated persistence context to be created that is not accessible through other `EntityManager` references within the same transaction.

An application-managed entity manager may be either a JTA entity manager (that uses a JTA data source configured in `persistence.xml`) or a resource-local entity manager (that uses a resource-local data source). A container-managed entity manager must be a JTA entity manager. JTA entity managers are only specified for use in Java EE containers.

Both container-managed entity managers and application-managed entity managers are required to be supported in Java EE Servlet containers and EJB containers. Within an EJB environment, container-managed entity managers are typically used. In Java SE environments and in Java EE application client containers, only application-managed entity managers are required to be supported.

For both transaction-scoped and extended persistence contexts, transaction rollback causes all *pre-existing* managed instances and removed instances to become detached. The instances' state will be the state of the instances at the point at which the transaction was rolled back. Transaction rollback typically causes the persistence context to be in an inconsistent state at the point of rollback. In particular, the state of version attributes and generated state, such as generated primary keys, may be inconsistent. Instances that were formerly managed by the persistence context may therefore not be reusable in the same manner as other detached objects. For example, they may fail when passed to the merge operation.

3.3.1 Contained-managed EntityManager

By default, the persistence context of a container-managed entity manager is transaction-scoped. A transaction-scoped persistence context begins when the container-managed entity manager is invoked inside an active JTA transaction, and there is no current persistence context already associated with the JTA transaction. The persistence context is created and then associated with the JTA transaction. The persistence context ends when the associated JTA transaction commits or rolls back, and all managed entities become detached. If the entity manager is invoked outside the scope of a transaction, any entities loaded from the database (as a result of invoking the find operation or executing a Query) will immediately become detached at the end of the method call.

A container-managed extended persistence context can only be initiated within a stateful session bean. It exists from the point at which the stateful session bean that declares an entity manager of type PersistenceContextType.EXTENDED is created, and is said to be *bound* to the stateful session bean. The extended persistence context is declared using the @PersistenceContext annotation or persistence-context-ref deployment descriptor in web.xml or ejb-jar.xml (see Section 8.1.2). The persistence context is closed by the container when the @Remove method of the stateful session bean completes (or the stateful session bean instance is otherwise destroyed). A typical usage of an extended persistence context in a stateful session bean is to model a work flow scenario that spans multiple user requests and synchronize the conversational state to the database for the duration of a user session.

When a container-managed entity manager is used (in Java EE environments), it is obtained by the application directly through dependency injection, or JNDI lookup. The application does not interact with the entity manager factory directly. The container manages the persistence context lifecycle and the creation and the closing of the entity manager instance. It must be noted that an entity manager (container-managed or application-managed) may not be shared among multiple concurrently executing threads. Entity managers may only be accessed in a single-threaded manner.

The `@PersistenceContext` annotation is used for entity manager injection. The `type` element specifies whether a transaction-scoped or extended persistence context is to be used (the default is transaction-scoped), and the `unitName` element may be specified to designate the name of the persistence unit (if omitted, it refers to the default persistence unit). The `name` element refers to the name by which the entity manager is to be accessed using JNDI lookup, and is not needed when dependency injection is used. The following code listings give examples on how container-managed entity managers can be obtained in various scenarios.

Listing 3-2 Obtain a container-managed and transaction-scoped entity manager through dependency injection in a stateless session bean or message-driven bean, using container-managed transaction.

```
package jpatest.ejb;

import java.util.List;
import javax.ejb.Stateless;
import javax.persistence.EntityManager;
import javax.persistence.PersistenceContext;
import javax.persistence.Query;

import jpatest.Vehicle;

@Stateless(mappedName = "VehicleSL")
public class VehicleSL implements VehicleSLLocal {
  @PersistenceContext(unitName = "jpaTestJtaPU")
  EntityManager em;
```

```
  public void createVehicle(Vehicle v) {
    em.persist(v);               // insert into database
  }

  public Vehicle updateVehicle(Vehicle v) {
    Vehicle v2 = em.merge(v); // merge v into managed state
    v2.setYear(2011);          // update year to 2011
    return v2;
  }

  public void deleteVehicle(Vehicle v) {
    em.remove(em.merge(v));     // merge v into managed state & delete
  }
}
```

> **Listing 3-3** Obtain a container-managed and transaction-scoped entity manager through JNDI lookup in a stateless session bean or message-driven bean, using container-managed transaction.

```
@Stateless
@PersistenceContext(name = "jpaTestJtaPC", unitName = "jpaTestJtaPU")
public class OrderSL implements OrderSLLocal {
  @Resource
  SessionContext ctx;

  public void createOrder(Order o) {
    EntityManager em = (EntityManager) ctx.lookup("jpaTestJtaPC");
    em.persist(o);
  }

  public Order addLineItem(int orderID, LineItem li) {
    EntityManager em = (EntityManager) ctx.lookup("jpaTestJtaPC");

    // find the order in the persistence context or bring it to the
    // persistence context, before we add the line item to it.
    Order order = em.find(Order.class, orderID);
    li.setOrder(order);
    order.getLineItems().add(li);
    return order;
  }

  public void deleteOrder(Order o) {
    EntityManager em = (EntityManager) ctx.lookup("jpaTestJtaPC");
```

```
    em.remove(em.merge(o));
  }
}
```

```
@PersistenceContext(name = "jpaTestJtaPC", unitName = "jpaTestJtaPU")
public class TestServlet extends HttpServlet {
  @Resource
  private UserTransaction ut;        // UserTransaction is thread-safe

  protected void doGet(HttpServletRequest req,
    HttpServletResponse resp) throws ServletException, IOException {

    InitialContext ctx = null;
    EntityManager em = null;
    try {
      Order order = new Order();
      // fill in order and related objects

      ctx = new InitialContext();
      ut.begin();
      em = (EntityManager) ctx.lookup("java:comp/env/jpaTestJtaPC");
      em.persist(order);
      ut.commit();
    } catch (Exception e) {
      e.printStackTrace();
    } finally {
      if (em != null && em.isOpen()) em.close();
    }
  }
}
```

In Listing 3-5, we demonstrate how an entity manager with extended persistence context is used in a stateful session bean. The persistence context starts when the bean instance is created, and exists until when the bean instance is removed or destroyed. During this interval, managed entities are cached in the persistence context unless they are explicitly detached or removed. It is used when an application wants to maintain a conservational state, during which managed entities remain managed in the persistence context. For example, after an *order* is initialized by calling the `init` method and created by calling the `create` method, the *order* instance remains managed in the persistence context until it is removed by calling the `deleteOrder` method or when the bean instance is destroyed. The advantage is that it eliminates the overhead of detaching and merging entity instances compared to transaction-scoped persistence contexts, but the downside is that it incurs some other overhead by caching managed entity instances for a long time, possibly for the duration of the stateful session bean.

Listing 3-5 Obtain a container-managed extended entity manager through dependency injection in a stateful session bean, using container-managed transaction.

```
@Stateful
@TransactionAttribute(TransactionAttributeType.REQUIRED)
public class OrderSF implements OrderSFLocal {
  @PersistenceContext(type = PersistenceContextType.EXTENDED,
    unitName = "jpaTestJtaPU"
  )
  EntityManager em;

  private Order order;

  public void init(Order order) {
    this.order = order;
  }

  public void createOrder() {
    // persist order and make order managed
    em.persist(order);
  }

  public List<Order> retrieveOrders(Timestamp orderTime) {
    // named query: queryOrders is defined in Listing 3-1.
    Query query = em.createNamedQuery("queryOrders");
    query.setParameter(1, orderTime, TemporalType.TIMESTAMP);
    List<Order> result = query.getResultList();

    // The list of orders remain managed in this extended persistent
    // context even after this method returns
    return result;
  }

  public void addLineItem(LineItem li) {
```

```
      li.setOrder(order);
      order.getLineItems().add(li);
   }

  public void deleteOrder() {
     // Object order remains managed in this extended persistent
     // context so that a call of em.merge(order) is not needed here.
     em.remove(order);
   }
}
```

A single container-managed persistence context may correspond to one or more JTA entity manager instances within the same persistence unit. The persistence context is propagated across the entity manager instances as the JTA transaction is propagated. Propagation of persistence contexts only applies within a local environment and does not apply to remote tiers.

If a stateful session bean instantiates another stateful session bean in the same EJB container which also has an extended persistence context, the extended persistence context of the first stateful session bean is inherited by the second stateful session bean and bound to it, and this rule recursively applies. If the persistence context has been inherited by any stateful session beans, the container does not close the persistence context until all such stateful session beans have been removed or otherwise destroyed.

To illustrate how persistence contexts are propagated, let us look at this example:

```
@Stateless
public class OrderSL implements OrderSLLocal {
  @PersistenceContext(unitName = "jpaTestJtaPU")
  EntityManager em;

  @EJB LineItemSLLocal lineItemSLLocal;

  public void addLineItem(Order ord, LineItem li) {
    em.merge(ord);
    lineItemSLLocal.addLineItem(ord, li);
  }
}

@Stateless
public class LineItemSL implements LineItemSLLocal {
  @PersistenceContext(unitName = "jpaTestJtaPU")
  EntityManager em;
```

```
public void addLineItem(Order order, LineItem li) {
    em.merge(li);
    li.setOrder(order);
    order.getLineItems().add(li);
  }
}
```

Suppose we call the method `OrderSL.addLineItem()`, then a JTA transaction starts since an EJB method has the default transaction attribute: `REQUIRED`. When the line `em.merge(ord)` inside the method is executed, a persistence context is created and associated with this JTA transaction. Now the execution comes to the next line: `lineItemSLLocal.addLineItem(ord, li)`. The same JTA transaction is propagated to the method `LineItemSL.addLineItem()`, and so is the persistence context. Then the line `em.merge(li)` in the `LineItemSL.addLineItem()` method merges the *li* object into the same persistence context that contains the *ord* object. Everything works as expected.

Now, let us change the transaction attribute to `REQUIRES_NEW` for the `addLineItem()` method in the `LineItemSL` bean as:

```
@Stateless
public class LineItemSL implements LineItemSLLocal {

  @TransactionAttribute(TransactionAttributeType.REQUIRES_NEW)
  public void addLineItem(Order order, LineItem li) {
    em.merge(li);
    li.setOrder(order);
    order.getLineItems().add(li);
  }
}
```

Then things will not work. The problem is that a new transaction is required for the method `LineItemSL.addLineItem()`, and a new persistence context will be created. Thus the *ord* and *li* objects are merged into two different persistence contexts.

To close this subsection, we give the definition of the annotation `@PersistenceContext`:

```
@Target({TYPE, METHOD, FIELD}) @Retention(RUNTIME)
public @interface PersistenceContext {
```

```
  String name() default "";                    // name for JNDI lookup
  String unitName() default "";                 // persistence unit name
  PersistenceContextType type default TRANSACTION;
  PersistenceProperty[] properties() default {};
}

public enum PersistenceContextType { TRANSACTION, EXTENDED }

@Target({}) @Retention(RUNTIME)
public @interface PersistenceProperty {
  String name();
  String value();
}

@Target({TYPE}) @Retention(RUNTIME)
public @interface PersistenceContexts {
  PersistenceContext[] value();
}
```

The optional `properties` element of `@PersistenceContext` may be used to specify properties for the container or persistence provider. Vendor-specific properties may be included in the set of properties, and are passed to the persistence provider by the container when the entity manager is created. Properties that are not recognized by a vendor will be ignored.

3.3.2 Application-Managed EntityManager

The scope of the persistence context of an application-managed entity manager is always extended. In this case, the `persist`, `remove`, `merge`, and `refresh` operations may be called regardless of whether a transaction is active. The effects of these operations will be committed to the database when the extended persistence context is enlisted in a transaction and the transaction commits. An application-managed persistence context exists when the entity manager is created using the `EntityManagerFactory.createEntityManager()` method and ends when the entity manager is closed by calling `EntityManager.close()`. If the `close` method is invoked when a transaction is active, the persistence context remains managed until the transaction completes. An application-managed persistence context is a standalone persistence context and is not propagated with the transaction. An application may have to pass an entity manager around in order for two Java classes to share the persistence context associated with the entity manager.

When an application-managed JTA entity manager is created outside the scope of the current JTA transaction, the application may associate the entity manager with the JTA transaction by calling the `EntityManager.joinTransaction()` method. When it is created inside a JTA transaction, it is automatically associated with the JTA transaction. For a resource-local entity manager, the only way to obtain a transaction is to call the `EntityManager.getTransaction()` method.

When an application-managed entity manager is used in Java EE or Java SE environments, the application must use the entity manager factory to obtain an entity manager and must manage the persistence context lifecycle itself.   Methods of the `EntityManagerFactory` interface are thread-safe.

An example is given in Section 1.2 on how to obtain an application-managed entity manager, which applies in both Java SE and Java EE environments. A resource-level transaction is obtained by calling the `getTransaction` method on the `EntityManager`.   In general, certain standard and vendor-specific properties may be utilized when creating an entity manager factory. Being able to dynamically supply database properties here allows the database password to be stored in some encrypted form and decrypted at run-time to obtain an entity manager factory. See Listing 3-6.

Listing 3-6 Application-managed entity manager with resource-local transaction in Java SE or Java EE environments. An entity manager instance is created and closed inside each method.

```java
public class BookDAO {
  private EntityManagerFactory emf = null;

  public BookDAO() {
    Map<String, String> props = new HashMap<String, String>();
    props.put("javax.persistence.jdbc.user", "username");
    props.put("javax.persistence.jdbc.password", "password");
    emf = Persistence.createEntityManagerFactory("jpaTestPU", props);
  }

  public void createBook(Book b) {
    EntityManager em = emf.createEntityManager();
    try {
      em.getTransaction().begin();
      em.persist(b);
      em.getTransaction().commit();
```

```
    } catch (Throwable t) {
      t.printStackTrace();
      em.getTransaction().rollback();
    } finally {
      em.close();
    }
  }

  public Book retrieveBook(int bookID) {
    EntityManager em = emf.createEntityManager();
    Book b = null;

    try {
      b = em.find(Book.class, bookID);
    } finally {
      em.close();
    }

    return b;
  }

  // make sure this method is called after use to release resources
  public void destroy() {
    if (emf != null && emf.isOpen()) emf.close();
  }
}
```

In Java EE environments, the @PersistenceUnit annotation may also be used to express a dependency on an entity manager factory and its associated persistence unit.

Listing 3-7 Application-managed entity manager with container-managed JTA transaction in a stateless session bean. Each business method creates and closes an entity manager.

```
@Stateless
public class BookSL implements BookSLLocal {
  @PersistenceUnit(unitName = "jpaTestJtaPU")
  private EntityManagerFactory emf;

  public Book createBook(Book book) {
    EntityManager em = emf.createEntityManager();
    em.persist(book);
    em.close();
```

```
      return book;          // remains managed until JTA transaction ends
  }

  public Book getBook(int id) {
    EntityManager em = emf.createEntityManager();
    Book book = em.find(Book.class, id);
    em.close();
    return book;
  }
}
```

Listing 3-8   Application-managed entity manager with container-managed JTA transaction in a stateful session bean. Session bean creates an entity manager right after the bean is constructed and closes the persistence context right before the stateful bean is destroyed.

```
@Stateful
public class BookSF implements BookSFLocal {
  @PersistenceUnit(unitName = "jpaTestJtaPU")
  private EntityManagerFactory emf;
  private EntityManager em;

  private Book book;

  @PostConstruct
  public void postConstruct() {
    em = emf.createEntityManager();
  }

  public void init(Book book) {
    this.book = book;
  }

  public Book createBook() {
    em.joinTransaction();              // join current JTA transaction
    em.persist(book);

    return book;
  }

  public Book getBook(int id) {
    Book book = em.find(Book.class, id);
    return book;
```

```
  }

  @PreDestroy
  public void destroy() {
    em.close();
  }
}
```

The `name` element of `@PersistenceUnit` refers to the name by which the entity manager factory is to be accessed using JNDI lookup, and is not needed when dependency injection is used. The optional `unitName` element refers to the name of the persistence unit as defined in the `persistence.xml` file. If omitted, it refers to the default persistence unit.

```
@Target({TYPE, METHOD, FIELD}) @Retention(RUNTIME)
public @interface PersistenceUnit{
  String name() default "";
  String unitName() default "";
}

@Target(TYPE) @Retention(RUNTIME)
public @interface PersistenceUnits {
  PersistenceUnit[] value();
}
```

From the code listings above, one can see that container-managed entity managers with container-managed transactions are much easier to use and are typically recommended over application-managed entity managers and application-managed transactions, unless such a container is not available such as in Tomcat or Java SE environments. With the help of the container, a developer can concentrate on the business logic, instead of managing the lifecycle of entity managers or the transaction. The downside of container-managed entity managers is that they require JTA data sources and JTA transactions, which may not be necessary when two-phase commit is not needed and could negatively impact the performance.

Finally, in this subsection, we list all the methods of the `EntityManagerFactory` interface and the `EntityTransaction` interface in Table 3.2 and Table 3.3.

Table 3.2 The `javax.persistence.EntityManagerFactory` interface and its methods.

Method Signature	High Level Description
`public EntityManager` `   createEntityManager();`	Create a new `EntityManager`. This method returns a new `EntityManager` instance each time it is invoked.

`public EntityManager`
`   createEntityManager(`
`   Map properties);`
	Create a new `EntityManager` with the specified Map of properties. This method returns a new `EntityManager` instance each time it is invoked.

`public CriteriaBuilder` `   getCriteriaBuilder();`	Return an instance of `CriteriaBuilder` for the creation of `CriteriaQuery` objects. See Chapter 7.
`public Metamodel` `   getMetamodel();`	Return an instance of `Metamodel` interface for access to the `metamodel` of the persistence unit. See Chapter 7.
`public boolean isOpen();`	Indicates whether the factory is open. Returns true until the factory has been closed.
`public void close();`	Close the factory, releasing any resources that it holds. After a factory instance is closed, all methods invoked on it will throw an `IllegalStateException`, except for `isOpen`, which will return false. Once an `EntityManagerFactory` has been closed, all its entity managers are considered to be in the closed state.
`public Map<String, Object>` `   getProperties();`	Get the properties and associated values that are in effect for the entity manager factory. Changing the contents of the map does not change the configuration in effect.
`public Cache getCache();`	Access the "second level cache" that is associated with the entity manager factory. See Section 3.7.
`public PersistenceUnitUtil` `get PersistenceUnitUtil();`	Return interface `PersistenceUnitUtil` providing access to utility methods for the persistence unit.

Table 3.3 The `javax.persistence.EntityTransaction` interface and its methods.

Method Signature	High Level Description
`public void begin();`	Start a resource-level transaction. It throws `IllegalStateException` if `isActive()` is true
`public void commit();`	Commit the current transaction, writing any unflushed changes to database. It throws `IllegalStateException` if `isActive ()` is false, and throws `RollbackException` if the commit fails.
`public void rollback();`	Roll back the current transaction. It throws `IllegalStateException` if `isActive ()` is false, and throws `PersistenceException` if an unexpected error condition is encountered.
`public void setRollbackOnly();`	Mark the current transaction so that the only possible outcome is for the transaction to roll back. It throws `IllegalStateException` if `isActive ()` is false.
`public boolean getRollbackOnly();`	Determine whether the current transaction has been marked for rollback. It throws `IllegalStateException` if `isActive ()` is false.
`public boolean isActive();`	Indicate whether a transaction is in progress. It throws `PersistenceException` if an unexpected error condition is encountered.

3.3.3 Find Entities

The `find` methods find and return an entity instance by its primary key. If the entity instance is contained in the persistence context, it is returned from there, without being fetched from the database or the second-level cache (see Section 3.7). If the entity instance does not exist in the database, null is returned. Persistent attributes (including relationships) that are configured for lazy-loading may not be loaded until they are first accessed.

The `getReference` method returns an entity reference or proxy by its primary key. However, the state of the reference or proxy may be lazily-fetched. Persistent attributes, including those that are even configured for eager-loading, may not be loaded until they are first accessed. If the entity instance with the given primary key does not exist in the database, the `EntityNotFoundException` will be thrown when the entity state other than the primary key is first accessed or when the `getReference` method is called.

A `find` method (provided it is invoked without a lock or invoked with `LockModeType.NONE`), and the `getReference` method are not required to be invoked within a transaction. In this case, if an entity manager with transaction-scoped persistence context is in use, the returned entity instance will be detached; if an entity manager with an extended persistence context is used, it will be managed. If they are invoked within a transaction, the returned entity instance will be in managed state. Invoking these methods and queries may be more efficient outside a transaction for a transaction-scoped entity manager, since the entity manager does not have to incur the overhead of managing the returned results.

The `getReference` method is typically used when creating a relationship from a child entity to a parent entity in a one-to-one or many-to-one child-parent relationship, in which the parent entity already exists in the database. In this case, since we only need to create the foreign key reference from the child to the parent, we do not need to fully-load the parent entity. Instead, using a reference or proxy of the parent entity will be sufficient.

For example, the following code creates a relationship from a child `LineItem` entity to a parent `Order` entity and we use the `getReference` method to retrieve a reference or proxy of the parent entity:

```
LineItem item = new LineItem();
item.setPrice(34.95);
item.setQuantity(100);

em.getTransaction().begin();
Order order = em.getReference(Order.class, orderId);
item.setOrder(order);
order.getLineItems().add(item);
em.persist(item);
em.getTransaction().commit();
```

In this process, the parent `Order` entity may not be fetched from the database, since all we need here is its primary key. The assumption here is that the primary key of the parent entity is already known. Thus, in this case, using the `getReference` method could be more efficient than a `find` method.

The downside is that the state of the entity returned by the `getReference` method may not be available after it is detached from the persistence context, and that lazy-fetching of the entity state when it is first accessed may require another trip to the database.

3.4 Locking and Concurrency

When concurrent transactions access the same data, locking is the way to ensure data consistency and integrity. JPA 1.0 supports only optimistic locking. In JPA 2.0, pessimistic locking is added. With the support of both optimistic locking and pessimistic locking, JPA should satisfy all the locking need for a typical application.

3.4.1 Optimistic Locking with Versioning

Optimistic locking using the `Version` attribute (field or property) is explained in Section 2.2.8. It ensures that update or delete to a database row corresponding to the state of an entity is made only when no intervening transaction has updated or deleted that database row since the entity state was last fetched from the database. When an intervening transaction has updated or deleted the same database row, instead of overwriting the update, JPA throws an `OptimisticLockException` and mark the transaction for rollback. Applications are strongly encouraged to enable optimistic locking for all entities that may be concurrently accessed or merged from a disconnected state. Failure to use optimistic locking may lead to inconsistent entity state and overwritten updates.

An entity is automatically enabled for optimistic locking if it has a persistent attribute mapped using the `@Version` annotation or its equivalent XML descriptor. When a non-relationship persistent field or property is changed, or when a relationship attribute owned by the entity is modified, JPA will increment the version value. For example, if an entity contains a unidirectional one-to-many relationship and this relationship is changed, then the version value on the entity object will be updated by JPA (even though no changes are made to the entity table). An application may read the state of its `Version` attribute, but must not set or update the version value, which is managed by JPA automatically. However, in bulk updates (see Section 5.3.8), the version value is permitted to be modified by the application.

When the `merge` operation of the entity manager is invoked on an entity, JPA examines the version attribute and throws an `OptimisticLockException` if the entity contains stale data -- that is, the database row corresponding to the entity has been updated or deleted since the entity became detached. It is also possible that such an exception is thrown later at flush or commit time.

When an `OptimisticLockException` occurs, an application typically refreshes the entity objects or reloads them in a new transaction and then retries the transaction. The user then needs to discard the previous work and repeat the process on the refreshed entity objects. If the process takes a lot of time and/or has to be repeated often, user experience may be negatively impacted. In this case, pessimistic locking may be considered, which is covered later in the section.

3.4.2 Optimistic Locking with Lock Mode

By default, JPA assumes that the underlying database is accessed using *read-committed* transaction isolation level. What it means is that any updates to an entity made inside a transaction will not be visible to another transaction until the changing transaction has committed successfully. Optimistic locking with versioning works with the read-committed isolation level to provide data-consistency checking when two or more concurrent users or processes modify the same data. To achieve the next level of locking constraint, which is *repeatable read* (a transaction gets the same result when querying the same data twice), JPA provides a mechanism for the developer to lock individual entity objects.

When locking selected entities, JPA uses lock modes to specify the level of locking and achieve the effect of *repeatable read* both optimistically and pessimistically. Six lock mode types are defined as:

```
public enum LockModeType
{
  READ,                            // same as OPTIMISTIC
  WRITE,                           // same as OPTIMISTIC_FORCE_INCREMENT
  OPTIMISTIC,                      // optimistic read lock
  OPTIMISTIC_FORCE_INCREMENT,      // force increment on version value
  PESSIMISTIC_READ,                // pessimistic read lock
  PESSIMISTIC_WRITE,               // pessimistic write lock
  PESSIMISTIC_FORCE_INCREMENT,     // force increment on version value
  NONE                             // no locking
}
```

Lock modes may be specified by means of the `EntityManager`'s `lock` method, the methods of the `EntityManager`, `Query`, and `TypedQuery` interfaces that allow lock

111

modes to be specified, and the `@NamedQuery` annotation. Specifying a lock mode other than `LockModeType.NONE` must be executed within a transaction. We talk about optimistic lock modes in this subsection and leave pessimistic lock modes to the next.

For example, the following code snippet locks an `Order` object optimistically to guarantee that it is not modified by another transaction. Otherwise, the transaction would fail.

```
@Stateless
public class OrderSL implements OrderSLLocal {

  public double getOrderPrice(int orderId) {
    double price = 0;

    // Find and lock the object optimistically to ensure
    // repeatable read
    Order order
      = em.find(Order.class, orderId, LockModeType.OPTIMISTIC);
    Timestamp t = order.getOrderTime();
    if (t.before(new Date())) {
      price = order.getPrice();
    }
    return price;
  }
}
```

Lock modes: `READ` and `WRITE` are introduced in JPA 1.0 and must be used on entities with a version attribute mapped. A `READ` lock checks the version attribute to ensure that the state of the entity object being locked does not change until the current transaction finishes; otherwise, an `OptimisticLockException` will be thrown. A `WRITE` lock checks and increments the version attribute and ensures the current transaction conflicts with any other transaction changing or locking the same entity object. A common use of the `READ` lock is when generating reports. You may not want other users to modify the data while you are reading the data for the reports. In this case, use the optimistic read lock while reading the data to generate the reports, as in the code snippet above.

The `WRITE` lock is useful when managing entity relationships. When a child entity is modified, the version of its parent is incremented if the parent is locked with the `WRITE` lock, regardless whether the parent object is modified or not. Suppose a user adds a book item to his `Order`. Since there is a one-to-many relationship from `Order` to `LineItem`, but the owner of this relationship is `LineItem`, modifying this relationship attribute will not cause the version of his `Order` object to be updated in his persistence context and in the database, although the transaction commits fine. Also assume that, in the same time, a system administrator tries to give this user's `Order` a 20% discount, which will commit successfully with the `Order` version value incremented in her persistence context and in the database. Thus the two copies of this user's `Order` object in the two persistence contexts will be in inconsistent state, with two different values for the `version` and `price` attributes.

The solution to resolve this issue is to use an optimistic `WRITE` lock to force an increment on the version value when the user adds the book item to his order. This will cause the administrator's update on the order to fail and an `OptimisticLockException` to be thrown. The correct code looks like this:

```
@Stateless
public class OrderSL implements OrderSLLocal {
  @PersistenceContext(unitName = "jpaTestJtaPU")
  EntityManager em;

  // User adds a new item to his order and the system updates the
  // version on his order object.
  public void addLineItem(int orderId, int quantity, double price) {
    Order order = em.find(Order.class, orderId);
    em.lock(order, LockModeType.OPTIMISTIC_FORCE_INCREMENT);

    LineItem li = new LineItem();
    li.setQuantity(quantity);
    li.setPrice(price);
    order.getLineItems().add(li);
    li.setOrder(order);
  }

  // If system administrator starts to modify the same order object at
  // the same time (after user started to call addLineItem, but before
  // his call commits), an OptimisticLockException will be thrown when
  // she commits her discount changes (assuming the user's change
  // already committed at this moment)
  public void performDiscount(int orderId, double percentage) {
    Order order = em.find(Order.class, orderId);
    List<LineItem> items = order.getLineItems();
    double price = 0;
    for (LineItem i : items) {
      price += i.getPrice();
    }
```

```
    price *= percentage;
    order.setPrice(price);
  }
}
```

Since JPA 2.0, the lock modes READ and WRITE are now synonyms of OPTIMISTIC and OPTIMISTIC_FORCE_INCREMENT, respectively. The latter are preferred for new applications. They are used for optimistic locking on versioned entities to prevent dirty read and non-repeatable read:

- **Dirty read**: Transaction T1 modifies a row. Another transaction T2 then reads that row and obtains the modified value, before T1 has committed or rolled back. Eventually transaction T2 commits successfully.

- **Non-repeatable read**: Transaction T1 reads a row. Another transaction T2 then modifies or deletes that row, before T1 has committed. T1 reads the same row again but gets the modified value or no value. Both transactions eventually commit successfully.

The prevention of dirty read and non-repeatable read is generally achieved by the entity manager acquiring a lock on the underlying database row. However, in the case of optimistic locking, long-term database read locks are typically not obtained immediately, but may be deferred until commit time. The difference between lock modes: OPTIMISTIC and OPTIMISTIC_FORCE_INCREMENT is that the latter also forces an update on the locked entity's version column. JPA does not require persistence providers to support these two lock modes on entities without the version attribute.

3.4.3 Pessimistic Locking

Optimistic locking is efficient and appropriate in dealing with moderate contentions among concurrent transactions. However, for dealing with high transaction contentions, pessimistic locking may be used by obtaining long-term database locks on selected entities.

Pessimistic locking guarantees that, once a transaction has obtained a pessimistic lock on an entity instance, no other transactions (including those from another application using the same underlying database) may successfully modify or delete that entity instance until the transaction has ended; if the pessimistic lock is an exclusive lock (with lock mode type: `PESSIMISTIC_WRITE` or `PESSIMISTIC_FORCE_INCREMENT`), only that same transaction may modify or delete that entity instance.

The three pessimistic lock modes: `PESSIMISTIC_READ`, `PESSIMISTIC_WRITE`, and `PESSIMISTIC_FORCE_INCREMENT` are used to immediately obtain long-term database locks to prevent dirty read and non-repeatable read. Such locks must be obtained immediately and retained until the transaction completes. The pessimistic read and write lock modes are supported on non-versioned entities as well as on versioned entities. A lock with `LockModeType.PESSIMISTIC_WRITE` can be obtained on an entity instance to force serialization among transactions attempting to update the entity data. It prevents other transactions from acquiring a `PESSIMISTIC_WRITE` or `PESSIMISTIC_READ` lock on the same entity object. It may also be used when querying data and there is a high likelihood of deadlock or update failure among concurrent updating transactions. The lock mode `PESSIMISTIC_WRITE` is typically translated by your JPA provider into a SQL `"SELECT FOR UPDATE"` statement on the database row corresponding to the locked entity, so that no other users or applications can update it. The following code snippet locks an `Order` object with `PESSIMISTIC_WRITE` for the duration of performing an update on it:

```
@Stateless
public class OrderSL implements OrderSLLocal {
  @PersistenceContext(unitName = "jpaTestJtaPU")
  EntityManager em;

  public void performDiscount(int orderId, double percentage) {
    Order order = em.find(Order.class, orderId);

    em.refresh(order, LockModeType.PESSIMISTIC_WRITE);
    List<LineItem> items = order.getLineItems();
    double price = 0;
    for (LineItem i : items) {
      price += i.getPrice();
    }
    price *= percentage;
    order.setPrice(price);
  }
}
```

A lock with lock mode `PESSIMISTIC_READ` can be used to query data requiring repeatable-read without blocking other transactions from reading the data. It prevents other transactions from acquiring a `PESSIMISTIC_WRITE` lock on the same entity object. The lock mode `PESSIMISTIC_FORCE_INCREMENT` also forces the version value to be incremented on versioned entities, even if the locked entity is not modified. However, its behavior on non-versioned entities is undefined, although some JPA implementations may reduce it to `PESSIMISTIC_WRITE`. When such locks cannot be obtained and the database locking failure results in transaction-level rollback, JPA throws `PessimisticLockException` and causes the current JTA transaction or `EntityTransaction` to be marked for rollback.

When a transaction locks an entity with `LockModeType.PESSIMISTIC_READ` and later updates that entity, JPA then converts the pessimistic read lock to an exclusive lock: `PESSIMISTIC_WRITE` or `PESSIMISTIC_FORCE_INCREMENT` when the entity is flushed to the database or at commit time.

Compared to optimistic locking, pessimistic locking uses more database resources, since it may require a database transaction and connection to be held open for the duration of the locking period. This is typically not desirable for interactive web applications. Also, pessimistic locking could cause concurrency issues and even deadlocks.

3.4.4 Lock Timeout

An application may wish to specify a timeout in milliseconds in pessimistic locking using the following standard property key string:

```
javax.persistence.lock.timeout          // timeout in acquiring a lock
```

This hint may be used with the `lock`, `find`, `refresh` methods of the `EntityManager` interface that allow lock modes to be specified, the `Query.setLockMode` method and the `@NamedQuery` annotation (see Section 5.2.1). The following code snippet gives an example:

```
Map<String, Object> p = new HashMap<String, Object>();
p.put("javax.persistence.lock.timeout", 60000);
Order o
  = em.find(Order.class, orderId, LockModeType.PESSIMISTIC_READ, p);
```

It may also be passed as a property to the following method: `Persistence.createEntityManagerFactory`, or used in the `properties` element of the `persistence.xml` file. For example,

```
<persistence-unit name="jpaTestPU" transaction-type="RESOURCE_LOCAL">
  <provider>org.eclipse.persistence.jpa.PersistenceProvider</provider>
  <properties>
    <property name="javax.persistence.lock.timeout" value="60000" />
  </properties>
</persistence-unit>
```

When used in the `createEntityManagerFactory` method, the `persistence.xml` file, and the `@NamedQuery` annotation, the timeout hint serves as a default value which can be selectively overridden in the methods of the `EntityManager` and `Query` interfaces. A timeout value of 0 is used to specify "no wait" locking.

However, it must be noted that this timeout hint may or may not be observed by your JPA implementation, depending on the database in use and the locking mechanisms used by the persistence provider, which may support the use of additional, vendor-specific locking hints.

3.4.5 Lock Scope

When an entity object is locked using pessimistic locking, JPA locks the database rows that correspond to non-collection-valued persistent attributes of the entity object. These include rows in secondary tables, and tables affected in a joined-table inheritance mapping. In addition, entity relationships for which the locked entity contains the foreign key will be locked (but not the state of the referenced entities , unless those entities are explicitly locked).

However, element collections and entity relationships for which the entity does not contain the foreign key will not be locked by default. Such entity relationships include those that are mapped to join tables and unidirectional one-to-many relationships for which the target entity contains the foreign key. To change this default behavior, the standard property `javax.persistence.lock.scope` must be specified with a value of `PessimisticLockScope.EXTENDED`. This property may be passed as an argument to the methods of the `EntityManager`, `Query`, and `TypedQuery` interfaces that allow lock modes to be specified or used with the `NamedQuery` annotation.

When an extended lock scope is set, element collections and entity relationships owned by the entity that are contained in join tables will be locked. Locking such a relationship or element collection generally locks only the rows in the join table or collection table for that entity relationship or element collection. Note that the state of entities referenced by such relationships will not be locked, unless those entities are explicitly locked.

To reverse the lock scope to the default, set the `javax.persistence.lock.scope` standard property to have the value of `PessimisticLockScope.NORMAL`.

3.5 Entity Listeners

For entity lifecycle events such as persist, load, update, or remove, JPA provides a mechanism to designate callback methods to receive notifications. These callback methods may perform common tasks such as logging, auditing, validating data, sending notifications after a database change, or generating data after an entity has been loaded. They are similar to database triggers. Table 3.4 lists the annotations to designate callback methods that are supported by JPA.

Table 3.4 Lifecycle callback methods supported by JPA.

Lifecycle Callback Methods	When It Is Performed
`@PrePersist`	Before the EntityManager persists an entity instance. If `merge` operation is applied to an entity and creates a new managed instance, this callback method is invoked after the entity state is copied to it.
`@PostPersist`	After an entity has been made persisted, or after database insert. Generated primary keys are available in this callback method.
`@PreRemove`	Before an entity instance is removed.
`@PostRemove`	After an entity instance is removed.
`@PreUpdate`	Before database update to entity data. It may occur when entity data is updated or when it is flushed to database.
`@PostUpdate`	After database update to entity data.
`@PostLoad`	After entity is loaded into the current persistence context from database, or after `refresh` operation is applied to it.

These callback methods may be defined in the entity class or its mapped super class, or defined in separate listener classes. As an example, let us define a callback method, annotated `@PrePersist`, to fill in the create timestamp field and the create user field when an entity is created, and another callback method, annotated `@PreUpdate`, to fill in the update timestamp field and the update user field when an entity is updated. There are two equivalent ways to achieve it. The first way is to define those methods on each entity class or mapped super class as in Listing 3-9.

> **Listing 3-9** Define `@PrePersist` and `@PreUpdate` callback methods on our entities' mapped super class.

```
@MappedSuperclass
public class BaseEntity implements Serializable {
  @Version
  protected int version;

  @Column(name="CREATE_USER")
  protected String createUser;

  @Column(name="CREATE_TIME")
  @Temporal(TemporalType.TIMESTAMP)
  protected Date createTime;

  @Column(name="UPDATE_USER")
  protected String updateUser;

  @Column(name="UPDATE_TIME")
  @Temporal(TemporalType.TIMESTAMP)
  protected Date updateTime;

  @PrePersist
  // This method is called automatically before entity is inserted
  // to the database
  public void insertAuditingField() {
    Timestamp currentTime = new Timestamp(new Date().getTime());
    setCreateTime(currentTime);
    setCreateUser("jpaUser");
    setUpdateTime(currentTime);
    setUpdateUser("jpaUser");
  }

  @PreUpdate
  // This method is called automatically before update is saved
  // to the database
  public void updateAuditingField() {
    Timestamp currentTime = new Timestamp(new Date().getTime());
    setUpdateTime(currentTime);
```

```
      setUpdateUser("jpaUser2");
   }
}
```

The second way is to define the callback methods on a listener class and designate it on each entity class or mapped super class using the @EntityListeners annotation, as in Listing 3-10.

Listing 3-10 Listener for filling out auditing fields defined in mapped super class using the annotation @EntityListeners.

```
package jpatest.util;

public class AuditingFieldListener {
  @PrePersist
  public void insertAuditingField(Object obj) {
    if (!(obj instanceof BaseEntity )) {
      return;
    }

    BaseEntity baseEntity = (BaseEntity) obj;

    Timestamp currentTime = new Timestamp(new Date().getTime());
    baseEntity.setCreateTime(currentTime);
    baseEntity.setCreateUser("jpaUser");
    baseEntity.setUpdateTime(currentTime);
    baseEntity.setUpdateUser("jpaUser");
  }

  @PreUpdate
  public void updateAuditingField(Object obj) {
    if (!(obj instanceof BaseEntity )) {
      return;
    }

    BaseEntity baseEntity = (BaseEntity) obj;

    Timestamp currentTime = new Timestamp(new Date().getTime());
    baseEntity.setUpdateTime(currentTime);
    baseEntity.setUpdateUser("jpaUser2");
  }
}
```

120

```
@EntityListeners(jpatest.util.AuditingFieldListener.class)
@MappedSuperclass
public class BaseEntity implements Serializable {  ...  }
```

Notice that the `@PrePersist` callback method is executed before each entity is persisted and the `@PreUpdate` callback method is executed before the entity is updated. The create user and update user fields are filled in as hard-coded constants here. In fact, the current user can be captured in the Servlet container by using a `Servlet` filter or the EJB container by using an interceptor, saved in some thread local variable, and accessed in the callback methods as the create or update user. See Section 8.1.5 for more details.

There is some difference in the method signature for the callback methods. When defined in the entity class or mapped super class, each callback method must not take any argument and must return void. On the each other hand, when defined in a listener class, it must take exactly one argument of type `Object` and return void; this argument represents the entity instance for which the lifecycle event is generated. It may be declared as the actual entity type as well. A listener class must be annotated with `@EntityListeners` or its equivalent XML descriptor.

A callback method must not be static or final, but may have public, private, protected, or package-level access. An entity listener must have a public no-argument constructor and be stateless. A single entity or listener class may not have more than one lifecycle callback method for the same lifecycle event. A callback method may be used for multiple callback events.

Generally speaking, callback methods address crosscutting concerns rather than business logic, and are recommended to be put in listener classes so that the entity class code will not be cluttered.

When there is more than one listener for an entity, they may be defined using a comma-separated list as:

```
@Entity
@EntityListeners({Listener.class, Listener2.class, Listener3.class})
public class Vehicle {  ...  }
```

When multiple entity listeners are defined for an entity, the order in which they are invoked is determined by the order in which they are specified in the @EntityListeners annotation. The XML descriptor may be used as an alternative to specify the invocation order of entity listeners or to override the order specified in annotations.

Default listener classes are defined in an orm.xml file and used for all entity classes in a persistence unit as in Listing 3-11. There is no mechanism to define default listeners using annotations.

Listing 3-11 An orm.xml file to define default listeners for a persistence unit.

```xml
<?xml version="1.0" encoding="UTF-8"?>
<entity-mappings version="2.0"
  xmlns="http://java.sun.com/xml/ns/persistence/orm"
  xmlns:xsi="http://www.w3.org/2001/XMLSchema-instance"
  xsi:schemaLocation="http://java.sun.com/xml/ns/persistence/orm
      http://java.sun.com/xml/ns/persistence/orm/orm_2_0.xsd">

  <persistence-unit-metadata>
    <persistence-unit-defaults>
      <schema>jpatest</schema>
      <access>FIELD</access>

      <entity-listeners>
        <entity-listener class="jpatest.util.AuditingFieldListener">
          <pre-persist method-name="insertAuditingField" />
          <pre-update method-name="updateAuditingField" />
        </entity-listener>
        <entity-listener class="jpatest.util.Listener2">
          ...
        </entity-listener>
      </entity-listeners>
    </persistence-unit-defaults>
  </persistence-unit-metadata>

  <named-query name="getAllOrders">
    <query>SELECT o FROM Order o</query>
  </named-query>
</entity-mappings>
```

The following rules apply to lifecycle callback methods:

- Lifecycle callback methods may throw unchecked (runtime) exceptions. A runtime exception thrown by a callback method that executes within a transaction causes that transaction to be marked for rollback.

- Lifecycle callback methods can invoke JNDI, JDBC, JMS, and enterprise beans.

- In general, a lifecycle callback method should not invoke `EntityManager` or `Query` operations, access other entity instances, or modify relationships within the same persistence context.

- When invoked from within a Java EE environment, the callback methods are executed in the enterprise naming context, transaction context, and security context of the invoking component.

Suppose we want to check the validity of the data before it is persisted to the database. We could put the validation logic in a `@PrePersist` callback method. When the data is not valid (for example, account minimum balance is not met), a runtime exception should be thrown from the callback method and the invalid data would not be committed to the database.

For an entity lifecycle event, multiple callback methods may be defined in the entity class, mapped super class, or listeners. In this case, the ordering of the invocation of these methods is as follows.

Default listeners, if any, are invoked first, in the order specified in the XML descriptor. Default listeners apply to all entities in the persistence unit, unless explicitly excluded by using the annotation `@ExcludeDefaultListeners` or its equivalent XML descriptor `exclude-default-listeners`. The lifecycle callback methods defined in entity listener classes for an entity class or mapped super class are invoked next, in the same order as specified in the `@EntityListeners` annotation.

If multiple entity classes or mapped super classes in an inheritance hierarchy define entity listeners, the listeners defined for a super class are invoked before the listeners defined for a subclass. The `@ExcludeSuperclassListeners` annotation or its equivalent XML element `exclude-superclass-listeners` may be applied to an entity class or mapped super class to exclude entity listener classes defined for super classes. An excluded listener may be reintroduced on an entity class by listing it in `@EntityListeners`. These annotations may be used as:

```
@Entity
@Table(name="ORDERS")
@ExcludeDefaultListeners
@ExcludeSuperclassListeners
@EntityListeners(jpatest.util.AuditingFieldListener.class)
public class Order extends BaseEntity { ... }
```

Lifecycle callback methods for the same lifecycle event defined on an entity class has lower priority than those defined in its super class, which in turn have lower priority than those defined in listener classes. Default listeners have highest priority. A class is permitted to override an inherited callback method of the same callback type, and in this case, the overridden method will not be invoked. The XML descriptor may be used to override the lifecycle callback method invocation order specified in annotations.

3.6 Bean Validation

JPA 2.0 adds support for Bean Validation. Entity classes, mapped super classes, and embeddable classes may be configured to include validation constraints, such as validation of a persistent field in certain range before being persisted to the database. These constraints may be specified using the annotations from the Bean Validation package: `javax.validation.constraints`, which is part of Java EE 6. If you want to use this feature in Java SE or Java EE 5, you will need to download a bean validation library that is compliant with JSR 303 (see Section 9.1). An example of such a library is Hibernate Validator (Section 9.8.2).

3.6.1 Validation Annotations

Validation annotations can be placed on persistent attributes, as in the following example:

```
package jpatest.entity;

import javax.validation.constraints.NotNull;
import javax.validation.constraints.Pattern;
import javax.validation.constraints.Size;

@Entity
public class Address extends BaseEntity {
  @NotNull
```

```
protected String city;

@NotNull
@Size(max=2, min=2, message="State name must have 2 characters")
protected String state;

@Pattern(regexp="^\\d{5}(-\\d{4})?$",
   message="Zip not in correct format"
)
@NotNull
@Column(name = "ZIP", length=5, nullable=false)
protected String zip;
}
```

Here the annotations @NotNull, @Size, and @Pattern specify that the city attribute cannot be null, state can have only 2 characters, and zip must be in the format specified by the regular expression "^\d{5}(-\d{4})?$". Note that "\d" is escaped by the backslash character. We have also specified a message that will be included in the ConstraintViolation exception if the constraint check fails. Validation checking may be performed automatically upon PrePersist, PreUpdate, and PreRemove lifecycle events (See below in Section 3.6.3), or programmatically as needed.

Table 3.5 lists the bean validation constraint annotations. Not shown in the table are the list versions, such as @Min.List and @NotNull.List for multiple @Min and @NotNull validations, respectively. See Java EE 6 Javadoc for more details (Section 9.1).

Table 3.5 Annotations from Bean Validation that may be used in JPA.

Bean Validation Annotations	High Level Description
@Min	The annotated attribute's minimum value. Supported types: byte, short, int, long, and their respective wrappers, and BigDecimal, BigInteger. Note: null elements are considered valid.
@Max	The annotated attribute's maximum value. Supported types: byte, short, int, long, and their respective wrappers, and BigDecimal, BigInteger. Note: null elements are considered valid.

@DecimalMin	The annotated attribute's minimum value. Supported types: `byte`, `short`, `int`, `long`, and their respective wrappers, and `String`, `BigDecimal`, `BigInteger`. Note: `null` elements are considered valid. Also `double` and `float` are not supported due to rounding errors.
@DecimalMax	The annotated attribute's maximum value. Supported types: `byte`, `short`, `int`, `long`, and their respective wrappers, and `String`, `BigDecimal`, `BigInteger`. Note: `null` elements are considered valid.
@Digits	The annotated attribute must be a number. Supported types: `byte`, `short`, `int`, `long`, and their respective wrappers, and `String`, `BigDecimal`, `BigInteger`. Note: `null` elements are considered valid.
@Size	The size of the annotated attribute. Supported types: `String` for string length, `Collection` for collection size, `Map` for map size, `Array` for array length, or `null`.
@Future	The annotated attribute must be a date in the future. Supported types: `java.util.Date`, `java.util.Calendar`, or `null`.
@Past	The annotated attribute must be a date in the past. Supported types: `java.util.Date`, `java.util.Calendar`, or `null`.
@Pattern	The annotated attribute must be a regular expression. Supported data types: `String`, or `null`.
@Null	The annotated attribute must be `null`. Accepts any type.
@NotNull	The annotated attribute must not be `null`. Accepts any type.
@AssertTrue	The annotated attribute must be `true`. Supported types are `Boolean`, `boolean`, or `null`.
@AssertFalse	The annotated attribute must be `false`. Supported types are `Boolean`, `boolean`, or `null`.

3.6.2 Validation Groups

It is often needed that certain validation constraints on the entity be restricted at different times (such as upon `PreDelete` events only). Validation groups provide a way for us to specify a subset of validations at a given time. A group must be defined in the same

126

way as a Java class or an interface, and it is specified on the `groups` element of an annotation.To illustrate the usage, we define two validation groups and specify them on certain constraints:

```
package jpatest.groups;

public interface Basic {
}

public interface Extended extends javax.validation.groups.Default {
}

@Entity
public class Address extends BaseEntity {
  @NotNull(groups=Basic.class)
  protected String street;

  @NotNull(groups={Basic.class, Extended.class})
  protected String city;

  @NotNull
  @Size(max=2, min=2, groups=Extended.class)
  protected String state;
}

@Entity
@GroupSequence({Customer.class, Basic.class, Extended.class})
public class Customer extends User {
  @Valid
  @NotNull(groups={Basic.class, Extended.class})
  @Embedded
  protected BankInfo bank;

  @NotNull(groups={Basic.class, Extended.class}) //part of two groups
  @OneToOne
  private Address address;
}
```

The `@NotNull` constraint defined on the `address` field in `Customer` belong to two groups: `jpatest.groups.Basic` and `jpatest.groups.Extended`. Each constraint can be part of one or more validation groups. The constraints without a group specified explicitly belong to the `Default` validation group, which is identified by the interface `javax.validation.groups.Default`. A subclass group includes any groups that it inherits. Instead of validating all constraints at once, validation can be done one group after another. By default, validations are done in no particular order, regardless of which groups they belong to. The sequential order of validation can be specified using the @GroupSequence annotation. The validation stops if one group cannot be validated successfully. The annotation @Valid indicates that the embedded attribute will also be validated.

3.6.3 Validation Configuration

JPA supports automatic validation of persistent attributes upon the lifecycle events: pre-persist, pre-update, and pre-remove. For example, before an Address instance is persisted to the database, JPA validates the state attribute to have a character length of 2. These validations occur immediately after all the PrePersist, PreUpdate, and PreRemove lifecycle callback methods have been executed, respectively. This will make sure that data is valid before being inserted or updated to the database and before being deleted.

There are three validation modes that a developer may configure in JPA. The validation-mode element of the persistence.xml file determines whether the automatic lifecycle event validation is in effect. The values of the validation-mode element are AUTO, CALLBACK, and NONE, with the default being AUTO. For example, to configure your persistence unit not to do validation, use the NONE value as in

```
<persistence-unit name="jpaTestPU" transaction-type="RESOURCE_LOCAL">
  <provider>org.eclipse.persistence.jpa.PersistenceProvider</provider>
  <validation-mode>NONE</validation-mode>
</persistence-unit>
```

If the AUTO validation mode is specified, or if the validation-mode element is not specified but a bean validation provider is present in the environment, JPA performs automatic validation for entities in the persistence unit. If a bean validation provider is not present in the environment, lifecycle event validation will not take place. If the CALLBACK validation mode is specified, JPA performs the lifecycle event validation. In this case, it is an error if there is no bean validation provider present in the environment.

The configuration in the persistence.xml file may be overridden using the property map key: javax.persistence.validation.mode, passed to the method createEntityManagerFactory with valid values: auto, callback, and none, as in

128

```
Map<String, String> props = new HashMap<String, String>();
props.put("javax.persistence.validation.mode","callback");
EntityManagerFactory emf =
  Persistence.createEntityManagerFactory("jpaTestPU", props);
```

For each lifecycle event type, a list of groups is targeted for validation. By default, the `Default` bean validation group will be validated on the `pre-persist` and `pre-update` events, and no group will be validated upon the `pre-remove` event. This default behavior may be overridden by specifying the target groups using the following validation properties in the `persistence.xml` file, or by passing these properties to the `createEntityManagerFactory` method, or as properties for the `@PersistenceUnit` annotation, or `persistence-unit` descriptor tag:

- `javax.persistence.validation.group.pre-persist`
- `javax.persistence.validation.group.pre-update`
- `javax.persistence.validation.group.pre-remove`

The value of a validation property must be a list of the target groups. The target groups must be specified using a comma-separated list of fully qualified class names. For example,

```
<persistence-unit name="jpaTestPU" transaction-type="RESOURCE_LOCAL">
  <provider>org.eclipse.persistence.jpa.PersistenceProvider</provider>
  <validation-mode>CALLBACK</validation-mode>
  <properties>
    <property name="javax.persistence.valiation.group.pre-persist"
              value="jpatest.groups.Basic,jpatest.groups.Extended"/>
  </properties>
</persistence-unit>
```

If the list of targeted groups is empty, no validation is performed. When validation is performed, but there are errors from the validation, JPA throws the `javax.validation.ConstraintValidationException`, and marks the transaction for rollback.

JPA guarantees that no unloaded attribute or association will be loaded due to the validation and that no entity will be validated more than once. Embeddable attributes are validated only if the `@Valid` annotation has been specified on them.

In Java EE 6 or later environments, a `ValidatorFactory` instance is made available by the Java EE container. In Java SE environments, if a bean validation provider is present on the classpath, JPA will instantiate a default `ValidatorFactory`, unless the application wishes to override this default behavior by passing a `ValidatorFactory` instance via the map to the `createEntityManagerFactory` method. The map key must be the standard property name: `javax.persistence.validation.factory`.

Besides supporting automatic validation, JPA also allows an application to do programmatic validation by directly calling the `validate` method of a validator instance passing an entity instance as the parameter. Below is some code showing how to do it:

```
ValidatorFactory factory = Validation.buildDefaultValidatorFactory();
Validator validator = factory.getValidator();
Address addr = ...;
validator.validate(addr);
```

In a Java EE container, a `Validator` instance may also be injected using the annotation `@Resource`.

3.7 Caching

Within a persistence context, managed entity instances are cached, which is called the *first-level cache* and is not shared by other persistence contexts or other users. JPA 2.0 adds the support for a *second-level cache*, which caches entity instances within a persistence unit and are shared by different persistence contexts and users. Although this is an optional feature in the JPA 2.0 specification, many JPA implementations such as Hibernate, EclipseLink, and OpenJPA support it. If a JPA implementation supports it, it must do so in the standard way. This section talks about the second-level cache, which is also referred to as the shared cache.

The *second-level cache* is typically used to enhance performance. JPA does not have to go to the database to retrieve cached entity instances. Instead, they may be retrieved from the cache, if configured so. However, use of a second-level cache may have side effect. The cached data seen by the application may not be up-to-date, and may result in "stale reads". A *stale read* is defined as the reading of entities that are older than at the point where the persistence context was started. Thus frequently-used and read-only entity objects are perfect for the second-level cache. If some objects are frequently-read, but infrequently modified, they may be good caching candidates.

3.7.1 Cache Configuration

The good thing is that JPA gives an application the flexibility to enable or disable caching. Whether the entities of a persistence unit will be cached is determined by the value of the `shared-cache-mode` element in the `persistence.xml` file, or equivalently, the value of the `javax.persistence.sharedCache.mode` property, which can be passed in when the entity manager factory is created. The cache mode element has five valid values: `ALL`, `NONE`, `ENABLE_SELECTIVE`, `DISABLE_SELECTIVE`, and `UNSPECIFIED`. A value of `ALL` causes all entities and entity-related state and data in the persistence unit to be cached, and a value of `NONE` causes caching to be disabled for all entities in the persistence unit. For example, the following fragment in `persistence.xml` enables caching for all entities in the persistence unit.

```
<persistence-unit name="jpaTestPU" transaction-type="RESOURCE_LOCAL">
  <provider>org.eclipse.persistence.jpa.PersistenceProvider</provider>
  <shared-cache-mode>ALL</shared-cache-mode>
  <validation-mode>AUTO</validation-mode>
</persistence-unit>
```

The values `ENABLE_SELECTIVE` and `DISABLE_SELECTIVE` are used in conjunction with the `@Cacheable` annotation (or its equivalent XML descriptor). The `@Cacheable` annotation specifies whether an entity should be cached if caching is enabled by the `shared-cache-mode` element in `persistence.xml`. In both cases, `@Cacheable(true)` means that the entity and its state are cached, and `@Cacheable(false)` means that the entity and its state must not be cached. The `@Cacheable` annotation is defined as:

```
@Target({TYPE}) @Retention(RUNTIME)
public @interface Cacheable {
  boolean value() default true;         // default is true
}
```

A value of `ENABLE_SELECTIVE` enables caching selectively, which only caches entities annotated with `@Cacheable(true)` (or specified equivalently in XML). In this case, JPA does not cache entities for which `@Cacheable(true)` or `@Cacheable` is not specified. This option is useful when we want to selectively enable caching for a small number of entities (by annotating them with `@Cacheable`) and the caching for the rest of entities in the persistence unit are disabled by default.

131

A value of `DISABLE_SELECTIVE` disables caching selectively. In this case, JPA only disables caching on entities for which `@Cacheable(false)` is specified. That is, JPA caches entities for which `@Cacheable(false)` is not specified. This option is useful when we want to selectively disable caching for a small number of entities (by annotating them with `@Cacheable(false)`) and the caching for the rest of entities are enabled by default.

If either the `shared-cache-mode` element is not specified in the `persistence.xml` file or the value of this element is `UNSPECIFIED`, and the property `javax.persistence.sharedCache.mode` is not specified, the behavior is not defined, and the persistence provider specific default may apply.

3.7.2 Cache Retrieve and Store Modes

When the caching of an entity is enabled, the default behavior is to use the cached entity objects when retrieving the entity data by the `find` methods and in query executions. The cached entity objects will be updated when new changes are committed to the database. If an object is not already in the cache, it will be inserted into the cache when it is first read from the database.

This default caching behavior can be changed by using the cache retrieve mode and cache store mode properties, which may be dynamically specified at the level of the persistence context by using the `setProperties` method of the `EntityManager`. Cache mode properties may also be specified for the `EntityManager`'s `find` and `refresh` methods, and the `Query` and `TypedQuery`'s `setHint` method, which overrides those specified for the persistence context. Cache mode properties apply only to entities, for which caching has been enabled.

The cache mode properties are `javax.persistence.cache.retrieveMode` and `javax.persistence.cache.storeMode`. These properties have the following meanings. The `retrieveMode` property specifies the behavior when data is retrieved by the `find` methods and by the execution of queries. This property is ignored by the `refresh` method, since it always causes data to be retrieved from the database, not the cache. The value `CacheRetrieveMode.USE` indicates that JPA uses the cache when reading entity data, which is the default behavior, and the value `CacheRetrieveMode.BYPASS` indicates that the second-level cache is bypassed all together and JPA retrieves the data from the database directly. For example, the following code sets the cache retrieve mode to bypass the second-level cache:

```
EntityManager em = ...;
em.setProperty("javax.persistence.cache.retrieveMode",
               CacheRetrieveMode.BYPASS);
```

The enumeration type CacheRetrieveMode is defined as:

```
public enum javax.persistence.CacheRetrieveMode {
  USE,      // Read entity data from the cache: this is the default.
  BYPASS    // Bypass the cache: get data directly from database.
}
```

The storeMode property specifies the behavior when data is read from the database and when data is committed into the database. The default CacheStoreMode.USE option places objects in the cache when read from and committed to the database. However, it does not refresh the cached objects when reading from the database. The value CacheStoreMode.REFRESH forces such a refresh, besides doing whatever the CacheStoreMode.USE option does. This refresh option is useful when cached objects may be changed in the database by another application or another server cluster node. The CacheStoreMode.BYPASS option simply causes objects not to be inserted into the cache when they are read from or committed to the database.

The enumeration type CacheStoreMode is defined as:

```
public enum javax.persistence.CacheStoreMode {
  // Insert/update entity data into cache when read from database and
  // when committed into database. This is the default. Does not
  // force refresh of already cached items when reading from database.
  USE,

  // Do not insert into cache.
  BYPASS,

  // Insert/update entity data into cache when read from database and
  // when committed into database. Force refresh of already cached
  // objects using data read from database.
  REFRESH
}
```

When reading data from the database, the storeMode property also applies to the refresh methods, besides the find methods and query executions. When the

`CacheStoreMode.REFRESH` option is set, the results from the `refresh` methods will update the shared cache. Below is an example:

```
Map<String, Object> p = new HashMap<String, Object>();
p.put("javax.persistence.cache.storeMode", CacheStoreMode.REFRESH);
em.refresh(order, p);
```

To close this subsection, we give an example on how to set the cache modes for a query:

```
Query q = em.createQuery("SELECT o FROM Order o");
q.setHint("javax.persistence.cache.storeMode",
          CacheStoreMode.REFRESH);
q.setHint("javax.persistence.cache.retrieveMode",
          CacheRetrieveMode.BYPASS);
List result = q.getResultList();
```

With these settings, this query will bypass the cache and go to the database directly to retrieve the data, but the retrieved data will be used to refresh the cache.

3.7.3 Cache API

The second-level cache can be accessed programmatically through the entity manager factory, as follows.

```
EntityManager em = ...;
EntityManagerFactory emf = em.getEntityManagerFactory();
Cache sharedCache = emf.getCache();
boolean b = sharedCache.contains(Order.class, 123); // object cached?
sharedCache.evict(Book.class);          // evict all cached Book objects
sharedCache.evict(Book.class, 123);     // evict a specific Book object
sharedCache.evictAll();                 // evict all cached objects
```

The `Cache` interface and its methods are listed in Table 3.6. Note that when an object is evicted from the cache, its related objects may still stay in the cache (unless they are evicted explicitly). For example, if an `Order` object with primary key 123 is evicted from the cache, this may leave its cached associated `LineItem` objects pointing to the uncached `Order` object. Later, if the `Order` object with primary key 123 is inserted into the cache as a result of a query execution, then those cached `LineItem` objects may not point to this newly cached `Order` object. Thus, be careful when evicting objects with relationships. It may be better off just evicting an object and its associated relationships all together.

Table 3.6 The `javax.persistence.Cache` *interface. It is used to interact with the second-level cache. If such as cache is not in use, the methods of this interface have no effect.*

Method Signature	High Level Description

```public boolean contains(```
    `Class cls,`
    `Object primaryKey);`
	Whether the cache contains data for the given entity. It always returns false if the second-level cache is not in use.

`public void evict(Class cls,` `Object primaryKey);`	Remove the data for the given entity with the given primary key from the cache.
`public void evict(Class cls);`	Remove the data for entities of the specified class (and its subclasses) from the cache.
`public void evictAll();`	Clear the whole cache.

3.8 Persistence Utilities

JPA 2.0 has added two utility interfaces: `PersistenceUnitUtil` and `PersistenceUtil` in the `javax.persistence` package. The methods provided in the interfaces may not be used very often by application developers, but are more for application frameworks or testing.

3.8.1 Load State

An entity instance is considered to be loaded if all fields/properties with `FetchType.EAGER` (whether explicitly specified or by default, including relationship and other collection-valued fields/properties) have been loaded from the database or assigned value by the application. Fields/properties with `FetchType.LAZY` may or may not have been loaded.

The `PersistenceUnitUtil.isLoaded(Object)` method can be used to determine the load state of an entity object. The method `isLoaded(Object, String)` gives the load state of a persistent attribute of an entity object, with the second parameter being the name of the attribute. It returns false if the attribute state (marked as `LAZY` or `EAGER`) has not been loaded, and true if it has been loaded. The following code snippet shows how they can be used:

```
EntityManagerFactory emf = em.getEntityManagerFactory();
PersistenceUnitUtil puUtil = emf.getPersistenceUnitUtil();
```

135

```
Order orderRef = em.getReference(Order.class, 123);
boolean b = puUtil.isLoaded(orderRef);
boolean bPrice = puUtil.isLoaded(orderRef, "price");

Order order = em.find(Order.class, 123);
boolean bli = puUtil.isLoaded(order, "lineItems");
List<LineItem> li = order.getLineItems();
boolean bli2 = puUtil.isLoaded(order, "lineItems");
```

The interface `PersistencUtil` also provides these two methods. They may be used as:

```
PersistenceUtil util = Persistence.getPersistenceUtil();
boolean b = util.isLoaded(em.getReference(Order.class, 123));
boolean b2 = util.isLoaded(em.find(Order.class, 123), "lineItems");
```

The difference is that `PersistenceUtil` is accessed not through the entity manager factory and may require persistence provider resolution. Thus `PersistenceUnitUtil` is potentially more efficient.

3.8.2 Entity Identifier

The `PersistenceUnitUtil.getIdentifier(Object)` method returns the identifier object for a given entity instance. If an entity has a composite primary key, an object of the composite primary key class will be returned. Note that a generated ID may not be available until after the database insert has occurred. Below is an example on how to use it:

```
EntityManagerFactory emf = em.getEntityManagerFactory();
PersistenceUnitUtil puUtil = emf.getPersistenceUnitUtil();
Order order = ... ;
Object id = puUtil.getIdentifier(order);
```

4 Advanced OR Mapping

Basic OR mapping is covered in Chapter 2. In this chapter, we talk about advanced mapping techniques. The first section covers composite primary keys and element collections. The second section deals with using maps for collections of relationship attributes and derived identities from parent to child entities. The third section is devoted to entity inheritance. Finally, the fourth section shows complete mapping code for a few sample entities. On first reading, the reader may want to browse through the main ideas and come back to it later when needed.

4.1 Entity Mapping

This section is a continuation of Section 2.2, in which we talk about mappings on a single entity class. The first two subsections deal with composite primary keys (vs. simple primary keys in Section 2.2.9), which occur more often in legacy databases. The third subsection is on element collections where a collection of basic type or embeddable class may be defined (vs. a collection of entities in Sections 2.3.2 and 2.3.3).

4.1.1 @IdClass

When a database table has a composite primary key, the corresponding entity has to be defined to have a composite ID. There are two annotations to achieve it: @IdClass or @EmbeddedId. This subsection talks about @IdClass, while the next subsection deals with @EmbeddedId.

Suppose that we change the database table ADDRESS to ADDRESS2 in such a way that it has a composite primary key with two columns: STREET_PK and ZIP_PK, and still has other columns: CITY and STATE. In this case, the ADDRESS_ID_PK column is no longer needed.

JPA requires that a primary key class, say, Address2PK (see Listing 4-2), be defined. Then the corresponding entity can be defined using the primary key class, as in Listing 4-1. The @IdClass annotation is needed on the entity to specify the primary key class, and each attribute corresponding to the composite primary key class must be annotated with @Id.

Listing 4-1 Address2.java: Entity for table ADDRESS2.

```java
import javax.persistence.Entity;
import javax.persistence.Id;
import javax.persistence.IdClass;

@Entity
@IdClass(Address2PK.class)
public class Address2 {
  @Id
  @Column(name = "STREET_PK", insertable=true,  nullable=false)
  private String street;

  private String city;
  private String state;

  @Id
  @Column(name = "ZIP_PK", insertable=true,  nullable=false)
  private String zip;

  public Address2() {
    super();
  }

  public Address2(String street, String zip) {
    this.street = street;
    this.zip = zip;
  }

  // getters and setters are omitted
}
```

Listing 4-2 Address2PK.java: Composite primary key class for entity Address2. Its attributes street and zip must have the same name and type as in the entity class Address2.

```java
import java.io.Serializable;

public class Address2PK implements Serializable {
  private String street;
  private String zip;

  public Address2PK() {   }
```

```
public Address2PK(String street, String zip) {
  this.street = street;
  this.zip = zip;
}

public String getStreet() {
  return street;
}

public String getZip() {
  return zip;
}

public boolean equals(Object obj) {
  if (!(obj instanceof Address2PK)) {
    return false;
  }
  Address2PK spk = (Address2PK) obj;
  return this.street.equals(spk.street) && this.zip.equals(spk.zip);
}

public int hashCode() {
  return this.street.hashCode() ^ this.zip.hashCode();
}
}
```

Notice that the ID class `Address2PK` does not define setter methods. It is a good practice, since primary key values of a managed entity cannot be changed. With this mapping for the entity and its `@IdClass` primary key, it can be used very intuitively:

```
Address2 address = new Address2("2922 Shell Drive", "48092");
address.setState("MN");
em.persist(address);
```

In fact, we may not directly use the ID class for many of the operations on the `Address2` entity. However, the `find` operation makes use of the primary key class:

```
Address2PK pk = new Address2PK("2922 Shell Drive", "48092");
Address2 newAddr = em.find(Address2.class, pk);
```

At runtime, JPA determines if two instances of the `Address2` entity are equal or not by copying the marked `@Id` fields into the corresponding fields of the `Address2PK` class and calling `Address2PK.equals()` method.

Notice that JPA requires that each entity instance be uniquely identifiable by its primary key. So the primary key class must provide methods: `equals()` and `hashCode()` for testing equality. Below are the full requirements for `@IdClass`:

- It must implement `java.io.Serializable`.
- It must provide valid implementation of `equals()` and `hashCode()` methods. The semantics of value equality for these methods must be consistent with that of their corresponding database records. After all, each entity instance represents a database record.
- It must be a public class and have a public no-argument constructor.
- The names and types of the fields/properties in the primary key class must be the same as in the entity class, if the primary key attributes have basic types. See Section 4.2.2 for scenarios where a primary key attribute may be of an entity type.
- The access type (field- or property-based) of the primary key class must be the same as that of the entity.

4.1.2 @EmbeddedId

In the previous subsection, the `@IdClass` is introduced to handle composite primary keys. This subsection provides an alternative by using the `@EmbeddedId` annotation. Assume we are using the same table `ADDRESS2` as in the previous subsection, where two columns: `STREET_PK` and `ZIP_PK` are used as the composite primary key. We now define a new entity `Address3` with an embedded primary key class `Address3PK` as in Listing 4-3 and Listing 4-4.

Listing 4-3 Address3.java: Entity definition using embedded primary key.

```
@Entity
@Table(name = "ADDRESS2")
public class Address3 {
  @EmbeddedId
  private Address3PK pk;        // embedded primary key

  private String city;
```

```
  private String state;

  public Address3() {
    super();
  }

  public Address3(Address3PK pk) {
    this.pk = pk;
  }

  public Address3PK getPk() {
    return pk;
  }

  public String getCity() {
    return this.city;
  }

  public void setCity(String city) {
    this.city = city;
  }

  public String getState() {
    return this.state;
  }

  public void setState(String state) {
    this.state = state;
  }
}
```

Listing 4-4 Address3PK.java: Definition of embedded primary key.

```
@Embeddable
public class Address3PK implements Serializable {
  @Column(name = "STREET_PK", insertable=true,  nullable=false)
  private String street;

  @Column(name = "ZIP_PK", insertable=true,  nullable=false)
  private String zip;

  public Address3PK() {   }
```

```java
  public Address3PK(String street, String zip) {
    this.street = street;
    this.zip = zip;
  }

  public String getStreet() {
    return street;
  }

  public String getZip() {
    return zip;
  }

  public boolean equals(Object obj) {
    if (!(obj instanceof Address3PK)) {
      return false;
    }
    Address3PK spk = (Address3PK) obj;
    return this.street.equals(spk.street) && this.zip.equals(spk.zip);
  }

  public int hashCode() {
    return this.street.hashCode() ^ this.zip.hashCode();
  }

}
```

The embedded primary key class must be annotated with @Embeddable. Also, similar to @IdClass, it must provide valid implementation of the methods equals() and hashCode(). Notice that the primary key fields: street and zip do not need to be repeated in the entity class Address3, since they are embedded inside the primary key field pk of type Address3PK. Due to this fact, the usage seems a little bit awkward:

```java
Address3PK pk = new Address3PK("2923 Shell Drive", "48093");
Address3 address = new Address3(pk);
em.persist(address);

Address3 addr = em.find(Address3.class, pk);
String zip = addr.getPk().getZip(); // vs. addr.getZip() with @IdClass
```

The two approaches: @IdClass and @EmbeddedId are equivalent, but with slightly different usage patterns. Which approach to take in a real application depends typically on your personal taste.

4.1.3 @ElementCollection and @CollectionTable

The annotations `@OneToMany` and `@ManyToMany` define a collection of related entities, but cannot be used for a collection of non-entities. The `@ElementCollection` annotation is introduced in JPA 2.0 to fill the gap, which is used to define a collection of elements having basic type or embeddable type. Such a collection has to be mapped by means of a collection table. The `@CollectionTable` annotation specifies the table that is used for the mapping of the element collection through a foreign key relationship.

For example, a `Customer` may have a number of string-valued nicknames (collection of basic type), and a set of `BankInfo` (collection of embeddable class; `BankInfo` is defined in Section 2.2.12):

```
@Entity
public class Customer {
  @Id
  @Column(name = "CUSTOMER_ID_PK")
  protected int customerId;

  @ElementCollection
  @CollectionTable(name="CUST_NICKNAME", joinColumns=@JoinColumn(
    name="CUST_ID_FPK", referencedColumnName="CUSTOMER_ID_PK")
  )
  protected Set<String> nickNames;

  @ElementCollection(fetch=FetchType.LAZY)
  @CollectionTable(name="CUST_BANK", joinColumns=@JoinColumn(
    name="CUST_ID_FPK", referencedColumnName="CUSTOMER_ID_PK")
  )
  protected List<BankInfo> bankInfos;
}
```

The optional `name` element of `@CollectionTable` specifies the name of the collection table. If omitted, it defaults to the concatenation of the following: name of the containing entity; "_"; name of the collection attribute. The collection table would default to CUSTOMER_NICKNAMES for the *nicknames* collection field, and to CUSTOMER_BANKINFOS for the `bankInfos` collection field.

The optional `joinColumns` element of `@CollectionTable` specifies how the collection table is related to the entity table using a foreign key. The `name` element of `@JoinColumn` indicates the name of the foreign key column in the collection table, and the `referencedColumnName` element refers to the referenced column name in the entity table, which defaults to its primary key column. When the `name` element is omitted, it defaults to the concatenation of the following: the name of the entity; "_"; the name of the referenced primary key column. The definition of `@JoinColumn` is given in Section 2.3.1.

The column names of a collection table are defaulted as follows. In the case of a basic type, the column name is derived from the name of the collection-valued field/property. In the case of an embeddable type, the column names are derived from the field/property names of the embeddable class. The structures of the two collection tables for the example above look as depicted in Figure 4-1:

```
CUST_NICKNAME:
CUST_ID_FPK
NICKNAMES
```

```
CUST_BANK:
CUST_ID_FPK
BANK_NAME_X
BANK_ACCOUNT_NUMBER
BANK_ROUTING_NUMBER
```

Figure 4-1 Structure of the two collection tables. The columns CUST_TD_FPK *and* NICKNAMES *form primary keys for the* CUST_NICKNAME *table. The columns* CUST_TD_FPK *and* BANK_NAME_X *form primary keys for the* CUST_BANK *table. If needed, other columns corresponding to the embeddable class may be part of the primary key.*

Of course, these derived column names may be overridden. In the case of a basic type, the `@Column` annotation is used on the collection-valued field/property. The value of the `table` element of `@Column` defaults to the name of the collection table. In the case of an embeddable type, the annotations `@AttributeOverride` and/or `@AttributeOverrides` must be used. The value of the `table` element of the `@Column` annotation used in `@AttributeOverride` also defaults to the name of the collection table. For example, we can change the column name from NICKNAMES to NICK_NAME_PK in the first collection table, and change the bank info column names to BANK_NAME_PK, ACCOUNT_NUMBER, and ROUTING_NUMBER in the second collection table as:

```
@Entity
public class Customer {
  @Id
  @Column(name = "CUSTOMER_ID_PK")
  protected int customerId;
```

```
@ElementCollection
@CollectionTable(name="CUST_NICKNAME", joinColumns=@JoinColumn(
  name="CUST_ID_FPK", referencedColumnName="CUSTOMER_ID_PK")
)
@Column(name = "NICK_NAME_PK", length=20, nullable=false)
protected Set<String> nickNames;

@ElementCollection(fetch=FetchType.LAZY)
@CollectionTable(name="CUST_BANK", joinColumns=@JoinColumn(
  name="CUST_ID_FPK", referencedColumnName="CUSTOMER_ID_PK")
)
@AttributeOverrides({
  @AttributeOverride(
    name="bankName", column=@Column(name="BANK_NAME_PK")),
  @AttributeOverride(
    name = "accountNumber",
    column = @Column(name ="ACCOUNT_NUMBER")),
  @AttributeOverride(
    name = "routingNumber",
    column = @Column(name = "ROUTING_NUMBER"))
})
protected Set<BankInfo> bankInfos;
}
```

Since element collection deals with basic types and embeddable classes, they cannot be managed by the entity manager separately from the parent entity. For example, when we persist or remove a Customer object, its associated nickNames and bankInfos will be persisted or removed automatically by the entity manager.

The @CollectionTable annotation itself is optional. When omitted, the default values of its elements apply. The definitions of the two annotations are:

```
@Target({METHOD, FIELD}) @Retention(RUNTIME)
public @interface CollectionTable {
  String name() default "";              // name of collection table
  String catalog() default "";
  String schema() default "";
  JoinColumn[] joinColumns() default {};
  UniqueConstraint[] uniqueConstraints() default {};
}

@Target({METHOD, FIELD}) @Retention(RUNTIME)
public @interface ElementCollection {
  Class targetClass() default void.class;
```

```
   FetchType fetch() default LAZY;
}
```

The `targetClass` element of `@ElementCollection` is typically not used when Java generics is used for defining the collection attribute. See Section 2.3.2 for an example on how to use this element.

The `@ElementCollection` annotation can be applied to persistent attributes in an entity or an embeddable class. If an embeddable class is contained within an element collection, it must not contain an element collection attribute. Also, such an embeddable class must not contain a relationship to an entity other than a many-to-one or one-to-one relationship. The embeddable class must be on the owning side of such a relationship, which must be mapped by a foreign key strategy.

4.2 Relationship Mapping

In Section 2.3, basic relationship mapping is presented. In this section, we talk about using maps for collections of related entities and using derived identities from parent entities to child entities.

4.2.1 @MapKey Annotations

For one-to-many and many-to-many relationships, the collection of related entity instances may be of type `java.util.Map`. By default, the key of the map is the (simple or composite) primary key of the related entity. The annotation `@MapKey` may be used to override the map key to any persistent attribute of the related entity using its `name` element. However, such an attribute is expected to be unique in the context of the relationship. For example, for the `Customer` to `Order` relationship, we may return a map with the `orderId` field as the map key and `Order` as map value:

```
@Entity
public class Customer extends User {
  @OneToMany(mappedBy = "customer", cascade = CascadeType.ALL)
  @MapKey(name = "orderId")
  protected Map<Integer, Order> orders;
}
```

The definition of `@MapKey` is:

```
@Target({METHOD, FIELD}) @Retention(RUNTIME)
public @interface MapKey {
  String name() default "";     // name of entity attribute for map key
```

}

There are a few similar annotations for a map relationship attribute that we are now ready to describe. They are `@MapKeyEnumerated`, `@MapKeyTemporal`, `@MapKeyColumn`, `@MapKeyClass`, and `@MapKeyJoinColumn`.

@MapKeyClass

The `@MapKeyClass` annotation is used to specify the type of the map key for associations of type `java.util.Map`. The map key can be a basic type, an embeddable class, or an entity. If the map is specified using Java generics, the `@MapKeyClass` annotation need not be specified; otherwise it must be specified. The annotation `@MapKeyClass` is not needed either when `@MapKey` is specified and vice versa. The `@MapKeyClass` annotation is used in conjunction with `@ElementCollection`, `@OneToMany` or `@ManyToMany`. Below are some examples:

```
@Entity
@Table(name="ORDERS")
public class Order extends BaseEntity {
  @OneToMany(mappedBy="order", targetClass=LineItem.class)
  @MapKeyClass(Integer.class)
  protected Map lineItems;
}

@Entity
public class Book extends BaseEntity {
  @ManyToMany
  @JoinTable(name = "BOOK_CATEGORY", ...)   // MapKeyClass defaults
  protected Map<Integer,Category> categories;
}
```

The annotation definition is:

```
@Target({METHOD, FIELD}) @Retention(RUNTIME)
public @interface MapKeyClass {
  Class value();                            // type of the map key
}
```

@MapKeyEnumerated, @MapKeyTemporal

The `@MapKeyEnumerated` annotation is used to specify the *enum* type for a map key whose basic type is an enumerated type. The `@MapKeyTemporal` annotation is used to specify the temporal type for a map key whose basic type is a temporal type: either `java.util.Date` or `java.util.Calendar`. The class of the map key can be specified using either Java generics or the `@MapKeyClass` annotation.

Both `@MapKeyEnumerated` and `@MapKeyTemporal` can be applied to an element collection or entity relationship of type `java.util.Map`, in conjunction with `@ElementCollection`, `@OneToMany`, or `@ManyToMany`. Their definitions are:

```
@Target({METHOD, FIELD}) @Retention(RUNTIME)
public @interface MapKeyEnumerated {
  EnumType value() default ORDINAL;     // default is ORDINAL
}

@Target({METHOD, FIELD}) @Retention(RUNTIME)
public @interface MapKeyTemporal {
  TemporalType value();                 // there is no default value
}
```

If the enumerated type is not specified or the `@MapKeyEnumerated` annotation is not used, the enumerated type is assumed to be ORDINAL. However, there is no default value for `@MapKeyTemporal`.

@MapKeyColumn

The values in a database column may be used as the map key as well. The `@MapKeyColumn` annotation is used to specify the mapping for the key column of a map whose map key is of a basic type. Its `name` element specifies the name of the map key column. If omitted, it defaults to the concatenation of the following: the name of the referencing relationship attribute; "_"; "KEY". For example,

```
@Entity
@Table(name="ORDERS")
public class Order extends BaseEntity {
  @OneToMany(mappedBy="order",
    cascade={CascadeType.PERSIST, CascadeType.REMOVE}
  )
  @MapKeyColumn(name="ORDER_ID_PK")
  protected Map<Integer, LineItem> lineItems;
}
```

The full annotation definition is:

```
@Target({METHOD, FIELD}) @Retention(RUNTIME)
```

```
public @interface MapKeyColumn {
  String name() default "";              // name of map key column
  boolean unique() default false;        // this column unique?
  boolean nullable() default false;      // this column nullable?
  boolean insertable() default true;     // included in SQL insert?
  boolean updatable() default true;      // included in SQL update?
  String columnDefinition() default "";
  String table() default "";        // table containing the column
  int length() default 255;         // length of string-valued column
  int precision() default 0;        // decimal precision
  int scale() default 0;            // decimal scale
}
```

The `table` element specifies the name of the table that contains the map key column. If the map key is for a one-to-many entity relationship using a foreign key mapping strategy, it defaults to the name of the primary table of the entity that is the value of the map. If the map key is for a one-to-many or many-to-many relationship using a join table, it is the name of the join table. If the map key is for an element collection, it is the name of the collection table. If `@MapKeyColumn` is not specified, the default values apply.

@MapKeyJoinColumn

The `@MapKeyJoinColumn` annotation is used to specify a mapping to an entity that is a map key. The map key join column is in the collection table, join table, or table of the target entity that is used to represent the map. Take the `Book-Category` many-to-many relationship as an example. Assume that for each book `Category`, there is a `Manager` for it (represented by a `MANAGER_ID` column) and an extra column `MANAGER_ID_FK` is added to the join table `BOOK_CATEGORY`. The following mapping gives a map of categories (and the managers for those categories), to which a book belongs. The map key is `Manager` and map value is `Category`.

```
@Entity
@Table(name="BOOK")
public class Book extends BaseEntity {
  @ManyToMany
  @JoinTable(name = "BOOK_CATEGORY",
    joinColumns=@JoinColumn(
      name="BOOK_ID_FPK", referencedColumnName="BOOK_ID_PK"),
    inverseJoinColumns=@JoinColumn(
      name="CATEGORY_ID_FPK", referencedColumnName = "CATEGORY_ID_PK")
  )
  @MapKeyJoinColumn(
    name="MANAGER_ID_FK", referencedColumnName = "MANAGER_ID")
```

```
    )
    protected Map<Manager, Category> categories;
}
```

The full definition of @MapKeyJoinColumn is given as:

```
@Target({METHOD, FIELD}) @Retention(RUNTIME)
public @interface MapKeyJoinColumn {
    String name() default "";
    String referencedColumnName() default "";
    boolean unique() default false;
    boolean nullable() default false;
    boolean insertable() default true;
    boolean updatable() default true;
    String columnDefinition() default "";
    String table() default "";
}
```

The optional name element defines the name of the foreign key column. If omitted, it defaults to the concatenation of the following: the name of the referencing relationship field/property of the referencing entity or embeddable; "_"; "KEY". The referencedColumnName element defines the name of the column referenced by this foreign key column. The referenced column is in the table of the target entity. If this element is missing, it is defaulted to refer to the primary key of the referenced table. Support for referenced columns that are not primary key columns of the referenced table is optional.

The table element refers to the name of the table that contains the foreign key column. If the map is for an element collection, it is the name of the collection table for the map value. If the map is for a one-to-many or many-to-many entity relationship using a join table, it is the name of the join table for the map value. If the map is for a one-to-many entity relationship using a foreign key mapping strategy, it is the name of the primary table of the entity that is the value of the map.

The remaining annotation elements refer to this foreign key column and have the same semantics as those of @Column.

If no @MapKeyJoinColumn annotation is specified, a single join column is assumed and the default values described above apply. For composite primary keys, the annotation

@MapKeyJoinColumns should be used. Its usage is the same as @JoinColumns (see Section 2.3.1) and is omitted here.

```
@Target({METHOD, FIELD}) @Retention(RUNTIME)
public @interface MapKeyJoinColumns {
  MapKeyJoinColumn[] value();
}
```

4.2.2 Derived Identities and @MapsId

The identity of an entity (called dependent entity) may be derived from the identity of another entity (called parent entity) when the dependent entity is the owner of a many-to-one or one-to-one relationship to the parent entity and a foreign key maps the relationship from dependent to parent.

For example, Address may be a parent entity and Apartment and House dependent entities. At a given address, there may be one house or many apartments, and their primary keys may be derived from that of the address. The ID of Apartment may be derived from the ID of Address, plus an apartment number, and Apartment is the owner of a many-to-one relationship to Address. The ID of House may be the same as or a variant of the ID of Address, and House is the owner of a one-to-one relationship to Address. The assumption here is that a foreign key mapping strategy is applied from a dependent entity to the parent entity.

The following rules apply governing how a dependent entity's ID may be derived from its parent's ID. They are introduced in JPA 2.0 and may be viewed as extensions to the rules in Sections 4.1.1 and 4.1.2, which apply more often in legacy databases.

Rule 1: The dependent entity uses an IdClass (Section 4.1.1) to represent its PK (primary key).

- The ID attribute (field or property) of the entity class and the corresponding attribute in the ID class must have the same name.

- If an ID attribute in the entity class is of basic type, the corresponding attribute in the ID class must have the same type.

- If an ID attribute in the entity class is a many-to-one or one-to-one relationship reference to a parent entity, the type of the corresponding attribute in the ID class must be the same Java type as the PK of the parent entity.

Rule 2: The dependent entity uses an EmbeddedID (Section 4.1.2) to represent its PK.

- The ID attribute in the embedded ID class corresponding to the relationship in the dependent entity must be of the same type as the PK of the parent entity.

- The relationship attribute in the dependent entity must be designated by the `@MapsId` annotation (explained later), which means that this attribute provides mapping information for its corresponding ID attribute.

Rule 3: The dependent entity has a single ID attribute, which is either the relationship attribute or a separate ID attribute.

- The PK of the dependent entity must be of the same type as that of the parent entity.

- Either the relationship attribute is annotated with `@Id`, or a separate ID attribute is specified and the relationship attribute is annotated with `@MapsId`.

We consider the following examples and show how to map the relationship from a dependent entity to a parent entity. The reader is encouraged to identify which rule above is applied to each case.

Example 1: Parent entity has simple PK and dependent entity forms many-to-one relationship to parent.

```
@Entity
public class Address {
  @Id
  @Column(name = "ADDRESS_ID_PK")
  protected int addressId;
}
```

Case (1a): Dependent entity has IdClass PK, which has one attribute that corresponds to parent entity's PK. In this case, the relationship field `Apartment1a.addrId` is annotated by `@Id`, and the PK field `Apartment1PK.addrId` in the ID class corresponding to the relationship field has the same Java type as the PK of `Address`. The IdClass `Apartment1PK` is annotated with `@Embeddable` so that it may be re-used in Case (1b).

```
@Embeddable
public class Apartment1PK implements Serializable {
  short aptNumber;
  int addrId;                    // match PK type of parent
}


@Entity
@IdClass(Apartment1PK.class)
@Table(name = "APARTMENT")
public class Apartment1a {
  @Id
  @Column(name="APT_NUM_PK")
  short aptNumber;        // match name & type of Apartment1PK.aptNumber

  @Id
  @ManyToOne
  @JoinColumn(
    name="ADDRESS_ID_FPK", referencedColumnName="ADDRESS_ID_PK"
  )
  protected Address addrId;   // match name of ApartmentPK1.addrId
}
```

Case (1b): Dependent entity has embeddable PK. The relationship field in the dependent entity is `Apartment1b.address`, which is annotated with `@MapsId`. Its corresponding PK field in the embedded ID class is `Apartment1PK.addrId`, which has the same type as the PK of the parent entity `Address`.

```
@Entity
@Table(name = "APARTMENT")
public class Apartment1b {
  @EmbeddedId
  @AttributeOverride(
    name = "aptNumber", column = @Column(name = "APT_NUM_PK")
  )
  protected Apartment1PK aptId;

  @MapsId("addrId")              // addrId is a field of Apartment1PK
  @ManyToOne                     //   that matches PK type of parent
  @JoinColumn(
    name="ADDRESS_ID_FPK", referencedColumnName="ADDRESS_ID_PK"
```

```
    )
    protected Address address;
}
```

The `@MapsId` annotation is used to designate a many-to-one or one-to-one relationship attribute that provides mapping for its corresponding embedded ID primary key of the dependent entity, an attribute within an embedded ID primary key of the dependent entity, or the simple primary key of the dependent entity. The `value` element of `@MapsId` is used to specify the name of the primary key attribute within the embedded ID class to which the relationship corresponds. The `value` element is not specified when the PK of the dependent entity is of the same Java type as the PK of the parent entity. The annotation is defined as:

```
@Target({METHOD, FIELD}) @Retention(RUNTIME)
public @interface MapsId {
    String value() default "";
}
```

Notice that the relationship attribute designated by `@MapsId` determines the mapping for the corresponding ID attribute. In this case, the relationship attribute `Apartment1b.address` determines that the ID attribute `addrId` (the `value` element in `@MapsId`) is mapped to column `ADDRESS_ID_FPK` in table `APARTMENT`. On the other hand, the embedded ID field `Apartment1PK.addrId` is not used to provide mapping information.

Example 2: Parent entity has IdClass PK and dependent entity forms many-to-one relationship to parent. We re-use the ID class `Address2PK` and entity class `Address2`, defined in Section 4.1.1.

```
@Entity
@IdClass(Address2PK.class)
public class Address2 {
    @Id @Column(name = "STREET_PK")
    String street;

    @Id @Column(name = "ZIP_PK")
    String zip;
}

@Embeddable
public class Address2PK implements Serializable {
```

154

```
  String street;
  String zip;
}
```

Case (2a): Dependent entity has IdClass PK. The ID attribute `Apartment2a.addrId` forms a many-to-one relationship to the parent. The type of the corresponding field `Apartment2PK.addrId` in the ID class has the same type as the parent entity PK.

```
@Embeddable
public class Apartment2PK implements Serializable {
  short aptNumber;
  Address2PK addrId;              // match PK type of parent
}

@Entity
@IdClass(Apartment2PK.class)
@Table(name = "APARTMENT2")
public class Apartment2a {
  @Column(name = "APT_NUM_PK")
  @Id short aptNumber;           // match Apartment2PK.aptNumber

  @Id
  @ManyToOne
  @JoinColumns({
    @JoinColumn(name="STREET_FPK", referencedColumnName="STREET_PK"),
    @JoinColumn(name="ZIP_FPK", referencedColumnName="ZIP_PK")
  })
  protected Address2 addrId;   // match name of Apartment2PK.addrId
}
```

Case (2b): Dependent entity has embedded PK. The PK field `addrId` in the embedded ID class corresponds to the relationship in the dependent entity and has the same type as the PK of the parent. The relationship attribute `Apartment2b.address` determines that the ID attributes: `street` and `zip` in `addrId` (the `value` element in `@MapsId`) are mapped to columns `STREET_FK` and `ZIP_FK`, respectively, in table `APARTMENT`.

```
@Entity
@Table(name = "APARTMENT2")
public class Apartment2b {
  @EmbeddedId
  @AttributeOverride(
    name = "aptNumber", column = @Column(name = "APT_NUM_PK")
  )
  protected Apartment2PK aptId;
```

155

```
  @MapsId("addrId")                // addrId is a field of Apartment2PK
  @ManyToOne                       //   that matches PK type of parent
  @JoinColumns({
    @JoinColumn(name="STREET_FPK", referencedColumnName="STREET_PK"),
    @JoinColumn(name="ZIP_FPK", referencedColumnName="ZIP_PK")
  })
  protected Address2 address;
}
```

Example 3: Parent entity has embedded PK and dependent entity forms many-to-one relationship to parent. We re-use the embedded ID class Address3PK and entity class Address3, defined in Section 4.1.2.

```
@Entity
@Table(name = "ADDRESS2")
public class Address3 {
  @EmbeddedId
  @AttributeOverrides( {
    @AttributeOverride(
      name = "street", column = @Column(name = "STREET_PK")),
    @AttributeOverride(
      name = "zip", column = @Column(name = "ZIP_PK"))
  })
  Address3PK pk;
}

@Embeddable
public class Address3PK implements Serializable {
  private String street;
  private String zip;
}
```

Case (3a): Dependent entity has IdClass PK. The ID field Apartment3a.addrId forms a many-to-one relationship to parent and its corresponding field Apartment3PK.addrId in the ID class has the same Java type as the PK of the parent entity Address3.

```
public class Apartment3PK implements Serializable {
  short aptNumber;
  Address3PK addrId;              // match PK type of parent
}

@Entity
```

```
@IdClass(Apartment3PK.class)
@Table(name = "APARTMENT2")
public class Apartment3a {
  @Id
  @Column(name = "APT_NUM_PK")
  protected short aptNumber;       // match Apartment3PK.aptNumber

  @Id
  @ManyToOne
  @JoinColumns({
    @JoinColumn(name="STREET_FPK", referencedColumnName="STREET_PK"),
    @JoinColumn(name="ZIP_FPK", referencedColumnName="ZIP_PK")
  })
  protected Address3 addrId;       // match name of Apartment3PK.addrId
}
```

Case (3b): Dependent entity has embeddable PK. The PK field `Apartment3PK.addrId` in the embedded ID class corresponding to the relationship has the same type as the PK of the parent entity `Address3`.

```
@Entity
@Table(name = "APARTMENT2")
public class Apartment3b {
  @EmbeddedId
  @AttributeOverride(
    name = "aptNumber", column = @Column(name = "APT_NUM")
  )
  protected Apartment3PK aptId;

  @MapsId("addrId")              // addrId is a field of Apartment3PK
  @ManyToOne                     //   that matches PK type of parent
  @JoinColumns({
    @JoinColumn(name="STREET_FPK", referencedColumnName="STREET_PK"),
    @JoinColumn(name="ZIP_FPK", referencedColumnName="ZIP_PK")
  })
  protected Address3 address;
}
```

In this case, the following JPQL queries are equivalent:

```
SELECT p FROM Apartment3b p WHERE p.aptId.addrId.zip = '48331'
SELECT p FROM Apartment3b p WHERE p.address.pk.zip   = '48331'
```

Example 4: Parent entity has simple PK and dependent entity forms one-to-one relationship to parent.

```
@Entity
public class Address {
  @Id
  @Column(name = "ADDRESS_ID_PK")
  protected int addressId;
}
```

Case (4a): Dependent entity has a single relationship attribute that is annotated with `@Id` and corresponds to the parent's PK. The PK of the dependent entity `House4a` is of type `int`, the same as the PK type of the parent.

```
@Entity
@Table(name = "HOUSE")
public class House4a {
  @Id
  @OneToOne
  @JoinColumn(
    name="ADDRESS_ID_FPK", referencedColumnName="ADDRESS_ID_PK"
  )
  protected Address addr;
}
```

The rules in this subsection are new features of JPA 2.0. Some of them have equivalents in JPA 1.0, but the usage may look awkward now. For example, in JPA 1.0, this mapping would have to be done as:

```
@Entity
public class House {
  @Id
  @Column(name = "ADDRESS_ID_FPK", updatable=false, insertable=false)
  protected int houseId;

  @OneToOne
  @PrimaryKeyJoinColumn(
    name="ADDRESS_ID_FPK", referencedColumnName="ADDRESS_ID_PK"
  )
  protected Address addr;
}
```

Since both the `houseId` and `addr` attributes are mapped to the same database column, only one of them needs to update the database. That is why we have marked the houseId attribute with `insertable` and `updatable` to `false`. In fact, the `houseId` attribute looks redundant here and is marked as read-only for easy access.

Case (4b): Dependent entity has a simple PK that has the same type as its parent's PK. The `@MapsId` annotation is applied to the relationship attribute and indicates that the primary key is mapped by this relationship attribute. The ID attribute `houseId` annotated by `@Id` is actually redundant and is defined here only for easy access. Thus any mapping such as `@Column` should not be defined on this attribute.

```
@Entity
@Table(name = "HOUSE")
public class House4b {
  @Id
  protected int houseId;          // overriding is not allowed here

  @MapsId
  @OneToOne
  @JoinColumn(
    name="ADDRESS_ID_FPK", referencedColumnName="ADDRESS_ID_PK"
  )
  protected Address addr;
}
```

Although both the ID attribute `houseId` and the relationship attribute `addr` are mapped to the same foreign key column in the HOUSE table, the ID attribute `houseId` is effectively a read-only mapping. This is what the `@MapsId` annotation buys us. The developer should do updates/inserts on the foreign key column through the relationship attribute `addr`, and the ID attribute `houseId` should be filled out automatically when a `House4b` entity is retrieved from the database.

In this case, the annotation `@PrimaryKeyJoinColumn` may also be used as in Case (4a), but `@MapsId` is preferred for derived identities.

Example 5: Parent entity has IdClass PK and dependent entity forms one-to-one relationship to parent. The dependent entity's PK is of the same type as that of the parent entity.

```
@Entity
@IdClass(Address2PK.class)
public class Address2 {
```

```
  @Id @Column(name = "STREET_PK")
  String street;

  @Id @Column(name = "ZIP_PK")
  String zip;
}

@Embeddable
public class Address2PK implements Serializable {
  String street;
  String zip;
}
```

Case (5a): Dependent entity has IdClass PK. The entity House5a has a single ID attribute that is the relationship attribute and is annotated with @Id. Both parent and child have the same ID class: Address2PK.

```
@Entity
@IdClass(Address2PK.class)
@Table(name = "HOUSE2")
public class House5a {
  @Id
  @OneToOne
  @JoinColumns({
    @JoinColumn(name="STREET_FPK", referencedColumnName="STREET_PK"),
    @JoinColumn(name="ZIP_FPK", referencedColumnName="ZIP_PK")
  })
  protected Address2 address;
}
```

Case (5b): Dependent entity has embedded PK. The entity House5b has a single ID attribute that is different from the relationship field. The relationship attribute is annotated @MapsId. Note again that the @MapsId relationship attribute provides the mapping for the PK of House5b. Thus it is not allowed to attempt to provide mapping on the housePK attribute.

```
@Entity
@Table(name = "HOUSE2")
public class House5b {
  @EmbeddedId
  Address2PK housePK;        // @AttributeOverride not allowed here

  @MapsId
```

```
  @OneToOne
  @JoinColumns({
    @JoinColumn(name="STREET_FPK", referencedColumnName="STREET_PK"),
    @JoinColumn(name="ZIP_FPK", referencedColumnName="ZIP_PK")
  })
  protected Address2 addr;
}
```

Example 6: Parent entity has embedded PK and dependent entity forms one-to-one relationship to parent. The dependent entity's PK is of the same type as that of the parent entity.

```
@Entity
@Table(name = "ADDRESS2")
public class Address3 {
  @EmbeddedId
  @AttributeOverrides( {
    @AttributeOverride(
      name = "street", column = @Column(name = "STREET_PK")),
    @AttributeOverride(
      name = "zip", column = @Column(name = "ZIP_PK"))
  })
  Address3PK pk;
}

@Embeddable
public class Address3PK implements Serializable {
  private String street;
  private String zip;
}
```

Case (6a): Dependent entity has IdClass PK. The entity `House6a` has a single ID attribute that must be the same as the PK class of the parent entity. The `@Id` annotation is applied to the relationship attribute.

```
@Entity
@Table(name = "HOUSE2")
@IdClass(Address3PK.class)
public class House6a {
  @Id
  @OneToOne
  @JoinColumns({
    @JoinColumn(name="STREET_FPK", referencedColumnName="STREET_PK"),
    @JoinColumn(name="ZIP_FPK", referencedColumnName="ZIP_PK")
```

```
  })
  protected Address3 address;
}
```

Case (6b): Dependent entity has EmbeddedID PK. The PK of entity `House` is of the same Java type as the PK of the parent entity and the `value` element in `@MapsId` is not specified. Since the `@MapsId` relationship attribute provides mapping for the PK of `House`, the attribute `House.pk` cannot be overridden by the `@AttributeOverride` annotation.

```
@Entity
@Table(name = "HOUSE2")
public class House {
  @EmbeddedId
  Address3PK pk;          // @AttributeOverride not allowed here

  @MapsId
  @OneToOne
  @JoinColumns({
    @JoinColumn(name="STREET_FPK", referencedColumnName="STREET_PK"),
    @JoinColumn(name="ZIP_FPK", referencedColumnName="ZIP_PK")
  })
  protected Address3 address;
}
```

This concludes our examples on derived identities. When a many-to-one or one-to-one entity relationship attribute corresponds to a primary key attribute in a dependent entity, the dependent entity cannot be persisted before the parent relationship is assigned, since the identity of the dependent entity is derived from the parent entity. Thus, always set the relationship attribute on the dependent entity before persisting it to the database. The following code snippet gives an example:

```
Address3PK pk = new Address3PK("2923 Shell Drive", "48093");
Address3 addr = new Address3(pk);
House6b hs = new House6b();
hs.setAddress(addr);            // set relationship attribute

em.getTransaction().begin();
em.persist(addr);
em.persist(hs);
em.getTransaction().commit();
```

4.3 Inheritance Mapping

JPA supports three different strategies of mapping entity inheritance. The single-table strategy assumes all entities in an inheritance hierarchy are mapped to the same table. The joined-table strategy maps the root of an entity hierarchy to a table, and each derived entity to a separate table, whose primary key points to the primary key of the root table. The third strategy maps each class of an entity hierarchy to a completely separate table.

In this section, we illustrate all three strategies using `Customer` in Figure 2-2 as the root entity, and `PreferredCustomer` and `GoldCustomer` as derived entities in the inheritance hierarchy.

4.3.1 Joined-Table Strategy

In the joined-table strategy, each entity has a separate table, but direct descendants of a parent class in the hierarchy have one-to-one relationship with the parent entity. The table for the parent class contains only columns common to its children, and the table for a child entity contains only columns specific to that child. The primary key of a child table is also a foreign key to the primary key of the parent table. In the parent table, a discriminator column must be identified and the value in this column is used to tell a given row contains the value for which entity in the inheritance hierarchy.

See Figure 4-2 for the table structure and some sample data for the `Customer` hierarchy. The root `CUSTOMER` table contains data common to entities in the hierarchy, and child tables `PREFERRED_CUSTOMER` and `GOLD_CUSTOMER` contain data only specific to their corresponding entities. All three tables share the same primary key values and each child table has a foreign key to the root table. The column `CUSTOMER_TYPE` in the root table is the discriminator column, whose value is used to tell which row in the root table contains data for which entity: P for a preferred customer, G for a gold customer, and C for a regular customer. For example, for customers with ID 200 and 300, their customer type is P and they are preferred customers. For a preferred customer, its inherited values are stored in the `CUSTOMER` table and type-specific values are stored in the `PREFERRED_CUSTOMER` table, with a foreign key linking them together. However, the customer with ID 100 has customer type C and all its values are stored in the root table, corresponding to an instance of the `Customer` root entity. Thus, for an instance of a child entity, its values are stored in two tables: inherited values from the parent class in the parent table and child-entity specific values in the child table.

163

PREFERRED_CUSTOMER table		
CUSTOMER_ID_FPK	DISCOUNT_RATE	EXPIRATION_DATE
200	0.20	2010-12-15
300	0.15	2015-05-13

CUSTOMER table			
CUSTOMER_ID_PK	NAME	...	CUSTOMER_TYPE
100	John Wang	...	C
200	Big Guy	...	P
300	Rich Girl	...	P
500	Lisa Smith	...	G

GOLD_CUSTOMER table		
CUSTOMER_ID_FPK	CARD_NUMBER	CREDIT_LIMIT
500	12345678	5000

Figure 4-2 Table structure for joined-table inheritance strategy. A child entity draws inherited values from root table.

To map such an inheritance hierarchy, we use annotation @Inheritance to specify the joined-table strategy and @DiscriminatorColumn to specify CUSTOMER_TYPE as the discriminator column. The mapping looks like this:

```
@Entity
@Table(name = "CUSTOMER")
@Inheritance(strategy = InheritanceType.JOINED)
@DiscriminatorColumn(name = "CUSTOMER_TYPE",
  discriminatorType = DiscriminatorType.STRING, length = 1
)
@DiscriminatorValue(value = "C")
public class Customer extends User {
  @Id
  @GeneratedValue(strategy = GenerationType.TABLE,
    generator = "CUST_SEQ_GEN"
  )
  @Column(name = "CUSTOMER_ID_PK", updatable=false)
  protected int customerId;

  @Column(name = "CUSTOMER_TYPE", nullable=false)
  @Enumerated(EnumType.STRING)
  protected CustomerType customerType;

  // other fields and getters/setters
}

@Entity
@Table(name="PREFERRED_CUSTOMER")
```

```
@DiscriminatorValue(value = "P")
@PrimaryKeyJoinColumn(
  name="CUSTOMER_ID_FPK",referencedColumnName="CUSTOMER_ID_PK"
)
public class PreferredCustomer extends Customer {
  @Column(name="DISCOUNT_RATE")
  protected double discountRate;

  @Column(name="EXPIRATION_DATE")
  @Temporal(TemporalType.DATE)
  protected Date expirationDate;

  // getters and setters for discountRate and expirationDate
}

@Entity
@Table(name = "GOLD_CUSTOMER")
@DiscriminatorValue(value = "G")
@PrimaryKeyJoinColumn(
  name="CUSTOMER_ID_FPK",referencedColumnName="CUSTOMER_ID_PK"
)
public class GoldCustomer extends Customer {
  @Column(name = "CARD_NUMBER")
  protected String cardNumber;

  @Column(name = "CREDIT_LIMIT")
  protected double creditLimit;

  // getters and setters for cardNumber and creditLimit
}
```

The @DiscriminatorValue annotation must be specified for each non-abstract entity in the hierarchy. When an object of type, say, GoldCustomer, is saved to the database, JPA then knows to set the value of the CUSTOMER_TYPE column to G. Also, each derived entity must use @PrimaryKeyJoinColumn to map it to the parent entity. For composite primary keys, use @PrimaryKeyJoinColumns.

Below is the full definition of the new annotations introduced in this section.

```
@Target({TYPE}) @Retention(RUNTIME)
public @interface Inheritance {
  InheritanceType strategy() default SINGLE_TABLE;
}
```

165

```
public enum InheritanceType { SINGLE_TABLE, JOINED, TABLE_PER_CLASS };

@Target({TYPE}) @Retention(RUNTIME)
public @interface DiscriminatorColumn {
  String name() default "DTYPE";
  DiscriminatorType discriminatorType() default STRING;
  String columnDefinition() default "";
  int length() default 31;
}

public enum DiscriminatorType { STRING, CHAR, INTEGER };

public @interface DiscriminatorValue {
  String value();
}
```

The advantage of the joined-table strategy is that the database table structure resembles the Java class structure and offers an elegant choice from the design perspective. The downside is that each polymorphic query and polymorphic association requires joining of multiple tables and its performance should not be as good as the single-table strategy (see next subsection). Even when inserting or updating a record, multiple SQL insert or update statements may be needed: one for the root table and one for each involved child table. Nevertheless, such performance overhead should be insignificant in many applications, and the joined-table strategy should be the first one to consider.

4.3.2 Single-Table Strategy

In the single-table strategy, all entities in the inheritance hierarchy are mapped to a single table, which contains a superset of all data stored in the class hierarchy. Similar to the joined-table strategy, a discriminator column is needed to distinguish the type of an object in this entity hierarchy.

To map the Customer class hierarchy in Figure 2-2 using the single-table strategy, we would need to create a table, say, CUSTOMER2 that has all the combined columns of tables CUSTOMER, PREFERRED_CUSTOMER and GOLD_CUSTOMER (minus the two redundant primary key columns in the child tables). The CUSTOMER_TYPE column is still needed as the discriminator column. See Figure 4-3 for details. Note that there are many NULL values in the table. For example, the customer with ID 100 and customer type C is a regular customer and thus does not have any values for the four columns corresponding to the child entities.

CUSTOMER2 table								
CUSTOMER_ID_PK	NAME	...	CUSTOMER_TYPE	DISCOUNT_RATE	EXPIRATION_DATE	CARD_NUMBER	CREDIT_LIMIT
100	John Wang	...	C	NULL	NULL	NULL	NULL
200	Big Guy	...	P	0.20	2010-12-15	NULL	NULL
300	Rich Girl	...	P	0.15	2015-05-13	NULL	NULL
500	Lisa Smith	...	G	NULL	NULL	12345678	5000

Figure 4-3 Table structure for single-table inheritance strategy. Root entity and derived entities share the same table.

The entities in the hierarchy, renamed to `Customer2`, `PreferredCustomer2`, and `GoldCustomer2`, can now be mapped to the CUSTOMER2 table, which looks like this:

```
@Entity
@Table(name = "CUSTOMER2")
@Inheritance(strategy = InheritanceType.SINGLE_TABLE)
@DiscriminatorColumn(name = "CUSTOMER_TYPE",
  discriminatorType = DiscriminatorType.STRING, length = 1
)
@DiscriminatorValue(value = "C")
public class Customer2 extends User {

  @Id
  @GeneratedValue(strategy = GenerationType.TABLE,
    generator = "CUST_SEQ_GEN"
  )
  @Column(name = "CUSTOMER_ID_PK", updatable=false)
  protected int customerId;

  @Column(name = "CUSTOMER_TYPE", nullable=false)
  @Enumerated(EnumType.STRING)
  protected CustomerType customerType;

  // other fields and getters/setters
}

@Entity
@DiscriminatorValue(value = "P")
public class PreferredCustomer2 extends Customer2 {

  @Column(name="DISCOUNT_RATE")
```

```
  protected double discountRate;

  @Column(name="EXPIRATION_DATE")
  @Temporal(TemporalType.DATE)
  protected Date expirationDate;

  // getters and setters for discountRate and expirationDate
}

@Entity
@DiscriminatorValue(value = "G")
public class GoldCustomer2 extends Customer2 {

  @Column(name = "CARD_NUMBER")
  protected String cardNumber;

  @Column(name = "CREDIT_LIMIT")
  protected double creditLimit;

  // getters and setters for cardNumber and creditLimit
}
```

The advantage of the single-table strategy is its simplicity and efficiency. No table joins are needed for polymorphic associations and queries. However, the disadvantages are that its corresponding table may contain many NULL values and certain data integrity constraints cannot be easily enforced. For example, we cannot impose a unique constraint on the CREDIT_NUMBER column due to the NULL values for entities other than GoldCustomer2. Such a constraint has to be typically enforced through a database trigger. Overall, if performance is a top concern, the single-table strategy should be seriously considered.

4.3.3 Table-Per-Class Strategy

The table-per-class strategy simply stores each concrete entity class in an inheritance hierarchy to a completely different table. All attributes of the class, including inherited attributes, are mapped to columns of the table for the class. No relationship exists between any of the tables and there is no need for a discriminator column either.

To implement our Customer, PreferredCustomer, and GoldCustomer entity hierarchy using this strategy, we need to create three tables CUSTOMER3, PREFERRED_CUSTOMER3, and GOLD_CUSTOMER3. See Figure 4-4 for all the columns of the three tables. We can see that child tables duplicate the columns in the parent table.

CUSTOMER3:	PREFERRED_CUSTOMER3:	GOLD_CUSTOMER3:
CUSTOMER_ID_PK	CUSTOMER_ID_PK	CUSTOMER_ID_PK
NAME	NAME	NAME
ADDRESS_ID_FK	ADDRESS_ID_FK	ADDRESS_ID_FK
PICTURE	PICTURE	PICTURE
INCOME	INCOME	INCOME
BANK_NAME	BANK_NAME	BANK_NAME
ACCOUNT_NUMBER	ACCOUNT_NUMBER	ACCOUNT_NUMBER
ROUTING_NUMBER	ROUTING_NUMBER	ROUTING_NUMBER
	DISCOUNT_RATE	CARD_NUMBER
	EXPIRATION_DATE	CREDIT_LIMIT

Figure 4-4 Table design for table-per-class strategy.

Note that the column CUSTOMER_TYPE is no longer needed, since data from different entities do not mix in the same table. The code for this mapping scenario looks like:

```
@Entity
@Table(name = "CUSTOMER3")
@Inheritance(strategy = InheritanceType.TABLE_PER_CLASS)
public class Customer3 extends User {

  @Id
  @GeneratedValue(strategy = GenerationType.TABLE,
    generator = "CUST_SEQ_GEN"
  )
  @Column(name = "CUSTOMER_ID_PK", updatable=false)
  protected int customerId;

  // other fields and getters/setters
}

@Entity
@Table(name="PREFERRED_CUSTOMER3")
public class PreferredCustomer3 extends Customer3 {

  @Column(name="DISCOUNT_RATE")
  protected double discountRate;

  @Column(name="EXPIRATION_DATE")
  @Temporal(TemporalType.DATE)
  protected Date expirationDate;

  // getters and setters for discountRate and expirationDate
}
```

169

```java
@Entity
@Table(name="GOLD_CUSTOMER3")
public class GoldCustomer3 extends Customer3 {

  @Column(name = "CARD_NUMBER")
  protected String cardNumber;

  @Column(name = "CREDIT_LIMIT")
  protected double creditLimit;

  // getters and setters for cardNumber and creditLimit
}
```

This table-per-class design seems to be simple and easy to understand. However, it is the worst strategy among the three from both relational and OO standpoints. JPA even makes its support optional for persistence providers. It does not have good support for polymorphic relationships and queries because each entity class is mapped to its own table. It typically requires that SQL UNION statements (or a separate SQL query per subclass) be issued for queries that are intended to range over the class hierarchy.

4.4 Sample Mapping

In this section, we show the complete mapping for the entity inheritance hierarchy for the three strategies: join-table, single-table, and table-per-class. The mapping for the base class `BaseEntity` and other related entities is shown in Section 2.4. Again, to save space, we just show the mapping and omit the getters and setters in these classes.

Listing 4-5 User.java: Mapped super class for Customer and its derived classes.

```java
@MappedSuperclass
public class User extends BaseEntity {
  protected String name;

  @OneToOne(cascade={CascadeType.PERSIST,CascadeType.REMOVE})
  @JoinColumn(
    name = "ADDRESS_ID", referencedColumnName="ADDRESS_ID_PK"
  )
  protected Address address;

  protected double income;
```

```
@Access(AccessType.PROPERTY)
@Lob
@Basic(fetch=FetchType.LAZY, optional=false)
@Column(name="PICTURE", columnDefinition="BLOB NOT NULL")
public byte[] getPicture() {
  return this.picture;
}
}
```

Listing 4-6 Customer.java: Base Customer entity for joined-table strategy.

```
@Entity
@Table(name = "CUSTOMER")
@TableGenerator(name = "CUST_SEQ_GEN",
   table = "SEQUENCE_GENERATOR_TB",
   pkColumnName = "SEQUENCE_NAME", valueColumnName = "SEQUENCE_VALUE",
   pkColumnValue = "CUSTOMER_SEQ"
)
@AssociationOverride(name="address", joinColumns=@JoinColumn(
  name = "ADDRESS_ID_FK", referencedColumnName="ADDRESS_ID_PK")
)
@Inheritance(strategy = InheritanceType.JOINED)
@DiscriminatorColumn(name = "CUSTOMER_TYPE",
  discriminatorType = DiscriminatorType.STRING, length = 1
)
@DiscriminatorValue(value = "C")
public class Customer extends User  {
  @Id
  @GeneratedValue(strategy = GenerationType.TABLE,
    generator = "CUST_SEQ_GEN"
  )
  @Column(name = "CUSTOMER_ID_PK", updatable=false)
  protected int customerId;

  @Column(name = "CUSTOMER_TYPE", nullable=false)
  @Enumerated(EnumType.STRING)
  protected CustomerType customerType;

  @Embedded
  @AttributeOverrides({
    @AttributeOverride(
      name = "bankName", column = @Column(name = "BANK_NAME")),
    @AttributeOverride(
```

```
      name = "accountNumber",
      column = @Column(name = "ACCOUNT_NUMBER")),
    @AttributeOverride(
      name = "routingNumber",
      column = @Column(name = "ROUTING_NUMBER"))
  })
  protected BankInfo bank;

  @OneToMany(mappedBy = "customer", cascade=CascadeType.ALL)
  @MapKey(name="orderId")
  protected Map<Integer, Order> orders; //inverse side of relationship

  @ElementCollection
  @CollectionTable(name = "CUST_NICKNAME",
    joinColumns = @JoinColumn(
      name = "CUST_ID_FPK", referencedColumnName = "CUSTOMER_ID_PK")
  )
  protected Set<String> nickNames;

  @ElementCollection(fetch = FetchType.LAZY)
  @CollectionTable(name = "CUST_BANK",
    joinColumns = @JoinColumn(
      name = "CUST_ID_FPK", referencedColumnName = "CUSTOMER_ID_PK")
  )
  protected List<BankInfo> bankInfos;
}
```

Listing 4-7 GoldCustomer.java: Derived entity class for joined-table strategy.

```
@Entity
@Table(name = "GOLD_CUSTOMER")
@DiscriminatorValue(value = "G")
@PrimaryKeyJoinColumn(
  name = "CUSTOMER_ID_FPK", referencedColumnName = "CUSTOMER_ID_PK"
)
public class GoldCustomer extends Customer {
  @Column(name = "CARD_NUMBER")
  protected String cardNumber;

  @Column(name = "CREDIT_LIMIT")
  protected double creditLimit;
}
```

Listing 4-8 PreferredCustomer.java: Derived entity class for joined-table strategy.

```
@Entity
@Table(name="PREFERRED_CUSTOMER")
@DiscriminatorValue(value = "P")
@PrimaryKeyJoinColumn(
  name = "CUSTOMER_ID_FPK", referencedColumnName = "CUSTOMER_ID_PK"
)
public class PreferredCustomer extends Customer {
  @Column(name="DISCOUNT_RATE")
  protected double discountRate;

  @Column(name="EXPIRATION_DATE")
  @Temporal(TemporalType.DATE)
  protected Date expirationDate;
}
```

Listing 4-9 Customer2.java: Base entity for single-table strategy.

```
@Entity
@Table(name = "CUSTOMER2")
@AssociationOverride(name="address", joinColumns=@JoinColumn(
  name = "ADDRESS_ID_FK", referencedColumnName="ADDRESS_ID_PK")
)
@Inheritance(strategy = InheritanceType.SINGLE_TABLE)
@DiscriminatorColumn(name = "CUSTOMER_TYPE",
  discriminatorType = DiscriminatorType.STRING, length = 1
)
@DiscriminatorValue(value = "C")
public class Customer2 extends User {
  @Id
  @GeneratedValue(strategy = GenerationType.TABLE,
    generator = "CUST_SEQ_GEN"
  )
  @Column(name = "CUSTOMER_ID_PK", updatable=false)
  protected int customerId;

  @Column(name = "CUSTOMER_TYPE", nullable=false)
  @Enumerated(EnumType.STRING)
```

```
  protected CustomerType customerType;

  @Embedded
  @AttributeOverrides({
    @AttributeOverride(
      name = "bankName", column = @Column(name = "BANK_NAME")),
    @AttributeOverride(
      name = "accountNumber",
      column = @Column(name = "ACCOUNT_NUMBER")),
    @AttributeOverride(
      name = "routingNumber",
      column = @Column(name = "ROUTING_NUMBER"))
  })
  protected BankInfo bank;
}
```

Listing 4-10 GoldCustomer2.java: Derived entity for single-table strategy.

```
@Entity
@DiscriminatorValue(value = "G")
public class GoldCustomer2 extends Customer2 {
  @Column(name = "CARD_NUMBER")
  protected String cardNumber;

  @Column(name = "CREDIT_LIMIT")
  protected double creditLimit;
}
```

Listing 4-11 PreferredCustomer2.java: Derived entity for single-table strategy.

```
@Entity
@DiscriminatorValue(value = "P")
public class PreferredCustomer2 extends Customer2 {
  @Column(name="DISCOUNT_RATE")
  protected double discountRate;

  @Column(name="EXPIRATION_DATE")
  @Temporal(TemporalType.DATE)
  protected Date expirationDate;
```

```
}
```

```
@Entity
@Table(name = "CUSTOMER3")
@AssociationOverride(name="address", joinColumns=@JoinColumn(
  name = "ADDRESS_ID_FK", referencedColumnName="ADDRESS_ID_PK")
)
@Inheritance(strategy = InheritanceType.TABLE_PER_CLASS)
public class Customer3 extends User {
  @Id
  @GeneratedValue(
    strategy = GenerationType.TABLE, generator = "CUST_SEQ_GEN"
  )
  @Column(name = "CUSTOMER_ID_PK", updatable=false)
  protected int customerId;

  @Embedded
  @AttributeOverrides( {
    @AttributeOverride(
      name = "bankName", column = @Column(name = "BANK_NAME")),
    @AttributeOverride(
      name = "accountNumber",
      column = @Column(name = "ACCOUNT_NUMBER")),
    @AttributeOverride(
      name = "routingNumber",
      column = @Column(name = "ROUTING_NUMBER"))
  })
  protected BankInfo bank;
}
```

```
@Entity
@Table(name="GOLD_CUSTOMER3")
@AssociationOverride(name="address", joinColumns=@JoinColumn(
  name = "ADDRESS_ID_FK", referencedColumnName="ADDRESS_ID_PK")
```

```
)
public class GoldCustomer3 extends Customer3 {
  @Column(name = "CARD_NUMBER")
  protected String cardNumber;

  @Column(name = "CREDIT_LIMIT")
  protected double creditLimit;
}
```

Listing 4-14 PreferredCustomer3.java: Derived entity for table-per-class inheritance strategy.

```
@Entity
@Table(name="PREFERRED_CUSTOMER3")
@AssociationOverride(name="address", joinColumns=@JoinColumn(
  name = "ADDRESS_ID_FK", referencedColumnName="ADDRESS_ID_PK")
)
public class PreferredCustomer3 extends Customer3 {
  @Column(name="DISCOUNT_RATE")
  protected double discountRate;

  @Column(name="EXPIRATION_DATE")
  @Temporal(TemporalType.DATE)
  protected Date expirationDate;
}
```

5 JPA Query Language

JPA introduces a string-based high level query language. It is called the Java Persistence Query Language (JPQL). Its syntax looks very much like the SQL language, but it is more intuitive to use. It works directly on JPA entities, and their states and relationships, with support of both static and dynamic queries. The main functionality of JPQL is to retrieve entity objects directly from the database based on certain search criteria. In addition, it has support for bulk updates and deletes.

The first two sections talk about the JPA `Query` interface and how to execute queries using the API. The third section explains the JPQL and its syntax. Then, the fourth section deals with native SQL queries. Finally, the fifth section gives an application example to see how JPQL is applied to a real-world problem.

5.1 The Query Interface

As shown in Section 3.1, the `EntityManager` interface has several methods for creating queries. Once a query is created, the `Query` interface is used to execute it and get the result. In Table 5.1, the `Query` interface and its methods are listed with some high level description. The link to the full Javadoc can be found in Section 9.1.

Table 5.1 The `javax.persistence.Query` interface. It can be used to query the database, perform bulk update, and execute native SQL queries.

Method Signature	High Level Description
`List getResultList();`	Execute a SELECT query and return the query results as an untyped List. It returns an empty list if no result is retrieved.
`Object getSingleResult();`	Execute a SELECT query that returns a single untyped result. It throws `NoResultException` if there is no result, and throws `NonUniqueResultException` if more than one result exists.
`int executeUpdate();`	Execute an UPDATE or DELETE statement. It should not be called on a SELECT statement or a criteria query. An active transaction is required. It returns the number of entities that are modified by the

	query.

`Query setMaxResults(`
`   int maxResult);`
 	
`int getMaxResults();`
	Set/get the maximum number of results to retrieve. The setter returns the same query instance.

`Query setFirstResult(`
`   int startPosition);`
 	
`int getFirstResult();`
	Set/get the zero-based position of the first result to retrieve.

`Query setHint(`
`   String hintName,`
`   Object value);`
 	
`Map<String, Object>`
`   getHints();`
	Set query hint. If a vendor-specific hint is not recognized, it is silently ignored. The second method gets the hints and associated values that are in effect for the query instance.

`<T> Query setParameter(`
`   Parameter<T> param,`
`   T value);`
 	
`Query setParameter(`
`   Parameter<Calendar>`
`   param,`
`   Calendar value,`
`   TemporalType tType);`
 	
`Query setParameter(`
`   Parameter<Date> param,`
`   Date value,`
`   TemporalType tType);`
	Bind the value of a parameter, and return the same query object.
	
	The second method binds an instance of `java.util.Calendar` to a Parameter object, while the third method binds an instance of `java.util.Date` to a Parameter object.
	
	The last two methods may specify the accuracy as `DATE`, `TIME`, or `TIMESTAMP`, for the third parameter.

`Query setParameter(`
`   String name,`
`   Object value);`
 	
`Query setParameter(`
`   String name,`
`   java.util.Date value,`
`   TemporalType tType);`
 	
`Query setParameter(`
`   String name,`
`   java.util.Calendar c,`
`   TemporalType tType);`
	These three methods set a named parameter and return the same query object. The last two methods may specify the accuracy as `DATE`, `TIME`, or `TIMESTAMP`, for the third parameter.
	
	Example:
	`Query q = em.createQuery("SELECT b FROM`
	`   Book b WHERE b.title = :bookTitle");`
	`q.setParameter("bookTitle", title);`
	`List<Book> books = q.getResultList();`

`Query setParameter(`
`   int position,`
`   Object value);`
	These three methods set a positioned parameter and return the same query object. The last two methods may specify the accuracy as `DATE`, `TIME`, or

`Query setParameter(`
`   int position,`
`   java.util.Date value,`
`   TemporalType tType);`
 	
`Query setParameter(`
`   int position,`
`   java.util.Calendar c,`
`   TemporalType tType);`
	`TIMESTAMP`, for the third parameter.
	
	Example:
	`Query q = em.createQuery("SELECT o FROM`
	`   Order o WHERE o.orderTime > ?1");`
	`Timestamp t = ...`
	`q.setParameter(1,t,`
	`                 TemporalType.TIMESTAMP);`
	`List<Order> orders = q.getResultList();`

`Set<Parameter<?>>`
`   getParameters();`
 	
`<T> Parameter<T>`
`   getParameter(`
`   String name,`
`   Class<T> type);`
 	
`Parameter<?>`
`   getParameter(`
`   String name);`
 	
`Parameter<?>`
`   getParameter(`
`   int position);`
 	
`<T> Parameter<T>`
`   getParameter(`
`   int position,`
`   Class<T> type);`
 	
`<T> T getParameterValue(`
`   Parameter<T> param);`
 	
`Object`
`   getParameterValue(`
`   String name);`
 	
`Object`
`   getParameterValue(`
`   int position);`
	The first method gets the query parameter objects, and returns empty set if the query has no parameters.
	
	The second method gets the parameter of the given name and type.
	
	Other methods are similar.
	
	The last two methods return the value that has been bound to the parameter.

`boolean`
`   isBound(`
`   Parameter<?> param);`
	Return a boolean indicating whether a value has been bound to the parameter.

`Query setFlushMode(` `   FlushModeType`	Set/get the flush mode for the query execution. The flush mode set here applies to the query, overwriting

`flushMode);`
 	
`FlushModeType`
`  getFlushMode();`
	the flush mode type in use for the entity manager.

`Query setLockMode(`
`  LockModeType`
`  lockMode);`
 	
`LockModeType`
`  getLockMode();`
	Set/get the lock mode type to be used for the query execution. They apply only to JPQL SELECT queries or Criteria queries.

`<T> T unwrap(` `  Class<T> cls);`	Return an object of the specified type to allow access to the provider-specific API.

The new interface `TypedQuery<X>` introduced in JPA 2.0 is very similar to the `Query` interface, except it is typed using Java Generics. The type parameter `X` is the query return type. This can be seen by just two methods, and other methods are omitted here:

```
public interface TypedQuery<X> extends Query {
  // Execute a SELECT query and return query results as a typed List.
  List<X> getResultList();

  // Execute a SELECT query and return a single typed result.
  X getSingleResult();
}
```

Table 5.2 shows the `Parameter` interface for typed input parameters. Then the next two tables: Table 5.3 and Table 5.4, show the `Tuple` and `TupleElement` interfaces, which are used for returning results in typed queries. Examples on how to use them are given in the next section and in Chapter 7.

Table 5.2 The `javax.persistence.Parameter<T>` interface. It is used to set or get a typed parameter for a query.

Method Signature	High Level Description
`String getName();`	Return the parameter name, or null if the parameter is not a named parameter or no name has been assigned.
`Integer getPosition();`	Return the parameter position, or null if the parameter is not a positional

	parameter.
`Class<T> getParameterType();`	Return the Java type of the parameter. Values bound to the parameter must be assignable to this type. This method is required to be supported for criteria queries only.

Table 5.3 The `javax.persistence.Tuple` *interface. It is used for extracting the elements of a query result tuple.*

Method Signature	High Level Description
`<X> X get(TupleElement<X> te);`	Get the value of the specified tuple element.
`<X> X get(String alias, Class<X> type);`	Get the value of the tuple element to which the specified alias has been assigned.
`Object get(String alias);`	Get the value of the tuple element to which the specified alias has been assigned.
`<X> X get(int i, Class<X> type);`	Get the value of the element at the specified position in the result tuple. The first position is 0.
`Object get(int i);`	Get the value of the element at the specified position in the result tuple. The first position is 0.
`Object[] toArray();`	Return the values of the result tuple elements as an array.
`List<TupleElement<?>> getElements();`	Return the tuple elements.

Table 5.4 The `javax.persistence.TupleElement<X>` *interface. It defines an element that is returned in a query result tuple.*

Method Signature	High Level Description
`Class<? extends X>`	Return the runtime Java type of the tuple

`getJavaType();`	element.
`String getAlias();`	Return the alias assigned to the tuple element, or null if no alias has been assigned.

5.2 Query Execution

The returned results from `Query` methods such as `getResultList` and `getSingleResult` contains `Object` or `Object[]`. All Primitive type values are wrapped into their corresponding Java wrapper classes. The methods of the `Query` interface return untyped objects, and an explicit or implicit cast to the desired type is needed.

The query method `getSingleResult` returns a single result, which could be an entity, a scalar, an embeddable, or a combination of them, depending on whether it has a single-select expression, or multiple-select expression. For example, Listing 5-1 gives a few queries that return such single results.

Listing 5-1 Examples on queries that return a single result.

```
// Return an entity single result which is the order with max orderId.
// MAX is JPQL maximum value function.
Query query = em.createQuery("SELECT o FROM Order o " +
  "WHERE o.orderId = (SELECT MAX(o2.orderId) FROM Order o2)");
Order order = (Order) query.getSingleResult();

// Return a scalar single result, which is the average price of
// orders billed.  The JPQL average function AVG is used, which always
// returns Double
Query query = em.createQuery(
  "SELECT AVG(o.price) FROM Order o WHERE o.status = :status");
query.setParameter("status", OrderStatus.BILLED);
Double price = (Double) query.getSingleResult();

// Query with multiple-select expression: o, o.customer.bank.bankName.
// Return a single result of type: Object[]: a combination of entity
// and scalar
Query query = em.createQuery(
  "SELECT o, o.customer.bank.bankName FROM " +
```

```
"Order o WHERE o.orderId = (SELECT MAX(o2.orderId) FROM Order o2)");
Object[] result = (Object[]) query.getSingleResult();
Order order = (Order) result[0];
String bank = (String) result[1];
```

The query method `getResultList` returns a list of results. Each element in the list can be an entity, a scalar, an embeddable, or a combination of them, depending on whether it has a single-select expression, or multiple-select expression. For example, Listing 5-2 gives a few queries that return such result lists.

Listing 5-2 Examples on queries that return a list of results.

```
// Single-select expression. Returns a list of Customers who ordered
// before today
Query query = em.createQuery(
  "SELECT o.customer FROM Order o WHERE o.orderTime < ?1");
query.setParameter(1, new Date(), TemporalType.TIMESTAMP);
List<Customer> resultList = query.getResultList();

// Single-select expression. Returns a list of prices with billed
// order status
Query query = em.createQuery(
  "SELECT o.price FROM Order o WHERE o.status = :status");
query.setParameter("status", OrderStatus.BILLED);
List<Double> resultList = query.getResultList();

// Multiple-select expression: o.customer, o.price. Returns a list
// of Object[]
Query query = em.createQuery(
  "SELECT o.customer, o.price FROM Order o WHERE o.orderTime < ?1");
query.setParameter(1, new Date(), TemporalType.TIMESTAMP);
List<Object[]> resultList = query.getResultList();
for (Object[] result: resultList) {
  Customer customer = (Customer) result[0];
  Double price = (Double) result[1];
}
```

The method `getResultList` retrieves a list of query results. If there is no result from the execution of the query, an empty list is returned. On the other hand, the method `getSingleResult` retrieves only one result. If no result exists, the `NoResultException` will be thrown. If there is more than one result, the

`NonUniqueResultException` will be thrown. However, these two exceptions will not cause the current transaction, if existed, to roll back.

A named parameter, such as ":`status`" above, of a JPQL query is an identifier that is prefixed by the ":" symbol. The parameter names passed to the `setParameter` methods of the `Query` API do not include this ":" prefix. Named parameters are case-sensitive, and can be used for JPQL queries and for criteria queries (although use of `Parameter` objects is preferred; see examples below).

Positional parameters are designated by the question mark (?) prefix followed by an integer, such as "?1" in the examples above. They must be numbered starting from 1. The same parameter can be used more than once in the query string. The ordering of the parameters within the query string need not conform to the order of the positional parameters.

Either positional or named parameters may be used in a query. This is a personal choice. However, positional and named parameters may not be mixed in a single query. All input parameters must be single-valued, except in `IN` expressions, which support the use of collection-valued input parameters (see Section 5.3.3).

Query parameters must be specified correctly. An `IllegalArgumentException` is thrown, if one of the following happens:

- A parameter instance is specified that does not correspond to a parameter of the query,
- A parameter name is specified that does not correspond to a named parameter of the query,
- A positional value is specified that does not correspond to a positional parameter of the query, or
- The type of the parameter is not valid for the query.

This exception may be thrown when the parameter is bound, or the execution of the query may fail.

JPA 2.0 introduces the `TypedQuery` and `Parameter` interfaces for better control on query result types and parameter types. Instances of the `Parameter` interface can be used for both `Query` and `TypedQuery`. For example,

```
import javax.persistence.Parameter;
import javax.persistence.TypedQuery;
import javax.persistence.criteria.CriteriaBuilder;

public class QueryTest {
  protected  void runTypedQueries(EntityManager em) {
    TypedQuery<Double> query = em.createQuery(
      "SELECT AVG(o.price) FROM Order o WHERE o.status = :status",
      Double.class);

    CriteriaBuilder cb = em.getCriteriaBuilder();
    Parameter<OrderStatus> os
      = cb.parameter(OrderStatus.class, "status");
    query.setParameter(os, OrderStatus.BILLED);
    Double price = query.getSingleResult();      // no type cast needed
  }
}
```

More details on the `CriteriaBuilder` interface will be given in Chapter 7.

The methods `getResultList` and `getSingleResult` are not required to be invoked within a transaction context, unless a lock mode has been specified for the query. When they are invoked without a transaction, the returned entities from the queries will be detached if an entity manager with transaction-scoped persistence context is used, and will be managed if an entity manager with an extended persistence context is used. In general, methods in the `Query` and `TypedQuery` interfaces other than the `executeUpdate` method are not required to be invoked within a transaction context, unless a lock mode has been specified for the query by invoking the `setLockMode` method or by specifying the lock mode in the `@NamedQuery` annotation.

Runtime exceptions other than `NoResultException`, `NonUniqueResultException`, `QueryTimeoutException`, and `LockTimeoutException` thrown by the methods of the query interfaces cause the current transaction to be marked for rollback. On database platforms where a query timeout causes transaction rollback, JPA throws the `PersistenceException`, instead of the `QueryTimeoutException`.

However, runtime exceptions thrown by the methods: `getParameters`, `getParameter`, `getParameterValue`, and `getLockMode` of the `Query` and

`TypedQuery` interfaces do not cause the current transaction to be marked for rollback. Also, runtime exceptions thrown by all methods of the `Tuple`, `TupleElement`, and `Parameter` interfaces do not cause the current transaction to rollback.

5.2.1 Named Queries

Named queries are static queries expressed in metadata using annotations or XML. In contrast, queries constructed at run-time are called dynamic queries as shown in Listing 5-1 and Listing 5-2. Named queries can be defined in JPQL using annotation `@NamedQuery` or in SQL using `@NamedNativeQuery`. Query names are scoped to the persistence unit. Certain naming convention is recommended in an application to avoid duplicated query names. The following is an example of the definition of a named query:

```
@Entity
@Table(name="ORDERS")
@NamedQuery(name="selectCustomerAndPrice",
  query= "SELECT o.customer, o.price FROM Order o " +
    "WHERE o.orderTime < ?1",
  hints={
    @QueryHint(
      name="javax.persistence.query.timeout", value="1000"),
    @QueryHint(
      name="javax.persistence.cache.retrieveMode", value="BYPASS")
  }
)
public class Order extends BaseEntity { ... }
```

It may be equivalently defined in XML as:

```
<named-query name="selectCustomerAndPrice">
  <query>
    <![CDATA[SELECT o.customer,o.price FROM Order o
           WHERE o.orderTime < ?1]]>
  </query>
  <hint name="javax.persistence.cache.retrieveMode" value="BYPASS" />
  <hint name="javax.persistence.query.timeout" value="1000" />
</named-query>
```

The code to execute such a named query looks like this:

```
List<Object[]> resultList
  = em.createNamedQuery("selectCustomerAndPrice")
  .setParameter(1, new Date(), TemporalType.TIMESTAMP)
  .getResultList();
```

186

```
for (Object[] result: resultList) {
  Customer c = (Customer) result[0];
  Double p = (Double) result[1];
}
```

The `@NamedQuery` annotation is used to specify a named query in JPQL. The `name` element is used by the `EntityManager` to refer to the query when creating a named query object. The `query` element must specify a query string in JPQL. The `lockMode` element specifies a lock mode for the results returned by the query. If a lock mode other than `NONE` is specified, the query must be executed within a transaction. The `hints` element may be used to specify standard or vendor-specific query hints. Notice that a named query is created using the method `createNamedQuery,` while a dynamic query is created using the method `createQuery.`

The `@NamedQuery` and `@NamedQueries` annotations can be applied to an entity or a mapped super class:

```
@Target({TYPE}) @Retention(RUNTIME)
public @interface NamedQuery {
  String name();
  String query();
  LockModeType lockMode() default NONE;
  QueryHint[] hints() default {};
}

@Target({}) @Retention(RUNTIME)
  public @interface QueryHint {
  String name();
  String value();
}

@Target({TYPE}) @Retention(RUNTIME)
public @interface NamedQueries {
  NamedQuery[] value ();
}
```

Below is an example illustrating the use of `@NamedQueries` to define multiple queries on an entity:

```
@Entity
@Table(name="ORDERS")
@NamedQueries({
```

```
@NamedQuery(name="selectOrderPrice",
  query="SELECT o.price FROM Order o WHERE o.status = :status"),
@NamedQuery(name="selectCustomer",
  query="SELECT o.customer FROM Order o WHERE o.orderTime < ?1")
})
public class Order extends BaseEntity {... }
```

The advantages of named queries are that they improve reusability of queries and can enhance performance since they are prepared once and used as many times as needed. Many developers prefer to define named queries in XML ORM files (see Chapter 6) so that query definitions are not scattered in entity classes and can be easily maintained.

5.2.2 Paginating Query Results

The methods setMaxResults and setFirstResult are used for paginating through a result list. There are times when thousands or millions of records can be returned from a query. Retrieving all of them at once could cause memory and performance problems. Instead, a limited number of records, say 50, can be retrieved and processed. After that, another 50 records are retrieved and processed, and so on. It is typically the case for a web application, where a page of records is displayed, the user hits the next button, and then another page of records is retrieved and displayed. The records for the first page may be retrieved as:

```
query.setMaxResults(50);    // maximum 50 records will be retrieved
query.setFirstResult(0);    // start position is 0 for first record
List<Object[]> resultList = query.getResultList();
```

Then the following code snippet retrieves the next 50 records:

```
query.setMaxResults(50);
query.setFirstResult(50);   // start position is 50 for 51st record
List<Object[]> resultList = query.getResultList();
```

The effect of applying setMaxResults or setFirstResult to a query involving fetch joins over collections is undefined. Fetch joins are introduced in Section 5.3.2.

5.2.3 Query Flush Mode

The flush mode setting determines how updates on the state of entities are flushed to the database and may affect the result of a query when the query is executed within a transaction. If FlushModeType.AUTO is set on the Query object by the method call setFlushMode, or if the flush mode setting for the persistence context is AUTO (the default) and a flush mode setting has not been specified for the `Query` object, JPA ensures that all updates to the state of all entities in the persistence context are visible to the processing of the query. That is, updates on entities may be flushed to the database automatically and the query may return these newly updated values. If `FlushModeType.COMMIT` is set, the effect of updates made to entities in the persistence context upon queries is unspecified.

If there is no transaction active, JPA does not flush updates on the state of entities to the database, and thus the flush mode setting does not affect query results in this case.

5.2.4 Query Lock Mode

The `setLockMode` method of the `Query` interface or the `lockMode` element of the `@NamedQuery` annotation may be used to lock the results of a query. In this case, a lock is obtained for each entity object returned by the query (including entity objects passed to constructors in the query `SELECT` clause; constructor expressions are covered in Section 5.3.5).

If the lock mode type is `OPTIMISTIC` or `OPTIMISTIC_FORCE_INCREMENT`, and the query returns scalar data (e.g., the non-collection values of entity fields or properties, including scalar data passed to constructors in the query `SELECT` clause, but not data passed to aggregate functions), any entities returned by the query will be locked. If the lock mode type is `PESSIMISTIC_READ`, `PESSIMISTIC_WRITE`, or `PESSIMISTIC_FORCE_INCREMENT`, and the query returns scalar data, the underlying database rows corresponding to such scalar data will be locked. However, the version columns for these entities will not be incremented unless the entities themselves are retrieved and updated.

If a lock mode other than `NONE` is specified for a query, the query must be executed within a transaction or the `TransactionRequiredException` will be thrown. Locking is supported for JPQL queries and criteria queries only. If the `setLockMode` or `getLockMode` method is invoked on a query that is not a JPQL `SELECT` query or a criteria query, the `IllegalStateException` may be thrown or the query execution will fail.

5.2.5 Query Timeout

The following query timeout hint is defined by JPA for use in query configuration:

```
javax.persistence.query.timeout        // time in milliseconds
```

This query hint may be used with the `Query.setHint` method, or the `@NamedQuery` and `@NamedNativeQuery` annotations. It may also be passed as a property to the `createEntityManagerFactory` method of the `Persistence` interface, or used in the `properties` element of the `persistence.xml` file. When used in the `persistence.xml` file, the `createEntityManagerFactory` method, or the annotations, the `timeout` hint serves as a default value which can be selectively overridden by using the `Query.setHint` method.

However, depending on the persistence provider and database in use, the hint may or may not be observed. A JPA implementation is permitted to support additional, vendor-specific query hints. Vendor-specific hints are ignored if they are not understood by your JPA implementation.

5.3 Java Persistence Query language

This section talks about the features of JPQL (Java Persistence Query Language) and illustrates its use through examples.

5.3.1 Statement Types

A JPQL statement can be either a select statement, an update statement, or a delete statement.

A select statement consists of a SELECT clause, a FROM clause, and optionally a WHERE clause, a GROUP BY clause, a HAVING clause, or an ORDER BY clause.

For example, the following query has the required SELECT and FROM clauses, and the optional WHERE clause to restrict the results that are returned by the query. It selects all the Order objects that have a non-empty line item collection.

```
SELECT DISTINCT o
FROM Order AS o
WHERE o.lineItems IS NOT EMPTY
```

This query navigates from the Order entity to the LineItem entity through the one-to-many relationship field o.lineItems. Navigation through such a relationship field is typical in a query. The dot (".") operator here as in o.lineItems is referred to as the navigation operator. The *identification variable o* is introduced for Order in the FROM clause and is used in `o.lineItems` to refer to the line item collection field of the order *o*. The keyword `AS` is optional in declaring identification variables.

Entities are designated in query strings by their entity names. The entity name is defined by the name element of the `@Entity` annotation (or the `entity-name` XML descriptor), and defaults to the unqualified name of the entity class. See Section 2.2.1 for an example. Entity names are scoped within the persistence unit and must be unique within the persistence unit. Also, queries can only use entities and embeddables defined in the same persistence unit.

Update and delete statements provide bulk operations over sets of entities. They are explained in details in Section 5.3.8.

The identifiers `SELECT`, `DISTINCT`, `FROM`, `AS`, `WHERE`, `GROUP BY`, `HAVING`, and `ORDER BY` are reserved identifiers or keywords in JPQL, which are case insensitive, although it is customary to use them in upper case. The full list of JPQL reserved identifiers is divided into a few categories and shown in Table 5.5.

Table 5.5 JPQL reserved identifiers or keywords. The meaning of these identifiers is explained throughout this section. As of JPA 2.0, `BIT_LENGTH`, `CHAR_LENGTH`, `CHARACTER_LENGTH`, `POSITION`, and `UNKNOWN` are not used, and they are reserved for future use.

Categories	Reserved identifiers
Clauses and statements	SELECT, UPDATE, DELETE, FROM, WHERE, GROUP, HAVING, ORDER, SET, BY, ASC, DESC
Joins	JOIN, INNER, OUTER, LEFT, FETCH
Conditions and operators	DISTINCT, OBJECT, NULL, TRUE, FALSE, NOT, AND, OR, BETWEEN, LIKE, ESCAPE, IN, AS, EMPTY, MEMBER, OF, IS, NEW, EXISTS, ALL, ANY, SOME, CASE, END, WHEN, THEN, ELSE, TYPE, CLASS, UNKNOWN
Functions	AVG, MAX, MIN, SUM, COUNT, ABS, SQRT, MOD, SIZE, INDEX, POSITION, CONCAT, SUBSTRING, TRIM, LEADING, TRAILING, BOTH, LOCATE, LOWER, UPPER, LENGTH, CHAR_LENGTH, CHARACTER_LENGTH, BIT_LENGTH, KEY, VALUE, ENTRY, CURRENT_DATE, CURRENT_TIME, CURRENT_TIMESTAMP, NULLIF, COALESCE

5.3.2 FROM Clause

The FROM clause defines the domain for a query, which consists of the names of entities that will be used in other clauses of the query. Identification variables may be declared in the FROM clause using the optional keyword AS. For example, the domain of the following query are the entities: Order and LineItem, and it introduces two identification variables *o* and *li*:

```
SELECT DISTINCT o
FROM Order AS o JOIN o.lineItems AS li
WHERE li.price > 50
```

This query joins the Order entity with the LineItem entity through the one-to-many relationship field Order.lineItems. The identification variable *li* evaluates to any LineItem object directly reachable from Order. The relationship field o.lineItems is a collection and the identification variable *li* refers to an element of this collection. This query selects all distinct orders that have at least one line item with price greater than 50.

An identification variable is case insensitive, but must be a valid Java identifier, which is a character sequence of unlimited length. It must begin with a Java identifier start character and other characters must be Java identifier part characters. A Java identifier start character is any character for which the method Character.isJavaIdentifierStart returns true. This includes the underscore (_) character and the dollar sign ($) character. A Java identifier part character is any character for which the method Character.isJavaIdentifierPart returns true. The question mark (?) character is reserved for use by JPQL for positional parameters.

An identification variable must not be a JPQL reserved identifier or have the same name as any entity in the same persistence unit. Also, it is recommended that SQL keywords not be used as identification variables in queries as they may be used as reserved identifiers in future releases of JPA.

Identification variable declarations are evaluated left to right in the FROM clause. It is sometimes necessary to introduce more than one identification variable for the same entity. The following query returns orders whose price is greater than the order price for 'John Wang':

```
SELECT DISTINCT o
FROM Order o, Order o2
WHERE o.price > o2.price AND o2.customer.name = 'John Wang'
```

An identification variable can only be declared in the FROM clause and always designates a reference to a single value (not a collection).

Path Expression

In the query above, the expression o.price is used to refer to the price attribute of the order *o*. Such an expression is called a *path expression*, which is an identification variable followed by the navigation operator (".") and a state field or an association field.

A path expression cannot evaluate to a collection. For example, if *o* designates Order, the path expression o.lineItems.book is illegal since navigation to lineItems results in a collection. To handle such a navigation, an identification variable may be declared in the FROM clause to range over the elements of the lineItems collection, as in the following query using the IN operator:

```
SELECT i.book
FROM Order o, IN(o.lineItems) i
WHERE i.quantity >= 5
```

This query returns all the books that have at least 5 copies being ordered in at least one line item. The argument to the IN operator must be a collection-valued path expression, which specifies a navigation to a collection-valued association field of an entity or embeddable class. The identification variable *i* above designates a member of the line item collection field. This query can be equivalently and preferably expressed in a join as:

```
SELECT i.book
FROM Order o JOIN o.lineItems i
WHERE i.quantity >= 5
```

For an association or collection field represented as java.util.Map, the identification variable refers to an element of the map value. The functions KEY, VALUE, and ENTRY may be used to refer to the map key, map value, and map entry, respectively. Identification variables qualified by the KEY, VALUE, or ENTRY functions are also considered path expressions. For example, the following query searches all the customers and selects their orders with map key greater than or equal to 2:

```
SELECT VALUE(o)
FROM Customer AS c JOIN c.orders AS o
WHERE KEY(o) >= 2
```

In the query above, the path expressions `KEY(o)` and `VALUE(o)` are the map key and map value of the orders map, respectively. The keyword `VALUE` is optional. Thus, `VALUE(o)` and `o` are equivalent in this query.

In navigating a path expression, if the value of a non-terminal field in the path expression is null, the path is considered to have no value, and this path expression will not be used for determining the query result.

Inner Join

The `JOIN` operator in JPQL has the same meaning as in SQL. It is used to create a Cartesian product and a join condition may be used in the `WHERE` clause to reduce the number of objects retrieved. Two entities are joined based on either their relationship fields or arbitrary persistent fields. The former is called a *relationship join* and the latter is called a *theta join*. For example, we may join *Order* and *LineItem* entities using the one-to-many relationship between them and retrieve only entities that match the join condition. Such joins are called *inner joins*. A few relationship inner join examples are given early in this subsection. The keyword `INNER` is optional and thus `INNER JOIN` and `JOIN` are synonymous. The following relationship inner join query joins three entities and retrieves all the distinct orders having at least one line item with a given book title:

```
SELECT DISTINCT o
FROM Order o JOIN o.lineItems l JOIN l.book b
WHERE b.title = 'Java Persistence with JPA'
```

A *theta join* is a generalized style of join whose join condition does not involve a foreign key relationship that is mapped to an entity relationship. This type of join is not used often in applications. Nevertheless, an example of *theta join* would be to join the `Address` entity with the `Book` entity using their IDs:

```
SELECT a, b
FROM Address a, Book b
WHERE a.addressId = b.bookId
```

Outer Join

Recall that a left outer join in SQL returns all records in the left table, plus matched records from the right table and null values for non-matching records. Similarly, a left outer join in JPQL retrieves results that satisfy the join condition, plus objects from the entity on the left side of the join condition that do not have matching objects from the entity on the right side. JPQL does not support right outer joins since they can be converted into left outer joins.

An outer join retrieves additional entities that do not match the join condition when the association between entities is optional. Suppose we want to retrieve all the books and their associated categories. However, the relationship between `Book` and `Category` is optional. That is, some books may not be classified into categories. If a book does not have any categories, `NULL` will be retrieved for the category value. A left outer join would be perfect to do the job:

```
SELECT b, c
FROM Book b LEFT OUTER JOIN b.categories c
WHERE b.title LIKE '%Java%'
```

The keyword `OUTER` is optional and thus `LEFT OUTER JOIN` and `LEFT JOIN` are synonymous. This query retrieves all the book entities that do not have a matching category, as well as the books that have matching categories. As a comparison, if an inner join is used here, it would retrieve only the books that have matching categories.

As another example, the following outer join query retrieves customers with and without matching orders, but sharing a given bank name:

```
SELECT c, o FROM Customer c LEFT JOIN c.orders o
WHERE c.bank.bankName = ?1
```

Fetch Join
A *fetch join* is an inner or outer join that enables the fetching of an association or element collection field as a side effect of the execution of a query. For example, the following query returns a list of customers with a given customer type. As a side effect, the associated orders for those customers are also retrieved, even though they are not explicitly part of the query result.

```
SELECT c FROM Customer c LEFT JOIN FETCH c.orders
WHERE c.customerType = ?1
```

Fetch joins are typically used on relationship or element collection fields mapped with lazy-loading, but you want to eagerly load them as a side effect of a specific query.

JPA does not permit us to specify an identification variable for the objects referenced by the right side of the FETCH JOIN clause, and hence references to the implicitly fetched entities or elements cannot appear elsewhere in the query. Also, the FETCH JOIN construct must not be used in the FROM clause of a subquery.

5.3.3 Conditional Expressions

This subsection describes language constructs that can be used in conditional expressions of the WHERE or HAVING clause of a query.

Literals

A string literal is a sequence of characters enclosed in single quotes, for example: 'John'. A string literal that includes a single quote is represented by two single quotes, for example: 'John''s book'. String literals in queries, like Java String literals, use Unicode character encoding.

Exact numeric literals support the use of Java integer literal syntax as well as SQL exact numeric literal syntax. Approximate literals support the use of Java floating point literal syntax as well as SQL approximate numeric literal syntax.

JPA currently does not support hexadecimal and octal numeric literals. *Enum* literals support the use of Java *enum* literal syntax. The fully qualified *enum* class name must be specified.

The boolean literals are TRUE and FALSE.

JPA also supports temporal literals using the JDBC escape syntax: a pair of curly braces encloses the literal and the beginning characters are either 'd' for date, 't' for time, or 'ts' for timestamp. The general formats are:

```
{d 'yyyy-mm-dd'}
{t 'hh-mm-ss'}
{ts 'yyyy-mm-dd hh:mm:ss.f'}
```

Below are two examples using temporal literals:

```
SELECT p FROM PreferredCustomer p
WHERE p.expirationDate < {d '2010-12-31'}
```

```
SELECT o FROM Order o
WHERE o.orderTime < {ts '2012-12-31 11:45:10.513'}
```

Operators

The operators supported by JPQL are listed below in order of decreasing precedence.

Operator Type	Operators
Navigational	.
Unary sign	+, -
Arithmetic	*, / (multiplication and division) +, - (addition and subtraction)
Relational	`=, >, >=, <, <=, <>, [NOT] BETWEEN, [NOT] LIKE, [NOT] IN, IS [NOT] NULL, IS [NOT] EMPTY, [NOT] MEMBER [OF], [NOT] EXISTS`

Logical	`NOT`
	 `AND`
	 `OR`

The operator `NOT` is used for negation and operator <> for checking inequality. The notation `[NOT]` using square braces means that the operator `NOT` can be optionally applied. Some examples in the `WHERE` clause using these operators are as follows.

```
WHERE order.price * 0.8 > lineItem.price

WHERE customer.name IS NOT NULL

WHERE CONCAT(customer.lastName, ',', customer.firstName) <> 'Su,Lisa'

WHERE TYPE(c) = GoldCustomer
```

The comparison operators: =, >, >=, <, <=, <> can only be applied to values of like types. Java primitive types and their corresponding wrapped classes can be directly compared. For numeric types, numeric promotion can be implicitly applied. For example, an integer and a `Double` can be compared to see which one is smaller. Care must be taken when comparing equality or inequality for floating types due to round-off errors. For example, if f and d are two floating point numbers, comparing the equality $f = d$ is typically a bad idea; instead use $ABS(f-d) < \varepsilon$, where ε is a reasonably small positive number, and `ABS` is the absolute value function (Section 5.3.4). Also, two null values are not considered to be equal.

Operator BETWEEN

The comparison operator [NOT] BETWEEN can be used in arithmetic expressions, string expressions, or date expressions to compare a path expression to lower and upper limits using the syntax:

pathExpression [NOT] BETWEEN lowerLimit AND upperLimit

Here *pathExpression, lowerLimit*, and *upperLimit* must be of the same data type. For example, the BETWEEN expression

order.price BETWEEN 50 AND 100

returns TRUE if order.price is greater than or equal to 50 and less than or equal to 100, and returns FALSE otherwise. The NOT BETWEEN expression

order.price NOT BETWEEN 50 AND 100

returns TRUE if order.price is less than 50 or greater than 100, and returns FALSE otherwise.

Operator IN

The comparison operator [NOT] IN can be used to compare whether a path expression exists in a list of values using the syntax:

pathExpression [NOT] IN (listOfValues)

The expression *listOfValues* can be a static list of comma-separated values, a dynamic list retrieved by a subquery, or a collection-valued input parameter. When it is a static list of comma-separated values, the data type must be string, numeric, enum, date, time and timestamp. If a value in an IN or NOT IN expression is NULL or unknown, the value of the expression is unknown.

For example, the IN expression

customer.userId IN ('wrobel', 'msmith', 'kwang')

returns TRUE if customer.userId is either wrobel, msmith, or kwang, and returns FALSE otherwise. The NOT IN expression

```
customer.userId NOT IN ('wrobel', 'msmith', 'kwang')
```

returns FALSE if customer.userId is either wrobel, msmith, or kwang, and returns TRUE otherwise.

Entity types can be compared using the IN operator. For example, the following query selects all the customers who are either a PreferredCustomer or GoldCustomer. The TYPE operator gives the Java type of its argument:

```
SELECT c
FROM Customer c
WHERE TYPE(c) IN (PreferredCustomer, GoldCustomer)
```

A subquery is a query within another query. Below is an example of a subquery using the IN operator:

```
SELECT DISTINCT o
FROM Order o JOIN o.lineItems l
WHERE l.book.title IN (
  SELECT b.title FROM Book b JOIN b.categories c
  WHERE c.categoryName ='Fiction')
```

A nice feature with JPQL is that it supports the use of collection-valued input parameters with the IN operator, which is not currently supported by JDBC. Below are two such examples:

```
Query q
  = em.createQuery("SELECT o FROM Order o WHERE o.orderId IN ?1");
List<Integer> orderIds = new ArrayList<Integer>();
orderIds.add(102);
orderIds.add(152);
q.setParameter(1, orderIds);
List<Order> resultList = q.getResultList();

TypedQuery<Customer> q = em.createQuery(
  "SELECT c FROM Customer c WHERE TYPE(c) IN :customerTypes",
  Customer.class);
List<Class<? extends Customer>> cc
  = new ArrayList<Class<? extends Customer>>();
cc.add(PreferredCustomer.class);
cc.add(GoldCustomer.class);
q.setParameter("customerTypes", cc);
```

```
List<Customer> resultList = q.getResultList();
```

The downside for using collection-valued input parameters is that such static-looking queries cannot be precompiled, since the number of elements in the collection is not known until run-time. However, for all the benefits it provides, such a downside seems to be minor in most scenarios.

Operator LIKE

The comparison operator [NOT] LIKE can be used to compare whether a string expression matches a given pattern using the syntax:

stringExpression [NOT] LIKE patternValue [ESCAPE escapeCharacter]

The expression *patternValue* must be a string literal or a string-valued input parameter, in which an underscore (_) stands for any single character, a percent (%) stands for any sequence of characters, and all other characters stand for themselves. Optionally, the expression *escapeCharacter* can be specified as a single-character literal or a character-valued input parameter to escape the special meaning of the underscore and percent characters in *patternValue*.

The following are some examples using the LIKE operator:

```
address.zip LIKE '48%8' returns TRUE for '488', '4808', and FALSE for '498'
address.zip LIKE '48_85' returns TRUE for '48085', and FALSE for '4885'
book.title LIKE '\_%' ESCAPE '\' returns TRUE for '_C', and FALSE for 'C++'
book.title NOT LIKE 'Java%' returns TRUE for 'C++', and FALSE for 'Java SE'
```

If the value of *stringExpression* or *patternValue* above is NULL or unknown, the value of the LIKE expression is unknown. If the *escapeCharacter* is specified and is NULL, the value of the LIKE expression is unknown.

Operator NULL

The comparison operator [NOT] NULL can be used to compare whether a single-valued path expression or an input parameter is NULL or not using the syntax:

expression IS [NOT] NULL

For example, the following query selects all books that have non-null titles:

200

```
SELECT b FROM Book b WHERE b.title IS NOT NULL
```

Operator EMPTY

The comparison operator [NOT] EMPTY can be used to compare whether a collection-valued path expression is empty (ie, has no elements or size is 0) using the syntax:

collectionValuedPathExpression IS [NOT] EMPTY

For example, the following query selects all orders that have at least one line item:

```
SELECT DISTINCT o FROM Order o WHERE o.lineItems IS NOT EMPTY
```

To appreciate what JPA does for such a simple-looking JPQL query, here is the SQL generated by EclipseLink:

```
SELECT DISTINCT t0.ORDER_ID_PK, t0.UPDATE_TIME, t0.PRICE,
       t0.ORDER_TIME, t0.CREATE_TIME, t0.STATUS, t0.CREATE_USER,
       t0.UPDATE_USER, t0.VERSION, t0.CUSTOMER_ID_FK
FROM jpatest.ORDERS t0
WHERE ((SELECT COUNT(*) FROM jpatest.LINE_ITEM t1
        WHERE (t1.ORDER_ID_FK = t0.ORDER_ID_PK)) > 0)
```

Operator MEMBER

The comparison operator [NOT] MEMBER [OF] can be used to compare whether an expression is a member of a collection-valued path expression using the syntax:

entityOrValueExpression [NOT] MEMBER [OF] collectionValuedPathExpression

The expression *entityOrValueExpression* is a single-valued path expression, identification variable, input parameter, or literal. The keyword OF is optional. For example, the following query selects orders that the input parameter is a member of the line item collection:

```
SELECT DISTINCT o FROM Order o WHERE :item MEMBER OF o.lineItems
```

If the collection-valued path expression designates an empty collection, the value of the MEMBER OF expression is FALSE and the value of the NOT MEMBER OF expression is TRUE. If the value of the *entityOrValueExpression* above in the collection member expression is NULL or unknown, the value of the collection member expression is unknown.

EXISTS Expression

An EXISTS expression tests whether a subquery contains any result. It is a predicate that is true only if the result of the subquery consists of one or more values and that is false otherwise. The syntax of an EXISTS expression is

```
[NOT] EXISTS (subquery)
```

For example, the following query uses the NOT EXISTS expression to select all the categories that do not have parent categories (that is, all root categories):

```
SELECT DISTINCT c
FROM Category c
WHERE NOT EXISTS (
   SELECT parentCategory
   FROM Category parentCategory
   WHERE parentCategory = c.parentCategory)
```

Similar to the situation in SQL, an EXISTS expression in JPQL is generally preferred over the IN expression in terms of performance, when there are a large number of records in the table.

ALL Expression

An ALL conditional expression is a predicate that is true if the comparison operation is true for all values in the result of the subquery or the result of the subquery is empty. An ANY conditional expression is true if the comparison operation is true for at least one value in the result of the subquery, and is false if the result of the subquery is empty or if the comparison operation is false for every value in the result of the subquery. The keyword SOME is synonymous with ANY.

The comparison operators that can be used with ALL, ANY, or SOME conditional expressions are =, <, <=, >, >=, <>. The result of the subquery must be like that of the other argument to the comparison operator in type. The syntax of an ALL or ANY expression is specified as follows:

```
{ ALL | ANY | SOME } (subquery)
```

For example, the following query selects line items whose price is greater than the list prices of all books (for an antique book, its line item price may be much higher than the price listed on the book):

```
SELECT li
```

```
FROM LineItem li
WHERE li.price > ALL (SELECT b.price FROM Book b)
```

And this query below selects categories whose create timestamp is later than the timestamp of all the books created by the same user:

```
SELECT c
FROM Category c
WHERE c.createTime > ALL (
  SELECT b.createTime
  FROM Book b
  WHERE b.createUser = c.createUser)
```

To select categories whose create timestamp is later than the timestamp of some of the books created by the same user, we need to use the ANY or SOME expression:

```
SELECT c
FROM Category c
WHERE c.createTime > ANY (
  SELECT b.createTime
  FROM Book b
  WHERE b.createUser = c.createUser)
```

Subqueries

A subquery is a query inside another query, which may be used in the WHERE or HAVING clause. As of JPA 2.0, subqueries are not supported in the FROM clause. A subquery is evaluated first and then the main query is retrieved based on the result of the subquery. The typical form for subqueries is:

```
{[NOT] IN | [NOT] EXISTS | ALL | ANY | SOME |} (subquery)
```

Several examples of subqueries are given above with the IN, EXISTS, or ALL expressions. Below are two more with comparison expressions. The first example selects customers whose average order price is greater than 100, while the second selects gold customers whose credit limit is at least twice as much as the average.

```
SELECT c
FROM Customer c
WHERE (SELECT AVG(o.price) FROM c.orders o) > 100

SELECT g
FROM GoldCustomer g
WHERE g.creditLimit > (
```

```
SELECT AVG(c.creditLimit) * 2.0 FROM GoldCustomer c)
```

5.3.4 Scalar Functions

Numeric, string, boolean, datetime, case, and entity type expressions result in scalar values. JPQL provides built-in functions for performing scalar operations. Scalar expressions may be used in the SELECT, WHERE, and HAVING clauses of a query. If the value of any argument to a functional expression is null or unknown, the value of the functional expression is unknown.

String Functions

JPQL provides the string functions as shown in Table 5.6.

Table 5.6 String functions provided by JPQL.

String Functions	Description
`CONCAT(string1, string2, ...)`	Returns a string that is a concatenation of its arguments.
`SUBSTRING(string, position, length)`	Returns a substring starting at `position` with given `length`. The last two arguments are integers. The third is optional; if not specified, the substring extends to the end of `string`. The first position of a string is denoted by 1.
`TRIM([ [LEADING | TRAILING | BOTH] [trimChar] FROM] string)`	Returns trimmed string after trimming specified character from `string`. Trimming can be LEADING, TRAILING, or BOTH (default is BOTH). If `trimChar` is not specified, it defaults to space (or blank); it must be a single-character literal or input parameter. Trimming other than the space character may not be supported by all databases.
`LOWER(string)`	Returns the string after converting each character to lower case, using the locale of the database.
`UPPER(string)`	Returns the string after converting each character to upper case, using the locale of the database.
`LENGTH(string)`	Returns the length of `string` in characters as an integer.

LOCATE(searchString, string [initialPosition])	Returns the position of searchString within string, starting the search at initialPosition. It returns the first position at which searchString was found as an integer, and 0 if not found. If initialPosition is omitted, it defaults to the beginning of string. Not all databases support the third argument. The first position in a string is 1.

Below are some examples illustrating the usage of these functions in a WHERE clause.

```
WHERE CONCAT (book.title, 's') = 'Java by Examples'
WHERE SUBSTRING (book.title, 1, 4) = 'Java'
WHERE TRIM (LEADING FROM book.title) = 'Java Persistence with JPA'
WHERE LOCATE ('Java', b.title) = 1
```

Arithmetic Functions

JPQL provides the arithmetic functions as shown in Table 5.7.

Table 5.7 Arithmetic functions provided by JPQL.

Arithmetic Functions	Description
ABS(arithmeticExpression)	Returns the absolute value of an arithmetic expression. It returns a nonnegative number (integer, float, or double) of the same type as arithmeticExpression.
SQRT(arithmeticExpression)	Returns the square root value of an arithmetic expression, as a double. The argument arithmeticExpression must be a nonnegative number.
MOD(arithmeticExpression1, arithmeticExpression2)	Returns the modulus of arithmeticExpression1 divided by arithmeticExpression2. It takes two integer arguments and returns an integer.
SIZE(collectionExpression)	Returns the number of elements in the collection-valued path expression as an integer, and 0 for an empty collection.

INDEX(identificationVariable)	Returns an integer corresponding to the position of its argument in an ordered list. It can only be applied to identification variables denoting types for which @OrderColumn has been mapped.

Below are some examples illustrating the usage of these functions:

```
SELECT li FROM LineItem li WHERE SQRT(li.price) >= 4.0
SELECT li FROM LineItem li WHERE MOD(li.quantity, 2) = 1
SELECT o FROM Order o WHERE SIZE(o.lineItems) >= 10

SELECT i FROM Order o JOIN o.lineItems i
WHERE o.price > 20 AND INDEX(i) BETWEEN 0 AND 9
```

In the select query above, o.lineItems is a list of LineItems mapped using an order column and the INDEX function is applied to the identification variable *i*, denoting such a list. This query selects the first 10 line items for those orders with prices greater than 20.

Datetime Functions

JPQL supports three datatime functions, which are CURRENT_DATE, CURRENT_TIME, and CURRENT_TIMESTAMP. They return the value of current date, time, and timestamp, respectively, on the database server. The following is an example illustrating how they may be used:

```
SELECT pc FROM PreferredCustomer pc
WHERE pc.expirationDate < CURRENT_DATE
```

Entity Type Expression

The TYPE operator returns the exact type of the argument. The Java class of the entity is used as an input parameter to specify the entity type. Below are some examples. In the third example, the named parameter :customerTypes must be a collection of customer types.

```
SELECT c FROM Customer c
WHERE TYPE(c) IN (PreferredCustomer, GoldCustomer)

SELECT c FROM Customer c
WHERE TYPE(c) IN (:customerType1, :customerType2)

SELECT c FROM Customer c
```

```
WHERE TYPE(c) IN :customerTypes

SELECT c FROM Customer c WHERE TYPE(c) <> GoldCustomer
```

Case Expression

A case expression uses keywords: CASE, WHEN, THEN, ELSE, END. The syntax is similar to the branch operation supported by many programming languages. The meaning is explained in the context of examples. The following two queries are equivalent and each illustrates a typical usage of the case expression. It increases a book price by 20% if the book's rating is 1, by 10% if the book's rating is 2 and by 3% otherwise.

```
UPDATE Book b
SET b.price =
CASE WHEN b.rating = 1 THEN b.price * 1.2
     WHEN b.rating = 2 THEN b.price * 1.1
     ELSE b.price * 1.03
END

UPDATE Book b
SET b.price =
CASE b.rating WHEN 1 THEN b.price * 1.2
              WHEN 2 THEN b.price * 1.1
              ELSE b.price * 1.03
END
```

The following two queries illustrate how a case expression may be used in the SELECT clause and inside another expression:

```
SELECT c.name,
  CASE WHEN TYPE(c) = PreferredCustomer THEN 'Preferred Customer'
       WHEN TYPE(c) = GoldCustomer THEN 'Gold Customer'
       ELSE 'Normal Customer'
  END
FROM Customer c WHERE c.name LIKE 'John%'

SELECT o.customer.name, i.book,
  CASE WHEN i.quantity > 10 THEN 'Large Order'
       WHEN i.quantity > 5  THEN 'Medium Order'
       ELSE 'Small or No Order'
  END
FROM Order o JOIN o.lineItems i
```

Similar to SQL, JPQL supports the NULLIF and COALESCE functions, which have the general forms:

```
NULLIF (expression1, expression2)
COALESCE (scalarExpression1 {, scalarExpression2}+ )
```

The NULLIF function takes two arguments and returns NULL if the two arguments are equal in value, and returns the first argument otherwise. For instance, NULLIF(5, 5) would return NULL, but NULLIF(5, 3) would return 5.

The COALESCE function takes a list of scalar parameters that are separated by commas. The function returns the value of the first input parameter that is not NULL. The parameters can have different data types.

5.3.5 SELECT Clause

The SELECT clause contains the query result, which may consist of one or more of the following elements: an identification variable, a single-valued path expression, a scalar expression, an aggregate expression, and a constructor expression.

We have seen many examples using the SELECT clause. In fact, have you ever seen many queries without a SELECT clause? Below we note additional rules about the SELECT clause.

- The SELECT clause must be specified to return only single-valued expressions, and thus this query is not valid:

  ```
  SELECT o.lineItems FROM Order AS o
  ```

- The DISTINCT keyword is used to specify that duplicate values must be eliminated from the query result. The result of DISTINCT over embeddable objects or map *entry* results is undefined.

- When multiple select expressions are used in the SELECT clause, the elements of the query result are of type Object[], and these elements correspond in order to the order of their specification in the SELECT clause and in type to the result type of each of the select expressions. When a single select expression is used, the elements of the query result are of type Object. Various examples illustrating this rule are given in Section 5.2.

- When selecting entities, the keyword OBJECT may be optionally used for compatibility with EJB 2 Query Language. The clause SELECT x and SELECT OBJECT(x) are synonymous. However, the keyword OBJECT is not recommended to use for new applications.

If a query result corresponds to an association field or state field whose value is null, that null value is returned in the query result. The IS NOT NULL construct can be used to eliminate such null values. Note that state field types defined in terms of Java numeric primitive types cannot produce NULL values in query results.

If the query result is an embeddable or a collection of it, the embeddable instances returned by the query will not be part of the state of any managed entity. For example, the following query returns a list of embeddables and new changes to them will have no effect on any persistent state:

```
SELECT DISTINCT c.bank FROM Customer c
WHERE SIZE(c.orders) >= 5
```

Constructor Expression

A *constructor expression* may be used in the SELECT list to return new instances of a standard or user-defined Java class. The specified class is not required to be an entity or to be mapped to the database. The constructor name must be fully qualified in the query. For example, new instances of the user-defined Java class jpatest.entity.OrderDetail are constructed below in the SELECT clause directly using the JPQL keyword NEW:

```
Query query = em.createQuery(
  "SELECT NEW jpatest.entity.OrderDetail(o.customer.name, o.price)
   FROM Order o WHERE o.orderTime < ?1");
query.setParameter(1, new Date(), TemporalType.TIMESTAMP);
List<OrderDetail> resultList = query.getResultList();
```

In this case, the constructor of the class jpatest.entity.OrderDetail is defined to take two arguments: a customer name and an order price. This query returns a list of such objects.

Aggregate Functions

JPQL provides aggregate functions which can be used in the SELECT clause of a query. These aggregate functions are shown in Table 5.8.

Table 5.8 Aggregate functions provided by JPQL.

Aggregate Functions	Description
AVG	Returns the average of all values of the field it is applied to, which must be numeric. The return type is always java.lang.Double.
COUNT	Returns the number of results in the query. The return type is always java.lang.Long.
MAX	Returns the maximum value of the state field it is applied to. The return type is the type of the state field to which it is applied to, which must be orderable (numeric, string, character, or date).
MIN	Returns the minimum value of the state field it is applied to. The return type is the type of the state field to which it is applied to, which must be orderable (numeric, string, character, or date).
SUM	Returns the sum of all values of the field it is applied to, which must be numeric. The return type is Long when applied to state fields of integral types (other than BigInteger); Double when applied to state fields of floating point types; BigInteger when applied to state fields of type BigInteger; and BigDecimal when applied to state fields of type BigDecimal.

Below we give a few examples using these aggregate functions. This query returns the average price for all orders with a given status:

```
SELECT AVG(o.price) FROM Order o WHERE o.status = ?1
```

The following query returns the total price of line items ordered by a given customer name and with a given status:

```
SELECT SUM(li.price)
FROM Order o JOIN o.lineItems li JOIN o.customer c
WHERE c.name = ?1 AND o.status = ?2
```

This query counts the number of orders for customers matching a given name pattern:

```
SELECT COUNT(o)
FROM Order o JOIN o.customer c
WHERE c.name LIKE 'John%'
```

Finally, we state a few general rules on the aggregate functions:

- Expressions involving aggregate operators must not be used in the WHERE clause.

- Aggregate functions ignore null values. That is, null values are eliminated before an aggregate function is applied. This is true even if the keyword DISTINCT is specified.

- If AVG, SUM, MAX, or MIN is used, but there are no values to which the aggregate function can be applied, the result of the aggregate function is NULL. If COUNT is used, but there are no values to which COUNT can be applied, the result of the aggregate function is 0.

- The argument to an aggregate function may be preceded by DISTINCT to specify that duplicate values are to be eliminated before the aggregate function is applied. The use of DISTINCT with COUNT is not supported for arguments of embeddable types or map entry types.

Polymorphic Queries

Suppose we want to find all customers whose name matches a given pattern and whose income is higher than a given threshold, we would construct a query like this one:

```
SELECT c FROM Customer c WHERE c.name LIKE ?1 AND c.income > ?2
```

The surprising effect is that this query returns a list of objects of type Customer, PreferredCustomer, and GoldCustomer, simply because entities PreferredCustomer and GoldCustomer are subclasses of entity Customer. That is, this query is polymorphic. In fact, all JPQL queries are polymorphic by default. In other words, the FROM clause of a query designates not only instances of the specified entities, but also instances of their subclasses that satisfy the query condition. The code to capture the retuned types may be written as:

```
Query query = em.createQuery(
  "SELECT c FROM Customer c WHERE c.name LIKE ?1 AND c.income >= ?2");
query.setParameter(1, "J%");
query.setParameter(2, 50000);
List<Customer> resultList = query.getResultList();

for (Customer c : resultList) {
```

```
    if (c instanceof PreferredCustomer) {
        // ...
    } else if (c instanceof GoldCustomer) {
        // ...
    } else {
        // ...
    }
}
```

As another example, the following query returns the average income of all customers, including subtypes such as preferred customers and gold customers, whose name starts with 'J' and whose picture is not null:

```
SELECT AVG(c.income) FROM Customer c
WHERE c.name LIKE 'J%' AND c.picture IS NOT NULL
```

What should we do if we do not want so much polymorphism? Well, as we may recall, in Section 5.3.4, entity type expressions are introduced, which may be used to restrict query polymorphism. The following query computes the average income only for gold customers:

```
SELECT AVG(c.income) FROM Customer c WHERE TYPE(c) = GoldCustomer
```

5.3.6 GROUP BY and HAVING

The GROUP BY clause enables grouping of result values according to given properties. The HAVING clause allows conditions to be specified that further restrict the query result. If a query contains a WHERE clause, GROUP BY clause, and HAVING clause, the effect is to apply the where clause first, and then form the groups, and finally filter them according to the HAVING clause.

The following are two examples. The first one selects order status, average price, and order count among new and billed orders grouped by order status. The second one retrieves the bank name and customer count among banks with more than 30 customers grouped by bank name.

```
SELECT o.status, AVG(o.price), COUNT(o)
FROM Order o
GROUP BY o.status
HAVING o.status IN (?1, ?2)

SELECT c.bank.bankName, COUNT(c)
FROM Customer c
```

```
GROUP BY c.bank.bankName
HAVING COUNT(c.bank.bankName) > 30
```

When the first query is executed, the two parameters must be set as:

```
query.setParameter(1, OrderStatus.BILLED);
query.setParameter(2, OrderStatus.NEW);
```

There are certain rules on the usage of these clauses:

- Any item that appears in the SELECT clause (other than as an aggregate function or as an argument to an aggregate function) must also appear in the GROUP BY clause. For grouping purposes, null values are treated the same. For example, in the second query above, all bank names with null value are treated as one group.

- If the HAVING clause is used, but there is no GROUP BY clause, the result will be treated as a single group, and the select list can only consist of aggregate functions. The use of HAVING without GROUP BY is not required to be supported by the JPA specification.

- The HAVING clause can contain aggregate functions or other query language operators over the attributes that are used for grouping. It is not required that an aggregate function used in the HAVING clause also be used in the SELECT clause.

- Grouping by an entity is permitted. In this case, the entity must contain no serialized state fields or LOB-valued state fields that might be eagerly fetched.

- Grouping by embeddables is not supported.

5.3.7 ORDER BY Clause

If we want the objects or values that are returned from a query to be in a particular order, the ORDER BY expression may be used. The order-by expression must evaluate to an orderable state field of an entity or embeddable class designated in the SELECT clause. The keyword ASC may be used to specify ascending ordering for an order-by item, while DESC for specifying descending ordering. If omitted, ascending ordering is the default.

The following two queries illustrate the use of the ORDER BY clause.

```
SELECT o.price, a.zip
FROM Customer c JOIN c.orders o JOIN c.address a
WHERE a.state = 'MI' AND a.city = 'Troy'
ORDER BY a.zip ASC, o.price DESC

SELECT SUM(o.price) AS p, a.zip
FROM Customer c JOIN c.orders o JOIN c.address a
GROUP BY a.zip
ORDER BY p DESC
```

When more than one order-by item is specified in the order-by expression, the left-to-right sequence of the order-by items determines the precedence, whereby the leftmost order-by item has highest precedence.

When null values are included for ordering, all null values must appear before all non-null values, or all null values must appear after all non-null values in the ordering, but JPA does not specify which. This is not a shortcoming for JPA as SQL has the same rules.

5.3.8 Bulk Updates

Suppose we want to update the order status for all customers matching certain criteria. One way to achieve this is to execute a query to retrieve a collection of such orders, iterate them through, update each of them, and finally commit the transaction so that JPA will save all the modified entity objects into the database. Notice this approach brings all such objects into the JVM and they stay in memory for certain period of time. When the number of such objects is large, it may consumer a lot of memory and potentially affects the performance of the application.

It is typically more efficient to perform bulk updates/deletes against a large number of records in a single operation, without having to retrieve all the records to the JVM and modify them individually. In this case, data are updated directly in the database. The Query interface allows us to perform such bulk updates and deletes via UPDATE and DELETE statements.

Update and delete statements provide bulk operations over sets of entities. Only one entity class (together with its subclasses, if any) is permitted with such a statement. An update statement has an UPDATE clause and a delete statement has a DELETE clause. Both may have an optional WHERE clause. For example, the following update statement sets the order status to BILLED and price to 10 for all customers whose name starts with 'John'.

```
UPDATE Order o
SET o.status = jpatest.entity.OrderStatus.BILLED, o.price = 10
WHERE o.customer.name LIKE 'John%'
```

All update and delete statements must be executed inside a transaction. It does not matter if it is a JTA or resource-local transaction, nor is it container-managed or application-managed. For example, the following code executes the update statement with an application-managed entity manager *em* and a resource-local transaction:

```
em.getTransaction().begin();
Query query = em.createQuery(
  "UPDATE Order o " +
  "SET o.status = jpatest.entity.OrderStatus.BILLED, o.price = 10 " +
  "WHERE o.customer.name LIKE ?1");
query.setParameter(1, "John%");
int updated = query.executeUpdate();
em.getTransaction().commit();
```

Notice that the `executeUpdate` method is used to execute an update or delete query, and it returns the number of records that have been updated/deleted. A sample delete statement can be written as:

```
DELETE FROM Order o WHERE o.customer.name LIKE ?1
```

A bulk delete applies only to objects of the specified entity and its subclasses and it does not cascade to related entities. Bulk updates may go directly to the underlying database, bypassing listeners and optimistic locking checks on the entities. Your application may need to write code to update the value of the version column and other fields that will otherwise be updated automatically by listeners. The persistence context is not synchronized with database changes either. For example, entities that are deleted by a bulk operation may continue to stay in the persistence context for some time. Thus care must be taken when executing bulk updates and deletes. Typically, they should be performed in their own transactions within a new persistence context, and you may want to refresh or re-retrieve these entities that might have been affected by bulk operations.

You are advised to check the exact behavior of your JPA persistence provider before performing bulk operations. Some providers try to do more than what the specification requires. For example, EclipseLink increments the version column when performing a bulk update, which can be seen by the SQL statement generated from the JPQL update above:

```
UPDATE ORDERS
SET STATUS = 2, VERSION = (VERSION + 1), PRICE = 10.0
WHERE EXISTS(
  SELECT t1.ORDER_ID_PK FROM CUSTOMER t0, ORDERS t1
  WHERE ((t0.NAME LIKE John%)
         AND (t0.CUSTOMER_ID_PK = t1.CUSTOMER_ID_FK)) )
```

If your persistence provider does not automatically update the version value on entities modified by a bulk update and you need to programmatically perform the change, below is an example on how to do it:

```
UPDATE Order o
SET o.price = 10, o.version = o.version + 1
WHERE o.customer.name LIKE 'John%'
```

5.3.9 Null Values

Null, unknown, and empty values can happen in JPQL more often than we think. When the target of a reference does not exist in the database, its value is regarded as NULL. When an operand in an arithmetic operation is NULL, the result of the arithmetic expression is unknown. When a string has length 0 or a collection of objects has size 0, it is regarded as EMPTY.

JPQL follows theses NULL value rules for the evaluation of conditional expressions:

* Arithmetic or comparison operations with a NULL value always yield an unknown value.
* Two NULL values are not considered equal, and the comparison yields an unknown value.
* Comparison or arithmetic operations with an unknown value always yield an unknown value.
* Operators IS NULL and IS NOT NULL convert a NULL value into TRUE and FALSE, respectively.
* Boolean operators use the three valued logic, as defined by Table 5.9.

Table 5.9 Definition of the AND, OR, and NOT operators on the three-valued logic, where T stands for TRUE, *F stands for* FALSE *, and U stands for* UNKNOWN.

AND	T	F	U	OR	T	F	U	NOT	
T	T	F	U	T	T	T	T	T	F
F	F	F	F	F	T	F	U	F	T
U	U	F	U	U	T	U	U	U	U

Notice that JPQL defines the empty string as a string with length 0, which is not equal to a NULL value. However, not all databases treat an empty string and NULL differently. Thus portable code cannot rely on the semantics of query comparisons involving the empty string and NULL value.

5.4 Native SQL Queries

As we learn more about JPQL, we tend to like it a lot since it is a high-level, feature-rich, and portable query language. It deals with Java entities and their relationships directly and applies to different databases. Also it has pretty much every feature we have wanted. Then, should we forget about native SQL completely?

Not quite. There are still some scenarios that we need to use native SQL. Currently JPQL does not support intersect and union of different queries, nor does it support statistical functions such as deviation and variance. Also, some databases provide special features that are not part of JPQL. For example, to generate a hierarchic list of categories together with their subcategories from the CATEGORY table, Oracle has the CONNECT BY and START WITH clauses (see reference [Lk] in Section 9.2), which may be used as:

```
SELECT CATEGORY_ID_PK, CATEGORY_NAME
FROM CATEGORY
START WITH CATEGORY_ID_PK = 12345
CONNECT BY PARENT_CATEGORY_FK = PRIOR CATEGORY_ID_PK
```

Fortunately, JPA provides the ability to execute native SQL queries and return entity objects, scalars, or a combination of both, the same as JPQL queries.

In this section, we explore JPA's support for native SQL queries. However, it is illustrated using simple examples, which can be executed in JPQL as well for easy comparison.

5.4.1 SQL Named Queries

A named native SQL query is statically configured using the `@NamedNativeQuery` annotation or its equivalent XML descriptor. It is very similar to a named JPQL query. The following is an example showing how it is configured and executed. We may be surprised to see that even native queries are polymorphic.

```
@Entity
@Table(name="ORDERS")
@NamedNativeQuery(
  name="nativeCustomerSQL",
  query="SELECT c.customer_id_pk, c.customer_type, c.name, c.income
         FROM customer c WHERE c.name LIKE ?1",
  resultClass=Customer.class
)
public class Order extends BaseEntity { ... }

Query query = em.createNamedQuery("nativeCustomerSQL");
query.setParameter(1, "John%");
List<Customer> resultList = query.getResultList();
for (Customer result: resultList) {
  if (result instanceof GoldCustomer) {
    // ...
  } else if (result instanceof PreferredCustomer) {
    // ...
  } else {
    // ...
  }
}
```

The `@NamedNativeQuery` annotation works pretty much like `@NamedQuery`, except that we must specify the entity classes for the returned values using either the `resultClass` or `resultSetMapping` element. The latter specifies a string referring to the name element of the `@SqlResultSetMapping` annotation. The native named query above can be equivalently specified as:

```
@Entity
@Table(name="ORDERS")
@NamedNativeQuery(
  name="nativeCustomerSQL",
  query="SELECT c.customer_id_pk, c.customer_type, c.name, c.income
         FROM customer c WHERE c.name LIKE ?1",
  hints={
    @QueryHint(name="javax.persistence.query.timeout", value="1000")},
```

```
      resultSetMapping="customerRSmapping"
)
@SqlResultSetMapping(name="customerRSmapping",
    entities=@EntityResult(entityClass=Customer.class,
                          discriminatorColumn="CUSTOMER_TYPE")
)
public class Order extends BaseEntity { ... }
```

The `discriminatorColumn` element of the `@SqlResultSetMapping` annotation specifies the database column name or the column alias in the SELECT clause that is used to determine the inheritance type of the entity class.

In fact, the `@SqlResultSetMapping` annotation may be used to specify multiple entities and scalars for the returned types of a native named or dynamic query. More examples are given in Section 5.4.3 for complicated result set mappings.

Unlike JPQL, named parameters are not supported in SQL native queries, and only positional parameters are allowed. Like JPQL, native queries are executed in the same way and JPA converts JDBC results into entity objects automatically.

To close this subsection, here is the full definition of the annotations `@NamedNativeQuery` and `@NamedNativeQueries`:

```
@Target({TYPE}) @Retention(RUNTIME)
public @interface NamedNativeQuery {
  String name();                            // name of query
  String query();                           // query definition
  QueryHint[] hints() default {};           // query hints
  Class resultClass() default void.class;   // class of returned entity
  String resultSetMapping() default "";     // SqlResultSetMapping name
}

@Target({TYPE}) @Retention(RUNTIME)
public @interface NamedNativeQueries {
  NamedNativeQuery[] value ();              // for multiple queries
}
```

And here is an example on how to configure multiple named native queries:

```
@NamedNativeQueries({
  @NamedNativeQuery(
    name="nativeCustomerSQL", query="...", hints={...},
```

```
    resultClass=Customer.class),
  @NamedNativeQuery(
    name="nativeCustomerSQL2", query="...", hints={...},
    resultSetMapping="customerRSmapping")
})
```

5.4.2 SQL Dynamic Queries

A dynamic SQL query may be constructed at run-time, typically by using string concatenation. Below is an example to show how such a query is constructed using the createNativeQuery method of the EntityManager interface:

```
Query query = em.createNativeQuery(
    "SELECT o.order_id_pk, o.price, o.order_time, o.status " +
    "FROM Orders o, Line_Item i " +
    "WHERE (i.order_id_fk = o.order_id_pk) AND i.price < ?1",
    Order.class);
query.setParameter(1, 300);
List<Order> resultList = query.getResultList();
```

Notice the first argument is a string representing a SQL query, possibly with positional parameters, and the second argument is the entity class for the returned results. Make sure the primary key columns are included in the SELECT clause in order to construct instances of the Order entity from the returned results.

Generally speaking, a SQL query may return multiple entities plus additional scalar values, and the annotation @SqlResultSetMapping or its equivalent XML descriptor is used to map names of the columns in the SQL SELECT clause. In the simplest case, the example above may also use this annotation as follows.

```
@Entity
@Table(name="ORDERS")
@SqlResultSetMapping(name="orderRSmapping",
  entities = @EntityResult(entityClass=Order.class)
)
public class Order extends BaseEntity { ... }

Query query = em.createNativeQuery(
    "SELECT o.order_id_pk, o.price, o.order_time, o.status " +
    "FROM Orders o, Line_Item i " +
    "WHERE (i.order_id_fk = o.order_id_pk) AND i.price < ?1",
    "orderRSmapping");
query.setParameter(1, 300);
```

```
List<Order> resultList = query.getResultList();
```

This version of the `createNativeQuery` method specifies the second argument as the name of a SQL result set mapping. More complex result set mappings are given in Section 5.4.3.

5.4.3 Result Set Mapping

As we have mentioned in the previous two subsections, the SQL result set mapping annotation may be used when returning multiple entities and scalars. However, the mapping is pretty involved and we dedicate this subsection to this topic. First, here is a simple native query returning a list of `Order` and `LineItem` entities:

```
@SqlResultSetMapping(name="orderLineItemRSmapping",
  entities ={ @EntityResult(entityClass=Order.class),
            @EntityResult(entityClass=LineItem.class)
  }
)

Query query = em.createNativeQuery(
  "SELECT o.order_id_pk, o.price, i.line_item_id_pk " +
  "FROM Orders o, Line_Item i " +
  "WHERE (i.order_id_fk = o.order_id_pk) AND i.price < ?1",
  "orderLineItemRSmapping");
query.setParameter(1, 300);
List<Object[]> resultList = query.getResultList();
for (Object[] result: resultList) {
  Order order = (Order)result[0];
  LineItem li = (LineItem) result[1];
}
```

You may want to specify all columns in the `SELECT` clause that are mapped to the entities, although your JPA implementation may work as long as you specify the primary key and foreign key columns of the returned entities.

Column aliases must be used in SQL `SELECT` clauses, when database column names from multiple tables in the `FROM` clause are the same, as these column names would otherwise appear indistinguishable in the result set. In this case, the SQL result set mapping must explicitly map the attributes of the entities to column aliases in the SQL `SELECT` clause. The annotation `@FieldResult` is used for this purpose, whose `name` element specifies the entity field/property name and `column` element specifies the column alias. For example, in the following query, the `PRICE` column appears in both `ORDERS` and

221

LINE_ITEM tables and column aliases are required for it. On the other hand, column aliases for ORDER_ID_PK and LINE_ITEM_ID_PK columns are optional:

```
@SqlResultSetMapping(name="orderLineItemRSmapping2",
  entities ={
    @EntityResult(entityClass=Order.class,
      fields={@FieldResult(name="orderId", column="ORDER_ID"),
              @FieldResult(name="price", column="ORDER_PRICE")}),
    @EntityResult(entityClass=LineItem.class,
      fields={@FieldResult(name="lineItemId", column="LI_ID"),
              @FieldResult(name="price", column="LI_PRICE")})
  }
)

Query query = em.createNativeQuery(
  "SELECT o.order_id_pk AS ORDER_ID, o.price AS ORDER_PRICE, " +
  "i.line_item_id_pk AS LI_ID, i.price AS LI_PRICE, i.quantity " +
  "FROM Orders o, Line_Item i " +
  "WHERE (i.order_id_fk = o.order_id_pk) AND i.price < ?1",
  "orderLineItemRSmapping2");
query.setParameter(1, 300);
List<Object[]> reultList = query.getResultList();
for (Object[] result: reultList) {
  Order order = (Order)result[0];
  LineItem li = (LineItem) result[1];
}
```

Scalar values may also be included in the query result by applying the @ColumnResult annotation, whose only element name specifies the database column name or column alias in the SQL SELECT clause for the column whose value is to be returned as a scalar. In the following example, the column represented by i.price in the SELECT clause is to be returned as a scalar. Its column alias LI_PRICE must be used for the name element of the @ColumnResult annotation (otherwise, use its corresponding database column name PRICE).

```
@SqlResultSetMapping(name="orderLineItemRSmapping3",
  entities ={@EntityResult(entityClass=Order.class)},
  columns  ={@ColumnResult(name="LI_PRICE") }
)

Query query = em.createNativeQuery(
  "SELECT o.order_id_pk, o.price, i.price AS LI_PRICE " +
  "FROM Orders o, Line_Item i " +
```

```
"WHERE (i.order_id_fk = o.order_id_pk) AND i.price < ?1",
"orderLineItemRSmapping3");
query.setParameter(1, 300);
List<Object[]> resultList = query.getResultList();
for (Object[] result: resultList) {
  Order order = (Order) result[0];
  Double price = (Double) result[1];
}
```

When the returned entity is the owner of a single-valued (one-to-one or many-to-one) relationship mapped by a composite foreign key, a @FieldResult element should be used for each of the foreign key columns. The @FieldResult annotation must use a dot (".") notation to indicate which column maps to each field/property of the target entity primary key. To illustrate how to do result set mappings in such scenarios, we introduce three new tables CUSTOMER5, PREFERRED_CUSTOMER5, and GOLD_CUSTOMER5, in the table design as described in Figure 5-1.

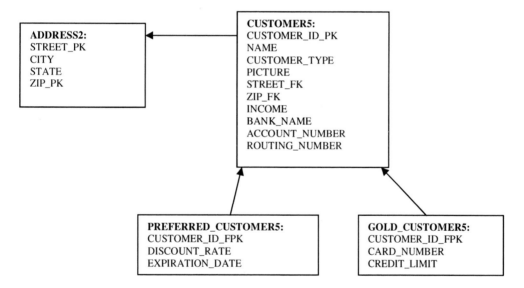

Figure 5-1 Table design for result set mapping with composite foreign keys. Table CUSTOMER5 has a composite foreign key to ADDRESS2, but forms a single-valued relationship to ADDRESS2.

The table `ADDRESS2` is introduced in Section 4.1.1 and Section 4.1.2, and two entities: `Address2` and `Address3`, both with composite primary keys, are mapped to this table. Entity `Customer5` is mapped to have an updatable one-to-one relationship to entity `Address2` and a read-only one-to-one relationship to entity `Address3`. Entities `Customer5`, `PreferredCustomer5,` and `GoldCustomer5` form an inheritance hierarchy using the joined-table strategy.

```
@Entity
@Table(name = "CUSTOMER5")
@Inheritance(strategy = InheritanceType.JOINED)
@DiscriminatorColumn(name = "CUSTOMER_TYPE",
  discriminatorType = DiscriminatorType.STRING, length = 1
)
@DiscriminatorValue(value = "C")
public class Customer5 extends BaseEntity {

    @OneToOne(cascade={CascadeType.PERSIST,CascadeType.REMOVE})
    @JoinColumns({
        @JoinColumn(name="STREET_FK", referencedColumnName="STREET_PK"),
        @JoinColumn(name="ZIP_FK", referencedColumnName="ZIP_PK")
    })
    protected Address2 address2;

    @OneToOne(cascade={CascadeType.PERSIST,CascadeType.REMOVE})
    @JoinColumns({
        @JoinColumn(name="STREET_FK", referencedColumnName="STREET_PK",
          insertable=false, updatable=false),
        @JoinColumn(name="ZIP_FK", referencedColumnName="ZIP_PK",
          insertable=false, updatable=false)
    })
    protected Address3 address3;

   // ...
}
```

The native query below makes use of result set mapping: *customer5Address2RSmapping*, which maps the field `address2.street` within `Customer5` to table column `STREET_PK`, and field `address2.zip` to table column `ZIP_PK`, using the dot notation:

```
@SqlResultSetMapping(name="customer5Address2RSmapping",
  entities ={
    @EntityResult(entityClass=Customer5.class,
      fields={@FieldResult(
```

```
                name="customerId", column="CUSTOMER_ID_PK"),
            @FieldResult(
                name="address2.street", column="STREET_PK"),
            @FieldResult(name="address2.zip", column="ZIP_PK")},
        discriminatorColumn="CUSTOMER_TYPE"),
      @EntityResult(entityClass=Address2.class)
  }
)

Query query = em.createNativeQuery(
  "SELECT c.customer_id_pk, c.customer_type, " +
  "       c.name,a.street_pk,a.zip_pk "+
  "FROM Customer5 c, Address2 a " +
  "WHERE c.street_fk = a.street_pk AND c.zip_fk = a.zip_pk",
  "customer5Address2RSmapping");
List<Object[]> resultList = query.getResultList();
for (Object[] result: resultList) {
  Customer5 cust = (Customer5) result[0];
  Address2 addr = (Address2) result[1];
}
```

The next result set mapping and native query shows how to map to composite foreign key with an embedded ID, using the dot notation:

```
@SqlResultSetMapping(name="customer5Address3RSmapping",
  entities ={
    @EntityResult(entityClass=Customer5.class,
      fields={@FieldResult(
                name="customerId", column="CUSTOMER_ID_PK"),
            @FieldResult(
                name="address3.pk.street", column="STREET_PK"),
            @FieldResult(
                name="address3.pk.zip", column="ZIP_PK")},
        discriminatorColumn="CUSTOMER_TYPE"),
      @EntityResult(entityClass=Address3.class)
  }
)

Query query = em.createNativeQuery(
  "SELECT c.customer_id_pk, c.customer_type, " +
  "       c.name,a.street_pk,a.zip_pk "+
  "FROM Customer5 c, Address2 a " +
  "WHERE c.street_fk = a.street_pk AND c.zip_fk = a.zip_pk",
  "customer5Address3RSmapping");
List<Object[]> resultList = query.getResultList();
```

```
for (Object[] result: resultList) {
  Customer5 cust = (Customer5) result[0];
  Address3 addr = (Address3) result[1];
}
```

When multiple SQL result set mappings are defined, they must be specified using the annotation @SqlResultSetMappings as the following example illustrates:

```
@SqlResultSetMappings({
  @SqlResultSetMapping(name="resultsetMapping1",
    entities ={ ... }, columns = { ... }),
  @SqlResultSetMapping(name="resultsetMapping2",
    entities ={ ... }, columns = { ... } )
})
```

Finally, we give the full definition of the annotations discussed in this subsection:

```
@Target({TYPE}) @Retention(RUNTIME)
public @interface SqlResultSetMappings {
  SqlResultSetMapping[] value();  // for multiple resultset mapping
}

@Target({TYPE}) @Retention(RUNTIME)
public @interface SqlResultSetMapping {
  String name();                         // resultset mapping name
  EntityResult[] entities() default {};  // for mapping entities
  ColumnResult[] columns() default {};   // for mapping scalars
}

@Target({}) @Retention(RUNTIME)
public @interface EntityResult {
  Class entityClass();
  FieldResult[] fields() default {};
  String discriminatorColumn() default "";      // for inheritance
}
```

The fields element of @EntityResult is used to map the columns specified in the SELECT list of the query to the fields/properties of the entity class. The discriminatorColumn element is used to specify the database column name (or its alias, if applicable) for the column in the SELECT list.

```
@Target({}) @Retention(RUNTIME)
public @interface FieldResult {
```

```
  String name();    // name of persistent field/property of entity
  String column();  // corresponding database column or its alias
}

@Target({}) @Retention(RUNTIME)
public @interface ColumnResult {
  String name();    // database column name or alias in SELECT list
}
```

5.5 Best Author Award

The online book-selling application has been a successful business and many customers
have come to order books from its website. Now we want to find the books with the most
number of copies sold and give the Best Author Award to those authors. As modeled in
Section 2.1, a customer may place many orders and each order may contain many line
items. Each line item can contain only one book, but possibly with many copies of the
book. It is possible that more than one book has sold the most number of copies.

The solution can be achieved in two steps:

1. Find the number that represents the most number of copies being sold among all
    books.
2. Find the authors whose books have been sold this many copies.

For Step 1, we select the quantities of sold copies per book among all line items in
decreasing order. The query would look like this:

```
SELECT SUM(j.quantity) AS q
FROM LineItem j
GROUP BY j.book.isbn ORDER BY q DESC
```

However, this query gives us the quantities sold for every book, which is more than we
really need. Since we are interested only in the largest of the quantities sold, getting the
first result of the query will be sufficient. This reminds us of the method: setMaxResults
on the query interface. So the following code achieves what we need for Step 1:

```
Long quantity = null;
Query query = em.createQuery(
  "SELECT SUM(j.quantity) AS q FROM LineItem j " +
  "GROUP BY j.book.isbn ORDER BY q DESC");
query.setMaxResults(1);
```

```
query.setFirstResult(0);
List<Long> resultList = query.getResultList();
quantity = resultList.get(0);
```

Now the variable *quantity* holds the largest number of all book quantities sold. In Step 2, we find the authors whose books have been sold the given largest number of copies. The following query should do the trick:

```
SELECT b FROM Book b
WHERE (?1 = (SELECT SUM(i.quantity) FROM LineItem i
             WHERE i.book.isbn = b.isbn GROUP BY i.book.isbn) )
```

The code to execute this query looks like the following:

```
Query query = em.createQuery("SELECT b FROM Book b WHERE " +
   "(?1 = (SELECT SUM(i.quantity) FROM LineItem i " +
        "WHERE i.book.isbn = b.isbn GROUP BY i.book.isbn) )");
query.setParameter(1, quantity);
List<Book> resultList = query.getResultList();
for (Book result : resultList) {
   System.out.println("Best Author Award to: " + result.getAuthor());
}
```

Guess, what result will this code snippet print out? Here it is:

```
Best Author Award to: Dr. Yang
```

He dreams.

6 XML Configuration and Mapping

JPA is flexible in the sense that metadata information can be configured in XML files. Persistence unit information may be configured in the `persistence.xml` file, which includes database access information, transaction type, the persistence provider to be used, what persistence classes are included, standard configuration properties such as query timeout and shared cache mode, and vendor-specific properties such as logging level. The `orm.xml` and other OR mapping files may contain configuration of listeners, sequence generators, named queries, and XML mapping for mapped super classes, entities, and embeddable classes, which override such information defined using annotations, if any.

The first section talks about how to do configuration in the `persistence.xml` file, while the second section deals with how to define OR mapping using XML instead of annotations.

6.1 XML Configuration

A persistence unit is a logical grouping of persistence classes, their mapping metadata (in the form of annotations and/or XML descriptors), and configuration information for the entity manager factory and its entity managers. A persistence unit is defined in a `persistence.xml` file. The `persistence.xml` file must be located in the META-INF subdirectory of a jar file or a directory on the class path. The jar file or directory whose META-INF subdirectory contains `persistence.xml` is termed the *root of the persistence unit*. A persistence unit must have a name. Multiple persistence units may be defined in one or more `persistence.xml` files, but must have unique names within the same scope (Section 6.1.4). The XML schema for the `persistence.xml` file may be found from the URL given in Section 9.1.

The root element of the `persistence.xml` file is the `persistence` element. It consists of one or more `persistence-unit` elements, each of which defines a persistence unit. The `persistence-unit` element consists of the `name` and `transaction-type` attributes and the following sub-elements: `description`, `provider`, `jta-data-source`, `non-jta-data-source`, `mapping-file`, `jar-file`, `class`, `exclude-unlisted-classes`, `shared-cache-mode`, `validation-mode`, and `properties`. Among those, only the `name` attribute is required.

Listing 6-1 gives a sample configuration file with two persistence units *"jpaTestPU"* and *"jpaTestJtaPU"*, and multiple OR mapping files and jar files.

Listing 6-1 persistence.xml: A sample configuration file with multiple persistence units.

```xml
<?xml version="1.0" encoding="UTF-8"?>
<persistence version="2.0"
  xmlns="http://java.sun.com/xml/ns/persistence"
  xmlns:xsi="http://www.w3.org/2001/XMLSchema-instance"
  xsi:schemaLocation="http://java.sun.com/xml/ns/persistence
     http://java.sun.com/xml/ns/persistence/persistence_2_0.xsd">

  <persistence-unit name="jpaTestPU"
                   transaction-type="RESOURCE_LOCAL">
    <description>A test persistence unit</description>
    <provider>org.eclipse.persistence.jpa.PersistenceProvider
    </provider>
    <non-jta-data-source>java:/jpaTestDS</non-jta-data-source>
    <mapping-file>META-INF/ormOrder.xml</mapping-file>
    <mapping-file>META-INF/ormCustomer.xml</mapping-file>
    <jar-file>order.jar</jar-file>
    <jar-file>customer.jar</jar-file>
    <class>jpatest.Vehicle</class>
    <class>jpatest.entity.Address</class>
    <class>jpatest.entity.Address2</class>
    <class>jpatest.entity.Address3</class>
    <class>jpatest.entity.Address3PK</class>
    <class>jpatest.entity.BankInfo</class>
    <class>jpatest.entity.BaseEntity</class>
    <class>jpatest.entity.User</class>
    <exclude-unlisted-classes/>
    <shared-cache-mode>ENABLE_SELECTIVE</shared-cache-mode>
    <validation-mode>CALLBACK</validation-mode>
    <properties>
      <property name="javax.persistence.lock.timeout" value="30000" />
      <property name="javax.persistence.validation.group.pre-persist"
               value="jpatest.groups.Basic,jpatest.groups.Extended"/>
      <property name="eclipselink.logging.level" value="FINEST" />
      <property name="eclipselink.target-server" value="JBoss" />
      <property name="eclipselink.target-database" value="Derby" />
    </properties>
  </persistence-unit>
```

```
<persistence-unit name="jpaTestJtaPU" transaction-type="JTA">
  <provider>org.eclipse.persistence.jpa.PersistenceProvider
  </provider>
  <jta-data-source>java:/jpaTestJtaDS</jta-data-source>
  <properties>
    <property name="eclipselink.logging.level" value="FINEST" />
    <property name="eclipselink.target-server" value="JBoss" />
    <property name="eclipselink.target-database" value="Derby" />
  </properties>
</persistence-unit>

</persistence>
```

In the persistence unit *"jpaTestPU"*, the element `non-jta-data-source` is used to designate a non-JTA data source, which means that resource-local entity managers are to be used for this persistence unit. Two OR mapping files are explicitly specified. If the default OR mapping file `META-INF/orm.xml` exists, JPA will automatically include it in the persistence unit. Two jar files: `order.jar` and `customer.jar` are listed for persistence classes and other metadata information such as named queries. If these jar files have the `orm.xml` files in their subdirectory `META-INF`, these `orm.xml` files will also be included for this persistence unit. See Example 4 in Section 6.1.2 for more explanation.

In the persistence unit *"jpaTestJtaPU"*, the element `jta-data-source` is used to designate a JTA data source, which implies that JTA entity managers are to be used. Persistence classes are included by the default, which are the ones located in the root of the persistence unit and others specified in the `META-INF/orm.xml` file, if existed.

6.1.1 Persistence Unit

In this section, we elaborate on the attributes and sub-elements of the `persistence-unit` element in the `persistence.xml` file.

The Name Attribute

The `name` attribute of the `persistence-unit` element defines the name of the persistence unit. The file in Listing 6-1 defines two persistence units with names *"jpaTestPU"* and *"jpaTestJtaPU"*, respectively. Persistence unit names must be unique within the same scope (Section 6.1.4). A persistence unit name is used to identify the persistence unit in the `@PersistenceContext` and `@PersistenceUnit` annotations

(Sections 3.3.1 and 3.3.2) and in creating an entity manager factory programmatically (Section 3.3.2).

The Transaction Type Attribute

The `transaction-type` attribute of the `persistence-unit` element specifies whether JTA entity managers or resource-local entity managers are used. Valid values for this attribute are `JTA` and `RESOURCE_LOCAL`. The transaction type `JTA` may be used in a Java EE container and requires a `JTA` data source (using the `jta-data-source` sub-element or being provided by the container). The transaction type `RESOURCE_LOCAL` may be used in both Java SE and Java EE environments. In a Java EE container, the transaction type `RESOURCE_LOCAL` assumes that a non-JTA data source will be provided (using the `non-jta-data-source` sub-element, for example). If this attribute is not specified, the default value is `JTA` in a Java EE environment, and is `RESOURCE_LOCAL` in a Java SE environment.

The Description Element

The `description` element provides optional descriptive information and comments about the persistence unit. It is meant for human readers and is ignored by JPA.

The Provider Element

The `provider` element specifies the fully qualified class name for the persistence provider. For example, the persistence providers for EclipseLink, Hibernate, and OpenJPA are respectively:

```
<provider>org.eclipse.persistence.jpa.PersistenceProvider</provider>
<provider>org.hibernate.ejb.HibernatePersistence</provider>
<provider>org.apache.openjpa.persistence.PersistenceProviderImpl
</provider>
```

When this optional element is omitted, it takes the default JPA implementation provided by your Java EE container. At most one persistence provider may be explicitly specified for a persistence unit.

The Data Source Elements

The data source elements are `jta-data-source` and `non-jta-data-source`. Use the former to specify the JNDI name for a JTA data source, and the latter for a non-JTA data source. It must be consistent with the value specified in the `transaction-type` attribute.

The Mapping File Element

The `mapping-file` element specifies an object relational mapping file which contains named queries, mapped super classes, entity classes, and embeddable classes, among other things (See Section 6.2). Repeat this element for multiple mapping files. The mapping files must be on the class path. These are in addition to the default OR mapping file `META-INF/orm.xml`.

When multiple mapping files are included in a persistence unit, the resulting mappings are obtained by combining all these mapping files. Notice that each jar file specified using the `jar-file` element may include a default `orm.xml` mapping file as well. The result is undefined if these mapping files contain overlapping information. The mapping from these files must be disjoint at the class level.

The Jar File Element

The `jar-file` element is used to specify a jar file that contains persistence classes and mapping metadata either annotated on these classes or defined in the `META-INF/orm.xml` file. Multiple jar files may be specified by repeating this element. Such jar files must be located relative to the directory or jar file that contains the root of the persistence unit. See Section 6.1.3 for various examples.

List of persistence classes

The `class` element is used to list a persistence class, which may be a mapped super class, an entity, or an embeddable class. Thus persistence classes for a persistence unit may be explicitly specified by the `class` elements, the `jar-file` elements, and the classes inside the mapping files. Persistence classes in the root of the persistence unit are included by default, unless the `exclude-unlisted-classes` element is specified. The `exclude-unlisted-classes` element may be used to exclude annotated persistence classes contained in the root of the persistence unit, but are not explicitly included.

In summary, the set of persistence classes that are managed by a persistence unit is defined by using one or more of the following:

- Annotated (using `@MappedSuperclass`, `@Entity`, or `@Embeddable`) persistence classes contained in the root of the persistence unit (unless the `exclude-unlisted-classes` element is specified)

- One or more object/relational mapping XML files specified using the `mapping-file` element (including the default `META-INF/orm.xml` files)

- One or more jar files specified using the `jar-file` element

- An explicit list of classes specified using the `class` element

The set of entities managed by the persistence unit is the union of these sources, with the mapping metadata annotations (or annotation defaults) for any given class being overridden by the XML mapping files if there are both annotations and XML mappings for that class. The minimum portable level of overriding is at the level of the persistent field or property. The classes, jar files, and mapping files that are named as part of a persistence unit must be on the classpath.

The `exclude-unlisted-classes` element is not intended for use in Java SE environments, where persistence classes found in the root of a persistence unit are automatically included.

The Cache Mode Element
The `shared-cache-mode` element determines whether second-level caching is in effect for the persistence unit. Valid values are `ALL`, `NONE`, `ENABLE_SELECTIVE`, `DISABLE_SELECTIVE`, and `UNSPECIFIED`. See Section 3.7 for their meanings.

The Validation Mode Element
The `validation-mode` element determines whether automatic validation is in effect for lifecycle events such as entity update or delete. Valid values are `AUTO`, `CALLBACK`, and `NONE`, with the default being `AUTO`. See Section 3.6 for their meanings.

The Properties Element
The `properties` element is used to specify both standard and vendor-specific properties and hints that apply to the persistence unit.

The following standard properties are intended for use in Java SE environments to connect to the database for the persistence unit:

- `javax.persistence.jdbc.driver`: fully qualified name of the JDBC driver class.

- `javax.persistence.jdbc.url`: driver-specific URL of the database.
- `javax.persistence.jdbc.user`: username used by database connection.
- `javax.persistence.jdbc.password`: password used by database connection.

The following standard properties and hints are intended for use in both Java EE and Java SE environments:

- `javax.persistence.lock.timeout`: value in milliseconds for pessimistic lock timeout. This is a hint only.
- `javax.persistence.query.timeout`: value in milliseconds for query timeout. This is a hint only.
- `javax.persistence.validation.group.pre-persist`: groups that are targeted for validation upon the pre-persist event. See Section 3.6.
- `javax.persistence.validation.group.pre-update`: groups that are targeted for validation upon the pre-update event. See Section 3.6.
- `javax.persistence.validation.group.pre-remove`: groups that are targeted for validation upon the pre-remove event. See Section 3.6.

Vendor-specific properties and hints may be defined within the `properties` element. If a persistence provider does not recognize such a property, it must silently ignore it.

6.1.2 Persistence Unit Examples

In this subsection, we show a few examples to illustrate how a persistence unit may be defined and how default values are applied.

Example 1:

```
<persistence-unit name="jpaTestPU"/>
```

This one line definition creates a persistence unit with name *"jpaTestPU"*. Any classes that are annotated with `@Entity`, `@Embeddable`, or `@MappedSuperclass` and that are located in the root of the persistence unit are included to the list of managed persistence classes. If the file `META-INF/orm.xml` exists, any classes that are referenced by it and mapping information contained in it are also included to the persistence unit.

Because the `transaction-type` attribute of the `persistence-unit` element and the data source element are not specified, the transaction type defaults to JTA in Java EE environments, where the data source must be provided by the container (for example, at application deployment). The transaction type defaults to RESOURCE_LOCAL in Java SE environments, where the data source must be provided by other means (for example, when programmatically creating the entity manager factory as in Section 3.3.2).

Since a persistence provider is not explicitly specified, a default provider is assumed. For example, in the JBoss application server, the Hibernate persistence provider (Section 9.8) is the default.

Example 2:

```
<persistence-unit name="jpaTestPU2" transaction-type="RESOURCE_LOCAL">
  <provider>org.eclipse.persistence.jpa.PersistenceProvider</provider>
  <non-jta-data-source>java:/jpaTestDS</non-jta-data-source>
  <mapping-file>ormOrder.xml</mapping-file>
  <mapping-file>ormCustomer.xml</mapping-file>
</persistence-unit>
```

This example creates a persistence unit with name *"jpaTestPU2"*. Any classes that are annotated with @Entity, @Embeddable, or @MappedSuperclass and that are located in the root of the persistence unit are included to the list of managed persistence classes. If the file META-INF/orm.xml exists, any classes that are referenced by it and mapping information contained in it are included to the persistence unit. In addition, persistence classes and mapping information contained in the mapping files ormOrder.xml and ormCustomer.xml are also included. These two mapping files must be on the classpath.

The provider element specifies the EclipseLink persistence provider (Section 9.3) and the data source element designates a non-JTA data source for the persistence unit. Application-managed non-JTA entity managers are to be used.

Example 3:

```
<persistence-unit name="jpaTestPU3" transaction-type="JTA">
  <provider>org.hibernate.ejb.HibernatePersistence</provider>
  <jta-data-source>java:/jpaTestJpaDS</jta-data-source>
  <jar-file>order.jar</jar-file>
  <jar-file>customer.jar</jar-file>
</persistence-unit>
```

This example creates a persistence unit with name *"jpaTestPU3"*, with a JTA data source.   Any classes that are annotated with   `@Entity`,   `@Embeddable`,   or `@MappedSuperclass` and that are located in the root of the persistence unit are included to the list of managed persistence classes.   If the file `META-INF/orm.xml` exists, any classes that are referenced by it and mapping information contained in it are included to the persistence unit. The two jar files: `order.jar` and `customer.jar` are searched for persistence classes and mapping information annotated or defaulted on them. If the file `META-INF/orm.xml` exists in the two jar files, they are also included in the persistence unit.

The `provider` element specifies the Hibernate JPA persistence provider (Section 9.8). Either container-managed or application-managed JTA entity managers are to be used.

Example 4:

```
<persistence-unit name="jpaTestPU4" transaction-type="RESOURCE_LOCAL">
  <provider>org.apache.openjpa.persistence.PersistenceProviderImpl
  </provider>
  <non-jta-data-source>java:/jpaTestDS</non-jta-data-source>
  <mapping-file>META-INF/orm.xml</mapping-file>
  <mapping-file>ormOrder.xml</mapping-file>
  <mapping-file>ormCustomer.xml</mapping-file>
  <jar-file>order.jar</jar-file>
  <jar-file>customer.jar</jar-file>
  <class>jpatest.Vehicle</class>
  <class>jpatest.entity.Address</class>
  <exclude-unlisted-classes/>
</persistence-unit>
```

This example creates a persistence unit with name *"jpaTestPU4"*, with a non-JTA data source and a resource-local transaction type.   The mapping files `META-INF/orm.xml`, `ormOrder.xml`, and `ormCustomer.xml` are read and persistence classes referenced by them and mapping information contained in them are added to the persistence unit. The two jar files: `order.jar` and `customer.jar` are searched for persistence classes and mapping information annotated or defaulted on them. If the file `META-INF/orm.xml` exists in the two jar files, they are also included in the persistence unit. The persistence classes `Vehicle` and `Address` are included as well. No other classes contained in the root of the persistence unit are included because of the `exclude-unlisted-classes` element. The files `ormOrder.xml`, `ormCustomer.xml`, `order.jar`, and `customer.jar` must exist on the class path.

The `provider` element specifies the OpenJPA persistence provider (Section 9.9). Application-managed non-JTA entity managers are to be used.

It should be noted that, if the `persistence.xml` file exists in the `META-INF` subdirectory of `order.jar` or `customer.jar`, this `persistence.xml` file will not be used to augment the persistence unit `"jpaTestPU4"` with the classes of the persistence unit whose root is `order.jar` or `customer.jar`.

6.1.3 Persistence Unit Structure

As mentioned early in this section, a persistence unit is defined in a `persistence.xml` file, and the jar file or directory whose `META-INF` subdirectory contains the `persistence.xml` file is termed the *root* of the persistence unit.

In Java EE environments, the root of a persistence unit must be one of the following:

- an EJB-JAR file;
- the `WEB-INF/classes` directory of a WAR file;
- a jar file in the `WEB-INF/lib` directory of a WAR file;
- a jar file in the EAR library directory;
- an application client jar file.

It is worth noting that JPA 1.0 supported the use of a jar file in the root of an EAR as the root of a persistence unit. This use is no longer supported and applications should use the EAR library directory instead.

The following examples illustrate possible structures of a persistence unit with the use of the `jar-file` element referencing additional persistence classes. These examples use the convention that a jar file with a name terminating in "PU" contains the `persistence.xml` file and that a jar file with a name terminating in "Entities" contains additional persistence classes.

Example 1:

```
app.ear
```

```
earRootPU.jar              (containing file META-INF/persistence.xml)
lib/earEntities.jar        (containing additional persistence classes)
```

The root of the persistence unit is the jar file `earRootPU.jar`, since the file `persistence.xml` is in its META-INF subdirectory. This persistence unit references additional persistence classes in the file `lib/earEntities.jar`. The `persistence.xml` file must contain the `jar-file` element as:

```
<jar-file>lib/earEntities.jar</jar-file>
```

Example 2:

```
app.ear
   lib/earLibPU.jar        (containing file META-INF/persistence.xml)
   lib/earEntities.jar     (containing additional persistence classes)
```

The root of the persistence unit is jar file `earLibPU.jar`, since the file `persistence.xml` is in its META-INF subdirectory. This persistence unit references additional persistence classes in the file `lib/earEntities.jar`. The `persistence.xml` file must contain the `jar-file` element as:

```
<jar-file>earEntities.jar</jar-file>
```

Example 3:

```
app.ear
   ejbjar.jar              (containing file META-INF/persistence.xml)
   lib/earEntities.jar     (containing additional persistence classes)
```

The root of the persistence unit is the jar file `ejbjar.jar`, since the file `persistence.xml` is in its META-INF subdirectory. This persistence unit references additional persistence classes in the file `lib/earEntities.jar`. The `persistence.xml` file must contain the `jar-file` element as:

```
<jar-file>lib/earEntities.jar</jar-file>
```

Example 4:

```
app.ear
   web.war
      WEB-INF/lib/warPU.jar   (containing META-INF/persistence.xml)
      WEB-INF/lib/warEntities.jar   (containing more persistence classes)
```

The root of the persistence unit is the jar file `warPU.jar`, since the file `persistence.xml` is in its `META-INF` subdirectory. This persistence unit references additional persistence classes in the file `WEB-INF/lib/warEntities.jar`. The `persistence.xml` file must contain the `jar-file` element as:

`<jar-file>warEntities.jar</jar-file>`

Example 5:

```
app.ear
   web.war
      WEB-INF/classes/META-INF/persistence.xml
      WEB-INF/lib/warEntities.jar   (containing more persistence classes)
```

The root of the persistence unit is the directory `classes/`, since the file `persistence.xml` is in its `META-INF` subdirectory. This persistence unit references additional persistence classes in the file `WEB-INF/lib/warEntities.jar`. The `persistence.xml` file must contain the `jar-file` element as:

`<jar-file>lib/warEntities.jar</jar-file>`

Example 6:

```
app.ear
   lib/earEntities.jar              (containing additional persistence classes)
   web.war
      WEB-INF/classes/META-INF/persistence.xml
```

The root of the persistence unit is the directory `classes/`, since the file `persistence.xml` is in its `META-INF` subdirectory. This persistence unit references additional persistence classes in the file `lib/earEntities.jar`. The `persistence.xml` file must contain the `jar-file` element as:

`<jar-file>../../lib/earEntities.jar</jar-file>`

Example 7:

```
app.ear
   lib/earEntities.jar      (containing additional persistence classes)
   web.war
      WEB-INF/lib/warPU.jar (containing file META-INF/persistence.xml)
```

The root of the persistence unit is the jar file `warPU.jar`, since the file `persistence.xml` is in its `META-INF` subdirectory. This persistence unit references additional persistence classes in the file `lib/earEntities.jar`. The `persistence.xml` file must contain the `jar-file` element as:

```
<jar-file>../../../lib/earEntities.jar</jar-file>
```

6.1.4 Persistence Unit Scope

In Java EE environments, an EJB-JAR, WAR, application client jar, or EAR can define one or more persistence units. When referencing a persistence unit using the *unitName* element of the annotations `@PersistenceContext` and `@PersistenceUnit`, or the `persistence-unit-name` element of the `persistence-context-ref` deployment descriptor in `web.xml` or `ejb-jar.xml`, the visibility scope of the persistence unit is determined by its point of definition.

A persistence unit that is defined inside an EJB-JAR, WAR, or application client jar is scoped only to that EJB-JAR, WAR, or application client jar, respectively.

A persistence unit that is defined at the level of the EAR is generally visible to all components in the application. However, if a persistence unit of the same name is defined by an EJB-JAR, WAR, or application client jar file within the EAR, the persistence unit of that name defined at EAR level will not be visible to the components defined by that EJB-JAR, WAR, or application client jar file unless the persistence unit name # syntax is used to specify the path name. In the following we provide two examples to illustrate the use of the # syntax.

Example 1:

```
app.ear
   lib/earLibPU.jar
```

```
ejbjar.jar
web.war
```

We assume that `earLibPU.jar` has a persistence unit with name *"jpaTestJtaPU"* and `ejbjar.jar` has also a persistence unit with the same name. The persistence unit *"jpaTestJtaPU"* defined from `earLibPU.jar` is automatically visible to the web module, and may be used as:

```
@PersistenceContext(name = "jpaTestJtaPC", unitName = "jpaTestJtaPU")
public class JpaTestServlet extends HttpServlet { ... }
```

However, if we want to refer to the persistence unit in the EJB module, the local persistence unit defined inside `ejbjar.jar` will take a higher precedence. If an EJB class packaged in `ejbjar.jar` wants to access the persistence unit *"jpaTestJtaPU"* defined from `earLibPU.jar`, the # syntax must be used as:

```
@Stateless
public class JpaBookSL implements JpaBookSLLocal {
  @PersistenceContext(unitName = "lib/earLibPU.jar#jpaTestJtaPU")
  EntityManager em;
}
```

Example 2:

```
app.ear
   lib/earLibPU.jar
   ejbjar.jar
   web.war
       WEB-INF/lib/warLibPU.jar
```

We assume that `earLibPU.jar` has a persistence unit with name *"jpaTestJtaPU"* and `warLibPU.jar` has also a persistence unit with the same name. Then the persistence unit *"jpaTestJtaPU"* defined from `earLibPU.jar` is automatically visible to the EJB module, and may be used as:

```
@Stateless
public class BookSL implements BookSLLocal {
  @PersistenceContext(unitName = "jpaTestJtaPU")
  EntityManager em;
}
```

However, if we want to refer to the persistence unit in the web module, the local persistence unit defined inside `warLibPU.jar` will take a higher precedence. If a web component packaged in `warLibPU.jar` wants to access the persistence unit *"jpaTestJtaPU"* defined from `earLibPU.jar`, the # syntax must be used as:

```
@PersistenceContext(name = "jpaTestJtaPC",
  unitName = "../../../lib/earLibPU.jar#jpaTestJtaPU"
)
public class TestServlet extends HttpServlet { ... }
```

Here we have assumed that `TestServlet` is packaged inside the `warLibPU.jar` file. The path name is relative to the referencing component: `warLibPU.jar`.

6.2 XML Mapping

XML object-relational mapping may serve as an overriding mechanism for annotations. On the other hand, it may also serve as an alternative to annotations; that is, an application may wish to use just XML mapping without any annotations. An XML mapping file may be the default `META-INF`/`orm.xml` or others specified using the `mapping-file` element in the `persistence.xml` file. The XML schema for OR mapping can be found from the URL given in Section 9.1.

The root element of an OR mapping file is the `entity-mappings` element. It consists of the following subelements (and in this order): `description`, `persistence-unit-metadata`, `package`, `schema`, `catalog`, `access`, `sequence-generator`, `table-generator`, `named-query`, `named-native-query`, `sql-result-set-mapping`, `mapped-superclass`, `entity`, and `embeddable`. All these subelements are optional.

The `persistence-unit-metadata` element contains metadata for the entire persistence unit. The result is undefined if it occurs in more than one mapping file within the same persistence unit. It has a subelement: `xml-mapping-metadata-complete`. When this subelement is specified, the complete set of mapping metadata for the persistence unit is contained in the XML mapping files (including default mapping values), and any annotations defined on the classes are ignored. In this case, any `metadata-complete` attributes within the `mapped-superclass`, `entity`, and `embeddable` elements are ignored. When the subelement `xml-mapping-metadata-complete` is omitted, the XML mapping descriptors override the annotations specified on the classes (including the default values).

243

The `package`, `schema`, `catalog`, and `access` elements apply to all of the `mapped-superclass`, `entity`, and `embeddable` elements defined in the same mapping file in which they occur.

The `sequence-generator`, `table-generator`, `named-query`, `named-native-query`, and `sql-result-set-mapping` elements are global to the persistence unit. The same persistence unit cannot have more than one sequence generator or table generator of the same name. Also, it cannot have more than one named query, named native query, or result set mapping of the same name.

The `mapped-superclass`, `entity`, and `embeddable` elements each define the mapping metadata for a persistent class. The mapping information contained in these elements may be complete or partial.

Listing 6-2 gives a sample XML mapping file with most of the above-mentioned elements. You may want to refer back to this example when you read the next few subsections.

Listing 6-2 Sample XML mapping file.

```xml
<?xml version="1.0" encoding="UTF-8"?>
<entity-mappings version="2.0"
  xmlns="http://java.sun.com/xml/ns/persistence/orm"
  xmlns:xsi="http://www.w3.org/2001/XMLSchema-instance"
  xsi:schemaLocation="http://java.sun.com/xml/ns/persistence/orm
      http://java.sun.com/xml/ns/persistence/orm/orm_2_0.xsd">

<description>override annotations</description>
<persistence-unit-metadata>
  <persistence-unit-defaults>
    <schema>jpatest</schema>    <!-- database schema for tables -->
    <access>FIELD</access>      <!-- map fields, not getters -->
    <entity-listeners>
      <entity-listener class="jpatest.util.AuditingFieldListener">
        <pre-persist method-name="insertAuditingField" />
        <pre-update method-name="updateAuditingField" />
      </entity-listener>
    </entity-listeners>
  </persistence-unit-defaults>
</persistence-unit-metadata>
```

```xml
</persistence-unit-metadata>

<named-query name="selectCustomerAndPrice">
  <query>
    <![CDATA[SELECT o.customer,o.price FROM Order o
             WHERE o.orderTime<?1]]>
  </query>
  <hint name="javax.persistence.cache.retrieveMode"
        value="BYPASS" />
  <hint name="javax.persistence.query.timeout" value="1000" />
</named-query>
<table-generator name="ADDRESS_SEQ_GEN" schema="JPATEST"
  table="SEQUENCE_GENERATOR_TB" pk-column-name="SEQUENCE_NAME"
  value-column-name="SEQUENCE_VALUE"
  pk-column-value="ADDRESS_SEQ" />

<mapped-superclass class="jpatest.entity.User">
  <attributes>
    <basic name="name" />
    <basic name="picture" fetch="LAZY" optional="false">
      <column name="PICTURE" column-definition="BLOB NOT NULL" />
      <lob />
    </basic>
    <one-to-one name="address" fetch="EAGER">
      <join-column name="ADDRESS_ID_FK"
                   referenced-column-name="ADDRESS_ID_PK" />
      <cascade>
        <cascade-persist />
        <cascade-remove />
      </cascade>
    </one-to-one>
  </attributes>
</mapped-superclass>

<entity class="jpatest.entity.Order">
  <table name="ORDERS" />
  <attributes>
    <id name="orderId">
      <column name="ORDER_ID_PK" />
      <generated-value generator="ORDER_SEQ_GEN" strategy="TABLE" />
    </id>
    <basic name="price" />
    <basic name="orderTime" optional="true">
      <column name="ORDER_TIME" updatable="true"
              insertable="true" />
    </basic>
```

```xml
    <basic name="status">
      <enumerated>ORDINAL</enumerated>
    </basic>
    <many-to-one name="customer" fetch="EAGER" optional="true">
      <join-column name="CUSTOMER_ID_FK"
                   referenced-column-name="CUSTOMER_ID_PK" />
    </many-to-one>
    <one-to-many name="lineItems" mapped-by="order" fetch="LAZY">
      <order-column name="LINE_ITEM_ID_PK" />
      <cascade>
        <cascade-persist />
        <cascade-remove />
        <cascade-merge />
      </cascade>
    </one-to-many>
  </attributes>
</entity>

<entity class="jpatest.entity.LineItem">
  <table name="LINE_ITEM" />
  <attributes>
    <id name="lineItemId">
      <column name="LINE_ITEM_ID_PK" />
      <generated-value generator="LM_SEQ_GEN" strategy="TABLE" />
    </id>
    <basic name="quantity" />
    <basic name="price" />

    <many-to-one name="book" fetch="EAGER" optional="true">
      <join-column name="BOOK_ID_FK"
                   referenced-column-name="BOOK_ID_PK" />
    </many-to-one>
    <many-to-one name="order" fetch="EAGER" optional="true">
      <join-column name="ORDER_ID_FK"
                   referenced-column-name="ORDER_ID_PK" />
    </many-to-one>
  </attributes>
</entity>

<entity class="jpatest.entity.Customer">
  <table name="CUSTOMER" />
  <inheritance strategy="JOINED" />
  <discriminator-value>C</discriminator-value>
  <discriminator-column name="CUSTOMER_TYPE"
                        discriminator-type="STRING" length="1" />
  <association-overrides>
```

```xml
    <association-override name="address">
      <join-columns>
        <join-column name="ADDRESS_ID_FK"
                    referenced-column-name="ADDRESS_ID_PK" />
      </join-columns>
    </association-override>
  </association-overrides>
  <attributes>
    <id name="customerId">
      <column name="CUSTOMER_ID_PK" />
      <generated-value generator="CUST_SEQ_GEN" strategy="TABLE" />
    </id>
    <basic name="customerType">
      <column name="CUSTOMER_TYPE" />
      <enumerated>STRING</enumerated>
    </basic>
    <embedded name="bank">
      <attribute-override name="bankName">
        <column name="BANK_NAME" />
      </attribute-override>
      <attribute-override name="accountNumber">
        <column name="ACCOUNT_NUMBER" />
      </attribute-override>
      <attribute-override name="routingNumber">
        <column name="ROUTING_NUMBER" />
      </attribute-override>
    </embedded>
    <one-to-many name="orders" mapped-by="customer" fetch="EAGER" />
  </attributes>
</entity>

<entity class="jpatest.entity.PreferredCustomer">
  <table name="PREFERRED_CUSTOMER" />
  <primary-key-join-column name="CUSTOMER_ID_FPK"
        referenced-column-name="CUSTOMER_ID_PK" />
  <discriminator-value>P</discriminator-value>
  <attributes>
    <basic name="discountRate">
      <column name="DISCOUNT_RATE" />
    </basic>
    <basic name="expirationDate">
      <column name="EXPIRATION_DATE" />
      <temporal>DATE</temporal>
    </basic>
  </attributes>
</entity>
```

247

```xml
<entity class="jpatest.entity.Category">
  <attributes>
    <id name="categoryId">
      <column name="CATEGORY_ID_PK" />
      <generated-value generator="CATEG_SEQ_GEN" strategy="TABLE" />
    </id>
    <basic name="categoryName">
      <column name="CATEGORY_NAME" />
    </basic>
    <many-to-one name="parentCategory" fetch="EAGER"
                 optional="true">
      <join-column name="PARENT_CATEGORY_FK"
                   referenced-column-name="CATEGORY_ID_PK" />
    </many-to-one>
    <one-to-many name="childCategories"
                 mapped-by="parentCategory" />
    <many-to-many name="books" mapped-by="categories">
      <order-by name="title ASC, price DESC" />
    </many-to-many>
  </attributes>
</entity>

<embeddable class="jpatest.entity.BankInfo">
  <attributes>
    <basic name="bankName">
      <column name="BANK_NAME_X" />
    </basic>
    <basic name="accountNumber">
      <column name="BANK_ACCOUNT_NUMBER" />
    </basic>
    <basic name="routingNumber">
      <column name="BANK_ROUTING_NUMBER" />
    </basic>
  </attributes>
</embeddable>

</entity-mappings>
```

6.2.1 Persistence Unit Defaults

This subsection elaborates on the subelements of the `persistence-unit-metadata` element. The `persistence-unit-metadata` element has two subelements: `xml-mapping-metadata-complete` and `persistence-unit-defaults`.

The element `xml-mapping-metadata-complete` is covered early in this section and controls whether the XML OR mapping is used to selectively override annotation values or it serves as a complete alternative to annotations.

The element `persistence-unit-defaults` has the following subelements: `schema`, `catalog`, `delimited-identifiers`, `access`, `cascade-persist`, and `entity-listeners`, which are explained below.

schema

The `schema` subelement specifies the database schema and applies to all entities, tables, secondary tables, join tables, collection tables, table generators, and sequence generators in the persistence unit.

The `schema` subelement may be overridden by any other `schema` subelement or attribute in the mapping metadata. In particular, it may be overridden by any of the following:

- The `schema` subelement explicitly specified in the `entity-mappings` element.
- The `schema` subelement explicitly specified in the `@Table` or `@SecondaryTable` annotation or any `schema` attribute on the `table` or `secondary-table` subelement of an `entity` element.
- The `schema` element explicitly specified in the `@TableGenerator` annotation or `table-generator` subelement.
- The `schema` element explicitly specified in the `@SequenceGenerator` annotation or `sequence-generator` subelement.
- The `schema` element explicitly specified in the `@JoinTable` annotation or `join-table` subelement.
- The `schema` element explicitly specified in the `@CollectionTable` annotation or `collection-table` subelement.

catalog

The `catalog` subelement specifies the database catalog and applies to all entities, tables, secondary tables, join tables, collection tables, table generators, and sequence generators in the persistence unit.

The `catalog` subelement may be overridden by any other `catalog` subelement or attribute in the mapping metadata. In particular, it may be overridden by any of the following:

- The `catalog` subelement explicitly specified in the `entity-mappings` element.
- The `catalog` subelement explicitly specified in the `@Table` or `@SecondaryTable` annotation or any `catalog` attribute on the `table` or `secondary-table` subelement of an `entity` element.
- The `catalog` subelement explicitly specified in the `@TableGenerator` annotation or `table-generator` subelement.
- The `catalog` element explicitly specified in the `@SequenceGenerator` annotation or `sequence-generator` subelement.
- The `catalog` element explicitly specified in the `@JoinTable` annotation or `join-table` subelement.
- The `catalog` element explicitly specified in the `@CollectionTable` annotation or `collection-table` subelement.

delimited-identifiers

Many mapping elements contain names of database objects or assume default names for database objects. For example, the `@Table` annotation or the `table` XML element of an entity contains the name of a database table object.

Regular identifiers (also known as undelimited identifiers) for names of database objects are restricted to letters, digits, underscore, and the dollar-sign symbol, and are case-insensitive. Delimited identifiers may include additional characters from the character set implied by the locale setting of the database. Delimited identifiers enable us to declare names that are otherwise identical to SQL keywords, such as TABLE, WHERE, DECLARE, and so on. Letters in delimited identifiers are case sensitive. In most databases, delimited identifiers are enclosed in double quotes (").

When specifying the `<delimited-identifiers/>` subelement within the `persistence-unit-defaults` element, all database table-, schema-, and column-level identifiers in use for a persistence unit are treated as delimited identifiers.

However, it is possible to specify on a per-name basis that the name of a database object is to be interpreted as a delimited identifier as follows:

- Using annotations, a name is specified as a delimited identifier by enclosing the name within double quotes, whereby the inner quotes are escaped by the backslash character, as in the examples,

```
@Table(name = "\"Book Orders\"")   // table name contains space
@Table(name = "\"book\"")      // table name in all small letters
@Table(name = "\"Book\"")      // table name has capital character
```

- When using XML descriptors, a name is specified as a delimited identifier by use of double quotes, as in the examples,

```
<table name="&quot;Book Orders&quot;"/>
<table name="&quot;book&quot;"/>
<table name="&quot;Book&quot;"/>
```

Note that, if `<delimited-identifiers/>` is specified and individual annotations or XML elements or attributes use escaped double quotes, the double-quotes appear in the name of the database identifier.

The `delimited-identifiers` subelement cannot be overridden in JPA 2.0.

access

The `access` subelement applies to all persistence classes in the persistence unit.

The `access` subelement may be overridden by any of the following:

- The use of any annotation specifying mapping information on the fields or properties of the entity class.
- Any `@Access` annotation on the entity class, mapped superclass, or embeddable class.
- Any `access` subelement of the `entity-mappings` element.
- Any `@Access` annotation on a field or property of an entity class, mapped superclass, or embeddable class.
- Any `access` attribute defined within an `entity`, `mapped-superclass`, or `embeddable` XML element.

- Any `access` attribute defined within an `id`, `embedded-id`, `version`, `basic`, `embedded`, `many-to-one`, `one-to-one`, `one-to-many`, `many-to-many`, or `element-collection` element.

cascade-persist

The `cascade-persist` subelement specifies the cascading policy for the `persist` operation and applies to all relationships in the persistence unit.

Specifying this subelement adds the cascade persist option to all relationships in addition to any settings specified in annotations or XML descriptors.

The `cascade-persist` subelement cannot be overridden in JPA 2.0, but this restriction may be removed in a future release.

entity-listeners

The `entity-listeners` subelement defines default entity listeners for the persistence unit. Specify each entity listener with a separate `entity-listener` descriptor within this subelement. These entity listeners are called before any other entity listeners for an entity unless the entity listener order is overridden by any of the following:

- The `entity-listeners` subelement within a `mapped-superclass` or `entity` element.
- The `@ExcludeDefaultListeners` annotation on the entity or mapped superclass.
- The `exclude-default-listeners` subelement within the corresponding `entity` or `mapped-superclass` element.

The `entity-listener` descriptor may contain subelements: `pre-persist`, `post-persist`, `pre-remove`, `post-remove`, `pre-update`, `post-update`, `post-load`, each of which defines a lifecycle callback method for the listener.

6.2.2 Access, Sequence, and Query

This subsection talks about the elements: `package`, `schema`, `catalog`, `access`, `sequence-generator`, `table-generator`, `named-query`, `named-native-query`, and `sql-result-set-mapping`. These elements are directly within the `entity-mappings` root tag.

package

The `package` subelement specifies the Java package of the classes listed within the subelements and attributes of the same mapping file only. This subelement may be overridden by specifying the fully qualified class name for a class.

schema

The `schema` subelement applies only to the entities, tables, secondary tables, join tables, collection tables, table generators, and sequence generators listed within the same mapping file.

The `schema` subelement may be overridden by any of the following:

- Any `schema` element explicitly specified in the `@Table`, `@SecondaryTable`, `@JoinTable`, or `@CollectionTable` annotation on an entity listed within the mapping file or any `schema` attribute on any `table` or `secondary-table` subelement defined within the `entity` element for such an entity.

- Any `schema` attribute on any `join-table` or `collection-table` subelement of an attribute defined within the `attributes` subelement of the `entity` element for such an entity.

- Any `schema` attribute of any `table-generator` or `sequence-generator` element within the mapping file.

catalog

The `catalog` subelement applies only to the entities, tables, secondary tables, join tables, collection tables, table generators, and sequence generators listed within the same mapping file.

The `catalog` subelement may be overridden by any of the following:

- Any `catalog` element explicitly specified in the `@Table`, `@SecondaryTable`, `@JoinTable`, or `@CollectionTable` annotation on an entity listed within the mapping file or any `catalog` attribute on any `table` or `secondary-table` subelement defined within the `entity` element for such an entity.

- Any `catalog` attribute on any `join-table` or `collection-table` subelement of an attribute defined within the `attributes` subelement of the `entity` element for such an entity.

- Any `catalog` attribute of any `table-generator` or `sequence-generator` element within the mapping file.

access

The `access` subelement applies to the persistence classes listed within the same mapping file.

The `access` subelement may be overridden by any of the following:

- The use of any annotation specifying mapping information on the fields or properties of the entity class.
- Any `@Access` annotation on the entity class, mapped superclass, or embeddable class.
- Any `@Access` annotation on a field or property of an entity class, mapped superclass, or embeddable class.
- Any `access` attribute defined within an `entity`, `mapped-superclass`, or `embeddable` XML descriptor.
- Any `access` attribute defined within an `id`, `embedded-id`, `version`, `basic`, `embedded`, `many-to-one`, `one-to-one`, `one-to-many`, `many-to-many`, or `element-collection` element.

sequence-generator

The `sequence-generator` subelement applies to the whole persistence unit. Thus the generators defined with this subelement must have unique names within the same persistence unit, even if they are defined in multiple mapping files. If a generator of the same name is defined using annotation, the generator defined by this subelement overrides that annotation. In the end, JPA combines all the generators defined using XML and annotation.

table-generator

The `table-generator` subelement applies to the whole persistence unit. Thus the generators defined with this subelement must have unique names within the same persistence unit, even if they are defined in multiple mapping files. If a generator of the same name is defined using annotation, the generator defined by this subelement overrides that annotation. In the end, JPA combines all the generators defined using XML and annotation.

named-query

The `named-query` subelement applies to the whole persistence unit. Thus the named queries defined with this subelement must have unique names within the same persistence unit, even if they are defined in multiple mapping files. If a named query of the same name is defined using annotation, the named query defined by this subelement overrides that annotation. In the end, JPA combines all the named queries defined using XML and annotation.

This is an example of a named query included inside a CDATA section and with two query hints:

```
<named-query name="selectCustomer">
  <query>
    <![CDATA[ SELECT o.customer FROM Order o
              WHERE o.orderTime < ?1 ]]>
  </query>
  <hint name="javax.persistence.cache.retrieveMode" value="BYPASS" />
  <hint name="javax.persistence.query.timeout" value="1000" />
</named-query>
```

named-native-query

The `named-native-query` subelement applies to the whole persistence unit. Thus the named native queries defined with this subelement must have unique names within the same persistence unit, even if they are defined in multiple mapping files. If a named native query of the same name is defined using annotation, the named native query defined by this subelement overrides that annotation. In the end, JPA combines all the named native queries defined using XML and annotation.

sql-result-set-mapping

The `sql-result-set-mapping` subelement applies to the whole persistence unit. Thus the SQL result set mappings defined with this subelement must have unique names within the same persistence unit, even if they are defined in multiple mapping files. If a SQL result set mapping of the same name is defined using annotation, the SQL result set mapping defined by this subelement overrides that annotation. In the end, JPA combines all SQL result set mappings defined using XML and annotation.

6.2.3 Persistence Classes

This subsection provide details on the elements: `mapped-superclass`, `entity`, and `embeddable`.

The `mapped-superclass` subelement defines a mapped superclass of the persistence unit. Multiple mapping files for the same persistence unit cannot contain entries for the same mapped superclass. The mapped superclass may or may not have been defined using the `@MappedSuperclass` annotation.

The `entity` subelement defines an entity of the persistence unit. Multiple mapping files for the same persistence unit cannot contain entries for the same entity. The entity class may or may not have been defined using the `@Entity` annotation.

The `embeddable` subelement defines an embeddable class of the persistence unit. Multiple mapping files for the same persistence unit cannot contain entries for the same embeddable class. The embeddable class may or may not have been defined using the `@Embeddable` annotation.

The subelements, attributes, and overriding rules of the `mapped-superclass`, `entity`, and `embeddable` elements are elaborated as follows.

metadata-complete

If the `metadata-complete` attribute of the `entity` (`mapped-superclass`, and `embeddable`, respectively) element is specified as true, any annotations on the `entity` class (`mapped-superclass`, and `embeddable` class, respectively) and its fields and properties, are ignored. When `metadata-complete` is specified as true and XML attributes or subelements of the element are omitted, the default values for those attributes and subelements are applied.

access

The `access` attribute defines the access type for the entity, mapped superclass, or embeddable. The `access` attribute overrides any access type specified by the `persistence-unit-defaults` element or `entity-mappings` element for the given entity, mapped superclass, or embeddable.

The access type for a field or property of the entity may be overridden by specifying the mapping for that field or property using the appropriate XML subelement within the `attributes` element.

Caution must be exercised in overriding an access type that was specified or defaulted using annotations, as this may cause the application to break.

cacheable

The `cacheable` attribute defines whether the entity should be cached or must not be cached when the `shared-cache-mode` element of the `persistence.xml` file is specified as `ENABLE_SELECTIVE` or `DISABLE_SELECTIVE`. This attribute overrides the `@Cacheable` annotation if it is specified for the entity.

The `cacheable` attribute does not apply to mapped superclasses and embeddable classes.

name

The `name` attribute defines the name for an entity. This `name` attribute overrides the entity name defined by the `name` attribute of the `@Entity` annotation (whether explicitly specified or defaulted).

Caution must be exercised in overriding the entity name, as this may cause the application to break.

The `name` attribute does not apply to mapped superclasses and embeddable classes.

table

The `table` subelement of the `entity` element overrides the `@Table` annotation (including the defaulted table value) on the entity. If a `table` subelement is present, but its attributes or subelements are not explicitly specified, their default values are applied.

The `table` subelement does not apply to mapped superclasses and embeddable classes.

secondary-table

The `secondary-table` subelement overrides all `@SecondaryTable` and `@SecondaryTables` annotations (including the defaulted values) on the entity. If a secondary-table subelement is present, but its attributes or subelements are not explicitly specified, their default values are applied.

The secondary-table subelement does not apply to mapped superclasses and embeddable classes.

primary-key-join-column

The primary-key-join-column subelement specifies a primary key column that is used to join the table of an entity subclass to the primary table for the entity superclass when the joined table inheritance strategy is used.

The primary-key-join-column subelement overrides all @PrimaryKeyJoinColumn and @PrimaryKeyJoinColumns annotations (including the defaulted values) on the entity. If a primary-key-join-column subelement is present, but some of its attributes or subelements are not explicitly specified, their default values are applied.

The primary-key-join-column subelement does not apply to mapped superclasses and embeddable classes.

id-class

The id-class subelement specifies the ID class for the entity or mapped super class and overrides any @IdClass annotation specified on the entity or mapped super class.

The id-class subelement does not apply to embeddable classes.

inheritance

The inheritance subelement specifies the inheritance strategy and overrides any @Inheritance annotation (including defaulted values) on the entity. If an inheritance subelement is present, but its strategy attribute is not explicitly specified, its default value is applied.

This subelement applies to an entity and its subclasses (unless otherwise overridden for a subclass by an annotation or XML element), but does not apply to mapped superclasses and embeddable classes.

Applications should use only a single inheritance strategy within an entity inheritance hierarchy. Mixing inheritance strategies within the same inheritance hierarchy is not supported by JPA.

discriminator-value

The `discriminator-value` subelement specifies the value of the discriminator for the entity in the inheritance hierarchy and overrides any `@DiscriminatorValue` annotations (including defaulted values) on the entity.

The `discriminator-value` subelement does not apply to mapped superclasses and embeddable classes.

discriminator-column

The `discriminator-column` subelement specifies the discriminator column for the entity in the inheritance hierarchy and overrides any `@DiscriminatorColumn` annotation (including defaulted values) on the entity. If a `discriminator-column` subelement is present, but some of its attributes are not explicitly specified, their default values are applied.

This subelement applies to an entity and its subclasses (unless otherwise overridden for a subclass by an annotation or XML element), but does not apply to mapped superclasses and embeddable classes.

sequence-generator

The `sequence-generator` subelement defines a sequence generator that is added to any generators defined in annotations and any other generators defined in XML. A generator defined by this subelement overrides any generator defined in annotations, if they have the same name.

If a `sequence-generator` subelement is present, but some of its attributes or subelements are not explicitly specified, their default values are applied. The generator defined by the `sequence-generator` subelement applies to the whole persistence unit. Multiple mapping files for the persistence unit cannot contain generators of the same name.

The `sequence-generator` subelement does not apply to mapped superclasses and embeddable classes.

table-generator

The `table-generator` subelement defines a table generator that is added to any generators defined in annotations and any other generators defined in XML. A generator defined by this subelement overrides any generator defined in annotations, if they have the same name.

If a `table-generator` subelement is present, but some of its attributes or subelements are not explicitly specified, their default values are applied. The generator defined by the `table-generator` subelement applies to the whole persistence unit. Multiple mapping files for the persistence unit cannot contain generators of the same name.

The `table-generator` subelement does not apply to mapped superclasses and embeddable classes.

attribute-override

The `attribute-override` subelement overrides any `@AttributeOverride` annotations for the same attribute name on the entity.

If an `attribute-override` subelement is present, but some of its attributes or subelements are not explicitly specified, their default values are applied.

The `attribute-override` subelement does not apply to mapped superclasses and embeddable classes.

association-override

The `association-override` subelement overrides any `@AssociationOverride` annotations for the same association name on the entity.

If an `association-override` subelement is present, but some of its attributes or subelements are not explicitly specified, their default values are applied.

The `association-override` subelement does not apply to mapped superclasses and embeddable classes.

named-query

The `named-query` subelement defines a named query that is added to the set of named queries defined in annotations, and other named queries defined in XML. A named query defined by this subelement overrides any named query defined in annotations, if they have the same name.

If a `named-query` subelement is present, but some of its attributes or subelements are not explicitly specified, their default values are applied. The named query defined by the `named-query` subelement applies to the whole persistence unit. Multiple mapping files for the persistence unit cannot contain named queries of the same name.

The `named-query` subelement does not apply to mapped superclasses and embeddable classes.

named-native-query

The `named-native-query` subelement defines a named query that is added to the set of named queries defined in annotations, and other named queries defined in XML. A named query defined by this subelement overrides any named query defined in annotations, if they have the same name.

If a `named-native-query` subelement is present, but some of its attributes or subelements are not explicitly specified, their default values are applied. The named query defined by the `named-native-query` subelement applies to the whole persistence unit. Multiple mapping files for the persistence unit cannot contain named queries of the same name.

The `named-native-query` subelement does not apply to mapped superclasses and embeddable classes.

sql-result-set-mapping

The `sql-result-set-mapping` defines a SQL result set mapping that is added to the set of SQL result set mappings defined in annotations, and other SQL result set mappings defined in XML. A SQL result set mapping defined by this subelement overrides any SQL result set mapping defined in annotations, if they have the same name.

If a `sql-result-set-mapping` subelement is present, but some of its attributes or subelements are not explicitly specified, their default values are applied. The SQL result set mapping defined by the `sql-result-set-mapping` subelement applies to the whole persistence unit. Multiple mapping files for the persistence unit cannot contain SQL result set mappings of the same name.

The `sql-result-set-mapping` subelement does not apply to mapped superclasses and embeddable classes.

exclude-default-listeners

The `exclude-default-listeners` subelement causes the default entity listeners to be excluded for the entity (or mapped superclass) and its subclasses, and applies whether or not the `@ExcludeDefaultListeners` annotation was specified on the entity (or mapped superclass).

The `exclude-default-listeners` subelement does not apply to embeddable classes.

exclude-superclass-listeners

The `exclude-superclass-listeners` subelement causes any superclass listeners to be excluded for the entity (or mapped superclass) and its subclasses, and applies whether or not the `@ExcludeSuperclassListeners` annotation was specified on the entity (or mapped superclass).

The `exclude-superclass-listeners` subelement does not apply to embeddable classes.

entity-listeners

The `entity-listeners` subelement defines entity listeners for the entity (or mapped superclass), which overrides any `@EntityListeners` annotation on the entity (or mapped superclass). Each `entity-listener` descriptor within this subelement defines an entity listener.

These listeners apply to the entity and its subclasses unless otherwise excluded.

The `entity-listeners` subelement does not apply to embeddable classes.

pre-persist, post-persist, pre-remove, post-remove, pre-update, post-update, post-load

These subelements define lifecycle callback methods and override such callback methods defined by the corresponding annotations on the entity (or mapped superclass).

These subelements do not apply to embeddable classes.

attributes

The `attributes` subelement contains mapping subelements for persistent fields and properties of the entity, mapped superclass, or embeddable. It may include only a subset of the persistent fields and properties. If the value of the `metadata-complete` attribute is `true`, the unspecified subelements will be defaulted according to the default rules. If `metadata-complete` is `false` or is not specified, only the mappings for the explicitly specified properties and fields will override those defined in annotations.

The `attributes` subelement may include the following mapping subelements.

- **id** The `id` subelement defines an ID field or property and overrides the annotation for the specified field or property. If an `id` subelement is present, but some of its attributes or subelements are not explicitly specified, their default values are applied. The `id` subelement does not apply to embeddable classes.

- **embedded-id** The `embedded-id` subelement defines an embedded ID field or property and overrides the annotation for the specified field or property. If an `embedded-id` subelement is present, but some of its attributes or subelements are not explicitly specified, their default values are applied. The `embedded-id` subelement does not apply to embeddable classes.

- **basic** The `basic` subelement defines basic mapping metadata for a field or property and overrides the annotation for the specified field or property. If a `basic` subelement is present, but some of its attributes or subelements are not explicitly specified, their default values are applied. The `basic` subelement applies to entities, mapped superclasses, and embeddable classes.

- **version** The `version` subelement defines the version field or property and overrides the annotation for the specified field or property. If a `version` subelement is present, but some of its attributes or subelements are not explicitly specified, their default values are applied. The `version` subelement does not apply to embeddable classes.

- **many-to-one** The `many-to-one` subelement defines a many-to-one association and overrides the annotation for the specified field or property. If a `many-to-one` subelement is present, but some of its attributes or subelements are not explicitly specified, their default values are applied. The `many-to-one` subelement applies to entities, mapped superclasses, and embeddable classes.

- **one-to-many** The `one-to-many` subelement defines a one-to-many association and overrides the annotation for the specified field or property. If a `one-to-many` subelement is present, but some of its attributes or subelements are not explicitly specified, their default values are applied. The `one-to-many` subelement applies to entities, mapped superclasses, and embeddable classes.

- **one-to-one** The `one-to-one` subelement defines a one-to-one association and overrides the annotation for the specified field or property. If a `one-to-one` subelement is present, but some of its attributes or subelements are not explicitly specified, their default values are applied. The `one-to-one` subelement applies to entities, mapped superclasses, and embeddable classes.

- **many-to-many** The `many-to-many` subelement defines a many-to-many association and overrides the annotation for the specified field or property. If a `many-to-many` subelement is present, but some of its attributes or subelements are not explicitly specified, their default values are applied. The `many-to-many` subelement applies to entities, mapped superclasses, and embeddable classes.

- **element-collection** The `element-collection` subelement defines an element collection and overrides the annotation for the specified field or property. If an `element-collection` subelement is present, but some of its attributes or subelements are not explicitly specified, their default values are applied. The `element-collection` subelement applies to entities, mapped superclasses, and embeddable classes.

- **embedded** The `embedded` subelement defines an embedded field or property and overrides the annotation for the specified field or property. If an `embedded` subelement is present, but some of its attributes or subelements are not explicitly specified, their default values are applied. The `embedded` subelement applies to entities, mapped superclasses, and embeddable classes.

- **transient** The `transient` subelement specifies a transient field or property and overrides the annotation for the specified field or property. The `transient` subelement applies to entities, mapped superclasses, and embeddable classes.

7 Metamodel and Criteria Queries

JPA 2.0 introduces criteria queries as an alternative way of constructing queries to JPQL. In contrast to string-based JPQL queries, criteria queries are constructed programmatically using an object-based approach. They are type safe in the sense that the compiler can verify for syntactic correctness and runtime errors can be reduced. The metamodel of a persistence unit refers to the persistence and mapping meta-information of managed classes in the persistence unit, which can be accessed programmatically. Metamodel information may be used in the construction of criteria queries.

The first section of this chapter shows two examples on how to construct criteria queries, utilizing entity metamodel information. The second section talks about the details of the metamodel API. Finally, the third section addresses the criteria API and shows how to construct complex criteria queries.

7.1 Introduction

JPQL provides a high-level and intuitive way of building queries on managed classes in a persistence unit. It is a well-loved feature of JPA. Just as nothing is perfect in this world, JPQL has some drawback too. The string-based nature of JPQL means that syntactic errors cannot be caught by the compiler, which become run-time errors.

For example, look at the following JPQL query and its execution:

```
Query query = em.createQuery("SELECT o FROM Order ");
List resultList = query.getResultList();
List<Order> orderList = (List<Order>) resultList;
```

These three lines of code will compile fine but cause a run-time error, since the identification variable *o* is not defined (it should be: `"SELECT o FROM Order o"`). However, a JPA provider cannot tell us this error at compile time and EclipseLink throws a run-time `MismatchedTokenException` in parsing the query string. The second line of the code above shows that a JPQL query returns an untyped list. We need to cast it to a list of the desired type (the third line).

The Criteria API provides a programmatical and object-based way of developing type-safe queries that a Java compiler can verify for syntactic correctness at compile time. Using this API, the JPQL query above can be equivalently written as:

```
import javax.persistence.TypedQuery;
import javax.persistence.criteria.CriteriaBuilder;
import javax.persistence.criteria.CriteriaQuery;
import javax.persistence.criteria.Root;
... ...

CriteriaBuilder cb  = em.getCriteriaBuilder();
CriteriaQuery<Order> cq = cb.createQuery(Order.class);
Root<Order> order = cq.from(Order.class);   // same as FROM clause
cq.select(order);                           // same as SELECT clause

TypedQuery<Order> typedQuery = em.createQuery(cq);
List<Order> resultList = typedQuery.getResultList();
```

Some explanations are in order. A `CriteriaBuilder` can be obtained from an entity manager or entity manager factory. A generic type `CriteriaQuery<Order>` is created by the `CriteriaBuilder`, passing the `Order` class as its argument, which means that this criteria query will return objects of type `Order`. The `from` method on the `CriteriaQuery` is equivalent to the FROM clause in JPQL. It forms the basis for the domain of the query, and returns a `Root<Order>` instance, which means that the query evaluates across all instances of the `Order` entity. The `select` method on the `CriteriaQuery` is equivalent to the SELECT clause in JPQL. These steps have achieved the same thing as the JPQL query: "`SELECT o FROM Order o`", but using a type-safe and object-based approach.

To execute such a criteria query, we pass it to the `createQuery` method of the entity manager to create an instance of `TypedQuery<Order>`. The `TypedQuery` has the same type parameter: `Order`, as specified for the `CriteriaQuery<Order>` during its construction by `CriteriaBuilder`. Finally, calling the `getResultList` method on the `TypedQuery<Order>` instance returns a typed list: `List<Order>`, without the need of a type cast.

In this process, a criteria query is constructed programmatically in an object-based and type-safe way. Every query expression is generically typed without type casting. Its main advantages are that it prohibits the construction of queries that are syntactically incorrect, and that it is generically typed. We now create another criteria query, which corresponds to the following JPQL query:

```
SELECT o FROM Order o WHERE o.price > 22
```

The code looks like this:

```
CriteriaBuilder cb = em.getCriteriaBuilder();
CriteriaQuery<Order> cq = cb.createQuery(Order.class);
Root<Order> order = cq.from(Order.class);

// the predicate for o.price > 22
Predicate condition = cb.gt(order.get(Order_.price), 22);
cq.where(condition);                          // same as WHERE clause

cq.select(order);
TypedQuery<Order> query = em.createQuery(cq);
List<Order> resultList = query.getResultList();
```

This criteria query calls its `where` method, corresponding to the `WHERE` clause in a JPQL query. The argument passed in is a predicate, which is a query expression evaluated to a boolean value. The `CriteriaBuilder` interface has many methods, one of which is the `gt` (short for greater than) method. It tests to see if its first argument is greater than its second argument. The first argument in this query expression

```
qb.gt(order.get(Order_.price), 22)
```

needs some attention. The class `Order_` is the metamodel class for entity `Order`, which can be generated by our JPA provider at development time. What it means is that the class `Order_` contains the meta-information for the `Order` entity class. Such meta-information includes the persistent attributes and their types of the `Order` entity class. In particular, the notation `Order_.price` denotes the `price` persistent attribute of entity `Order`, and `order.get(Order_.price)` denotes the value of the `price` attribute in the `order` query expression. The expression `order.get(Order_.price)` evaluates to a `Double` if the `price` attribute of entity `Order` has type `Double` or `double`.

The compiler would report an error if we write a type-mismatched expression such as:

```
qb.gt(order.get(Order_.price), "twenty two").
```

In contrast, the following JPQL query string:

```
SELECT o FROM Order o WHERE o.price > 'twenty two'
```

will compile happily, but cause a run-time error.

The `CriteriaBuilder` interface plays a critical role in constructing criteria queries. It is used to create not only criteria queries, but also query expressions (with the help of metamodel information). Details of the Metamodel API are discussed in the next section and those of the Criteria API are given in the section following it.

7.2 Metamodel API

In the previous section, we encountered the construct `Order_.price`. The class `Order_` is a metamodel class for the managed class `Order`, and `Order_.price` refers to the `price` attribute of `Order`. For the entity `Order`, defined in Listing 2-2, our JPA provider may generate the static metamodel class `Order_` as shown in Listing 7-1.

Listing 7-1 Order_.java: The static metamodel class for the managed class Order.java.

```
package jpatest.entity;

import java.sql.Timestamp;
import javax.annotation.Generated;
import javax.persistence.metamodel.ListAttribute;
import javax.persistence.metamodel.SingularAttribute;
import javax.persistence.metamodel.StaticMetamodel;
import jpatest.entity.Customer;
import jpatest.entity.LineItem;
import jpatest.entity.OrderStatus;

@Generated("EclipseLink - Tue Dec 15 09:55:30 EST 2009")
@StaticMetamodel(Order.class)
public class Order_ extends BaseEntity_ {
  public static volatile SingularAttribute<Order, Double> price;
  public static volatile SingularAttribute<Order, OrderStatus> status;
  public static volatile
    SingularAttribute<Order, Timestamp> orderTime;
  public static volatile SingularAttribute<Order, Customer> customer;
  public static volatile ListAttribute<Order, LineItem> lineItems;
  public static volatile SingularAttribute<Order, Integer> orderId;
}
```

This is called a *canonical metamodel* class, since it is generated according to the rules in the JPA 2.0 specification. In particular, all fields of this class are `static`, `public`, and `volatile`. The name of the class is obtained by appending "_" to the name of the original managed class, and this class must be annotated with `@StaticMetamodel`. Our JPA provider must be able to generate the source code for the metamodel classes, such as `Order_.java`, at development time, so that we can refer to the persistent attributes and relationships of `Order` at compile time, in a strongly typed manner. Typically, each JPA provider makes use of the Annotation Processor facility in Java SE 6.0. See Section 9.3.1 or 9.5.1 on how to generate static metamodel classes using the EclipseLink JPA implementation.

The metamodel field `Order_.price` has type `SingularAttribute<Order, Double>`. The first type parameter is `Order`: the type of the original managed class, and the second type parameter is: `Double`: the type or the primitive wrapper of the `price` attribute in the original managed class `Order`. For a collection attribute, the corresponding type would be one of the following types: `CollectionAttribute<Order, E>`, `SetAttribute<Order, E>`, `ListAttribute<Order, E>`, and `MapAttribute<Order, K, E>`, where `E` is the type of the elements in the collection, set, list, or is the type of the map value, and `K` is the type of the map key in entity `Order` (for a map attribute). In the case of the `lineItems` attribute in `Order_.java`, it has type: `ListAttribute<Order, LineItem>`, since the corresponding `lineItems` attribute in `Order.java` has type `List<LineItem>`.

See Figure 7-1 for the class diagram on standard JPA metamodel attribute interfaces, all of which have type parameters using Java generics.

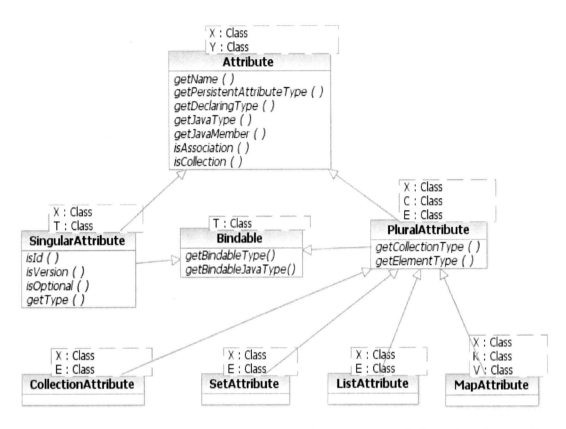

Figure 7-1 Class diagram for metamodel attribute types, including singular attributes and collection attributes. They are all packed in `javax.persistence.metamodel`. *The symbols: X, Y, etc, represent type parameters in Java generics.*

In Figure 7-2, we show standard JPA metamodel types for entities, mapped super classes, embeddable classes, and their related types. At run-time, these types and their attributes can be programmatically discovered and accessed, similar to the Java Reflection API for dynamically inspecting normal Java classes and interfaces for their meta-data information. The metamodel of a persistence unit can be accessed through an entity manager instance or the entity manager factory. See Listing 7-2 for sample code showing how to discover the meta persistence information (attributes and relationships) for the `Order` entity.

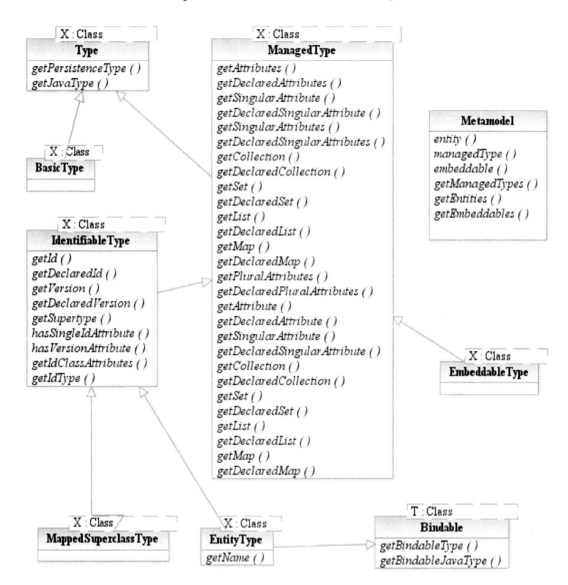

Figure 7-2 Class diagram on JPA metamodel types for entities, mapped superclasses, embeddables, and some related types.

Listing 7-2 Sample code for accessing metamodel information programmatically for entity Order.

```java
Metamodel mm = em.getMetamodel();
EntityType<Order> orderMM = mm.entity(Order.class);

// Get ID type for this entity: Integer
Type<?> idType = orderMM.getIdType();
System.out.println("id type = " + idType.getJavaType());

SingularAttribute<? super Order, Double> price
  = orderMM.getSingularAttribute("price", Double.class);

// Persistent attribute type for "price": BASIC
String priceAttributeName = price.getPersistentAttributeType().name();

// Declaring Java type: jpatest.entity.Order
Class c = price.getDeclaringType().getJavaType();

// Get the version attribute
SingularAttribute<? super Order, Integer> version
  = orderMM.getVersion(int.class);

// Get the plural attribute for "lineItems"
ListAttribute<? super Order, LineItem> lineItems
  = orderMM.getList("lineItems", LineItem.class);

// Get the set of all singular attributes for the Order entity
Set<SingularAttribute<? super Order, ?>> sa
  = orderMM.getSingularAttributes();
for (SingularAttribute<? super Order, ?> s : sa) {
  String attributeName = s.getName();  // eg: price, customer

  Boolean isId = s.isId();              // is this attribute an ID
  Boolean isVersion = s.isVersion();   // is this attribute Version

  // sample values: BASIC, ONE_TO_MANY, EMBEDDED, ELEMENT_COLLECTION
  PersistentAttributeType ap = s.getPersistentAttributeType();

}

// Get the set of all plural attributes (eg, Set, Map) for the Order
// entity
Set<PluralAttribute<? super Order, ?, ?>> pa
  = orderMM.getPluralAttributes();
```

274

```
for (PluralAttribute<? super Order, ?, ?> p : pa) {
  CollectionType ct = p.getCollectionType();
  Type<?> elemType = p.getElementType();
}

// Get the set of all attributes for the Order entity
Set<Attribute<? super Order, ?>> attributes = orderMM.getAttributes();
```

One potential use of the metamodel information is to discover an entity's persistence information at runtime and perform certain sanity checks inside a callback listener method, before an entity is persisted, updated, or deleted from a database. Another potential use is to define information of a persistence unit dynamically and programmatically. However, the JPA 2.0 metamodel API is still very limited in these aspects. For example, it does not provide OR mapping information of managed classes. The metamodel currently even does not tell us to which database table column an entity attribute is mapped. Such features may be added in a future release.

7.3 Criteria Queries

We devote this section to the Criteria API and show how to construct various parts of criteria queries.

7.3.1 Criteria Query Creation

A `CriteriaQuery` object is created by one of the following methods of the `CriteriaBuilder` interface:

```
CriteriaQuery<Object> createQuery();
<T> CriteriaQuery<T> createQuery(Class<T> resultClass);
CriteriaQuery<Tuple> createTupleQuery();
```

The first method above returns an instance of type `Object` or `Object[]`. The second method takes a class parameter for the query return type. The third is equivalent to the second one with the `Tuple.class` parameter passed in: `createQuery(Tuple.class)`, which is used when the SELECT clause of the query returns multiple expressions in a strongly typed manner.

We show the class diagram in Figure 7-3 for `AbstractQuery`, `CriteriaQuery`, and `Subquery` interfaces. It is worth noting that these interfaces are not derived from `Query` or `TypedQuery`. Instead, they are passed to the `createQuery` method of the entity manager to create a `Query` or `TypeQuery`, in a strongly typed manner. We have seen the `select`, `from`, and `where` methods on these interfaces, similar to the `SELECT`, `FROM`, and `WHERE` clauses of a JPQL query. In addition, the `orderBy`, `groupBy`, and `having` methods correspond to the `ORDER BY`, `GROUP BY`, and `HAVING` clauses of JPQL queries.

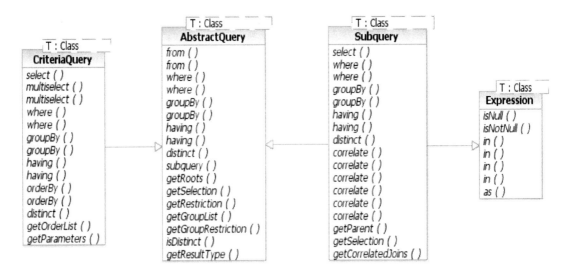

Figure 7-3 Class structure for `AbstractQuery, CriteriaQuery,` *and* `Subquery`.

7.3.2 Query Roots and Path Expressions

A `CriteriaQuery` object defines a query over one or more entity, embeddable, or basic types. The root objects of a criteria query are entities, from which other types are reached by path navigation. Query roots form the basis for defining the domain of the query. Path expressions are used to navigate from query roots and thus query roots are a special kind of path expressions. The class diagram for query roots and path expressions is shown in Figure 7-4.

A query root is created and added to the query by invoking the `from` method of the `AbstractQuery` interface (inherited by both `CriteriaQuery` and `Subquery`). The argument to the `from` method is the entity class or `EntityType` instance for the entity. The result of the `from` method is a `Root` object. A query may have more than one root and each call to the `from` method adds another root to the query. Adding a query root creates a Cartesian product between the entity type of the added root and those of the other roots.

For example, the following JPQL selects all distinct Address objects for which there is a valid Customer:

```
SELECT DISTINCT a FROM Address a, Customer c WHERE a = c.address
```

The equivalent criteria query will have two query roots and may be constructed as:

```
CriteriaBuilder cb = em.getCriteriaBuilder();
CriteriaQuery<Address> cq = cb.createQuery(Address.class);
Root<Address> a = cq.from(Address.class);
Root<Customer> c = cq.from(Customer.class);
cq.select(a).distinct(true);
cq.where(cb.equal(a, c.get(Customer_.address)));

TypedQuery<Address> q = em.createQuery(cq);
List<Address> resultList = q.getResultList();
```

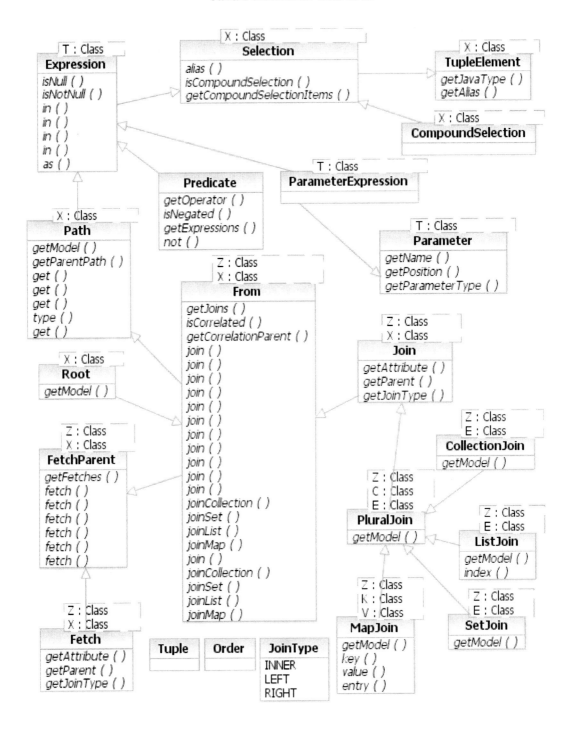

Figure 7-4 Class hierarchy for query expressions.

The `get` method of the `Path` interface is used for path navigation. The argument to the `get` method is an instance of `SingularAttribute`, or collection-valued attribute: `CollectionAttribute`, `SetAttribute`, `ListAttribute`, and `MapAttribute` of the corresponding metamodel class. For example, the following criteria query has a chained path expression (we always show its equivalent JPQL query first for comparison and easy understanding):

```
SELECT c.name FROM Customer c JOIN c.orders o
WHERE c.bank.bankName LIKE '%Bank%'

CriteriaBuilder cb = em.getCriteriaBuilder();
CriteriaQuery<String> cq = cb.createQuery(String.class);
Root<Customer> cust = cq.from(Customer.class);
Join<Customer, Order> item = cust.join(Customer_.orders);
Path<String> path = cust.get(Customer_.bank).get(BankInfo_.bankName);
cq.where(cb.like(path, "%Bank%"));
cq.select(cust.get(Customer_.name));

TypedQuery<String> q = em.createQuery(cq);
List<String> resultList = q.getResultList();
```

The criteria query above has a few path expressions. Similar to a `Query` instance, a `Path` instance may be chained as in:

```
cust.get(Customer_.bank).get(BankInfo_.bankName).
```

Below is an example with a local path variable *price* defined and used in the select and where clauses:

```
SELECT AVG(i.price) FROM LineItem i
WHERE i.price > 2.0 AND i.price < 200.0

CriteriaBuilder cb = em.getCriteriaBuilder();
CriteriaQuery<Double> cq = cb.createQuery(Double.class);
Root<LineItem> i = cq.from(LineItem.class);
Path<Double> price = i.get(LineItem_.price);
cq.select(cb.avg(price));
cq.where(cb.and(cb.gt(price, 2.0), cb.lt(price, 200.0)));

TypedQuery<Double> q = em.createQuery(cq);
```

```
Double result = q.getSingleResult();
```

The following is an example with a path expression derived from a map-valued association or element collection that returns a `MapJoin` object (this query also uses a `multiselect` method to select more than one item):

```
SELECT c.name, o.price
FROM Customer c JOIN c.orders o
WHERE KEY(o) > 2

CriteriaBuilder cb = em.getCriteriaBuilder();
CriteriaQuery<Tuple> cq = cb.createQuery(Tuple.class);
Root<Customer> c = cq.from(Customer.class);
MapJoin<Customer, Integer, Order> o = c.join(Customer_.orders);
cq.where(cb.gt(o.key(), 2));
cq.multiselect(c.get(Customer_.name), o.get(Order_.price));

TypedQuery<Tuple> q = em.createQuery(cq);
List<Tuple> resultList = q.getResultList();
for (Tuple tuple : resultList) {
  String custName = tuple.get(0, String.class);
  Double price = tuple.get(1, Double.class);
}
```

When evaluating a path expression, if the value of a non-terminal `Path` instance is null, the path is considered to have no value and it will not be used to determine the query result. This is exactly the same as in JPQL.

7.3.3 FROM Clause

The `from` method of the `AbstractQuery` interface is used to create the equivalent of the FROM clause of a JPQL query. In this subsection, we show how the inner, outer, and fetch joins contribute to the creation of the FROM clause.

The `join` and related methods (including `joinMap`, `joinList`) of the `From` interface extend the query domain by creating a join with a related class. The result of a `join` method is a `Join` object. Each invocation of a `join` method creates a new `Join` instance. The `join` methods are used to form inner and outer joins and can be applied on instances of `Root` and `Join` types. The argument to the `join` methods is an instance of `SingularAttribute`, or one of collection-valued `PluralAttribute` instances of the corresponding metamodel class. By default, a `join` method defines an inner join. Outer joins are defined by specifying a `JoinType` argument.

Chapter 7   Metamodel and Criteria Queries

Below is an example that creates an inner join between three entities:

```
SELECT o FROM Order o JOIN o.lineItems i JOIN i.book b
```

```
CriteriaBuilder cb = em.getCriteriaBuilder();
CriteriaQuery<Order> cq = cb.createQuery(Order.class);
Root<Order> order = cq.from(Order.class);
Join<Order, LineItem> item = order.join(Order_.lineItems);
Join<LineItem, Book> book = item.join(LineItem_.book);
cq.select(order);
```

To create a left outer join, the argument `JoinType.LEFT` may be used:

```
SELECT o FROM Order o LEFT OUTER JOIN o.lineItems i
WHERE i.price > 5
```

```
CriteriaBuilder cb = em.getCriteriaBuilder();
CriteriaQuery<Order> cq = cb.createQuery(Order.class);
Root<Order> o = cq.from(Order.class);
Join<Order, LineItem> i = o.join(Order_.lineItems, JoinType.LEFT);
cq.select(o);
```

```
Predicate condition = cb.gt(i.get(LineItem_.price), 5);
cq.where(condition);
```

A join that involves a Map-valued association is given in the previous subsection.

A fetch join may be constructed by using one of the `fetch` methods in the FetchParent interface (inherited by Root, Join, and Fetch interfaces). A `fetch` method can be applied on a Root, Join or Fetch instance and it returns a Fetch object. Fetch objects are not Path expressions and cannot be referenced elsewhere in the query. In particular, a `fetch` method cannot be used in a subquery. The following is an example of an outer fetch join with an input parameter:

```
SELECT o FROM Order o LEFT JOIN FETCH o.lineItems
WHERE o.orderTime < :today
```

```
CriteriaBuilder cb = em.getCriteriaBuilder();
CriteriaQuery<Order> cq = cb.createQuery(Order.class);
Root<Order> order = cq.from(Order.class);
order.fetch(Order_.lineItems, JoinType.LEFT);
cq.select(order);
```

281

```
ParameterExpression<Timestamp> today = cb.parameter(Timestamp.class);
Predicate condition = cb.lessThan(order.get(Order_.orderTime), today);
cq.where(condition);

TypedQuery<Order> q = em.createQuery(cq);
q.setParameter(today, new Timestamp(new Date().getTime()));
```

7.3.4 SELECT Clause

The select and multiselect methods of the CriteriaQuery interface are used to create the equivalent of the SELECT clause of a JPQL query. These two methods have the following signatures:

```
CriteriaQuery<T> select(Selection<? extends T> selection);
CriteriaQuery<T> multiselect(Selection<?>... selections);
CriteriaQuery<T> multiselect(List<Selection<?>> selectionList);
```

The difference is that the select method takes only one Selection object, while the multiselect methods may take multiple such objects. Both methods may be used interchangeably in most cases. However, when the select method is applied for multiple selection items, the tuple, array, and construct methods of the CriteriaBuilder interface are used to aggregate multiple selection items into a CompoundSelection instance. These methods have the following signatures:

```
CompoundSelection<Tuple> tuple(Selection<?>... selections);
CompoundSelection<Object[]> array(Selection<?>... selections);
<Y> CompoundSelection<Y> construct(Class<Y> resultClass,
                                   Selection<?>... selections);
```

For example, consider this JPQL query:

```
SELECT c.name, o.price
FROM Customer c JOIN c.orders o
WHERE o.orderTime < CURRENT_TIMESTAMP
```

It can be translated into a criteria query using a multiselect method:

```
CriteriaQuery<Tuple> cq = cb.createQuery(Tuple.class);

Root<Customer> c = cq.from(Customer.class);
MapJoin<Customer, Integer, Order> o = c.join(Customer_.orders);
cq.multiselect(c.get(Customer_.name), o.get(Order_.price));
```

```
cq.where(cb.lessThan(o.get(Order_.orderTime), cb.currentTimestamp()));
```

Equivalently, using the `tuple` and `select` methods can achieve the same thing:

```
CriteriaQuery<Tuple> cq = cb.createQuery(Tuple.class);
Root<Customer> c = cq.from(Customer.class);
MapJoin<Customer, Integer, Order> o = c.join(Customer_.orders);
cq.select(cb.tuple(c.get(Customer_.name), o.get(Order_.price)));
cq.where(cb.lessThan(o.get(Order_.orderTime), cb.currentTimestamp()));
```

It is worth noting that the method `lt` on the `CriteriaBuilder` interface is for comparing numeric values and `lessThan` for other values. The `Tuple` interface is used to denote a row of data, whose elements are a list of `TupleElement` instances.

If you prefer to use `Object[]` as the return type with a `multiselect` method, the query above may be written as:

```
CriteriaQuery<Object[]> cq = cb.createQuery(Object[].class);

Root<Customer> c = cq.from(Customer.class);
MapJoin<Customer, Integer, Order> o = c.join(Customer_.orders);
cq.multiselect(c.get(Customer_.name), o.get(Order_.price));
cq.where(cb.lessThan(o.get(Order_.orderTime), cb.currentTimestamp()));
```

This may be equivalently re-written using `select` together with the `array` method as:

```
CriteriaQuery<Object[]> cq = cb.createQuery(Object[].class);

Root<Customer> c = cq.from(Customer.class);
MapJoin<Customer, Integer, Order> o = c.join(Customer_.orders);
cq.select(cb.array(c.get(Customer_.name), o.get(Order_.price)));
cq.where(cb.lessThan(o.get(Order_.orderTime), cb.currentTimestamp()));
```

The `select` and `multiselect` methods of the `CriteriaQuery` interface can also be used to handle the so-called constructor expressions. For example, consider this JPQL query:

```
SELECT NEW jpatest.entity.OrderDetail(o.customer.name, o.price)
FROM Order o WHERE o.orderTime < CURRENT_TIMESTAMP
```

It can be translated into a criteria query using a `multiselect` method:

```
CriteriaQuery<OrderDetail> cq = cb.createQuery(OrderDetail.class);
Root<Order> o = cq.from(Order.class);
cq.multiselect(o.get(Order_.customer).get(Customer_.name),
  o.get(Order_.price));
cq.where(cb.lessThan(o.get(Order_.orderTime), cb.currentTimestamp()));
```

Equivalently, using the `construct` and `select` methods can achieve the same thing:

```
CriteriaQuery<OrderDetail> cq = cb.createQuery(OrderDetail.class);
Root<Order> o = cq.from(Order.class);
cq.select(cb.construct(OrderDetail.class,
  o.get(Order_.customer).get(Customer_.name), o.get(Order_.price)));
cq.where(cb.lessThan(o.get(Order_.orderTime), cb.currentTimestamp()));
```

Recall that aliases may be assigned to selection items in SQL or JPQL queries such as this one:

```
SELECT o.price AS price, i.quantity AS q
FROM Order o JOIN o.lineItems i
WHERE SIZE(o.lineItems) < 5
```

We can do the same in criteria queries by setting aliases from invoking the `alias` method on the `Selection` interface. The aliases may be extracted later from the query result using the `Tuple` interface. Invoking the `alias` method results in a new `Selection` object with the given alias. Below is the criteria query equivalent to the JPQL query above:

```
CriteriaQuery<Tuple> cq = cb.createQuery(Tuple.class);
Root<Order> o = cq.from(Order.class);
Join<Order, LineItem> i = o.join(Order_.lineItems);
cq.multiselect(o.get(Order_.price).alias("price"),
               i.get(LineItem_.quantity).alias("q"));
cq.where(cb.lessThan(cb.size(o.get(Order_.lineItems)), 5));

TypedQuery<Tuple> query = em.createQuery(cq);
List<Tuple> resultList = query.getResultList();
for (Tuple result : resultList) {
  Double price = result.get("price", Double.class);
  Integer quantity = result.get("q", Integer.class);
}
```

7.3.5 WHERE Clause

The `where` method of the `CriteriaQuery` and `Subquery` interfaces is used to restrict the result of a query. Each invocation of the `where` method results in a new `WHERE` clause for the generated SQL statement, discarding the previous values. The argument to the `where` method can be either zero or more `Predicate` instances or an `Expression<Boolean>` instance.

A predicate can be simple or compound. A simple predicate is created by invoking either one of the `isNull`, `isNotNull`, and `in` methods of the `Expression` interface, or one of the conditional methods of the `CriteriaBuilder` interface. A compound predicate is constructed by one of the methods: `and`, `or`, `not`, on the `CriteriaBuilder` interface. Passing multiple arguments to `where` is equivalent to applying the `and` method to the arguments first. See Table 7-1 for all conditional methods on the `CriteriaBuilder` interface and their corresponding JPQL equivalents.

Table 7-1 Conditional methods on the `CriteriaBuilder` interface and their corresponding JPQL operators. These conditional methods return a `Predicate` object.

CriteriaBuilder method	JPQL Operator	CriteriaBuilder method	JPQL Operator
and()	AND	isEmpty()	IS EMPTY
or()	OR	isNotEmpty()	IS NOT EMPTY
not()	NOT	isMember()	MEMBER OF
equal()	=	isNotMember()	NOT MEMBER OF
notEqual()	<>	exists()	EXISTS
lt(), lessThan()	<	not(exists())	NOT EXISTS
le(), lessThanOrEqualTo()	<=	like()	LIKE
gt(), greaterThan()	>	notLike()	NOT LIKE
ge(), greaterThanOrEqualTo()	>=	in()	IN
isNull()	IS NULL	not(in())	NOT IN
isNotNull()	IS NOT NULL	isTrue()	IS TRUE
between()	BETWEEN	isFalse()	IS FALSE

As an example, the following criteria query has the `isNotEmpty` predicate method:

```
SELECT o FROM Order o WHERE o.lineItems IS NOT EMPTY

CriteriaQuery<Order> cq = cb.createQuery(Order.class);
Root<Order> o = cq.from(Order.class);
cq.select(o);
cq.where(cb.isNotEmpty(o.get(Order_.lineItems)));
```

This criteria query below has a compound predicate passed to the `where` method:

```
SELECT i FROM Order o JOIN o.lineItems i
WHERE o.price > 2 AND INDEX(i) BETWEEN 0 AND 10

CriteriaQuery<LineItem> cq = cb.createQuery(LineItem.class);
Root<Order> o = cq.from(Order.class);
ListJoin<Order, LineItem> i = o.join(Order_.lineItems);
cq.select(i);
cq.where(cb.and(cb.gt(o.get(Order_.price), 2),
                cb.between(i.index(), 0, 10)));
```

Note that the `conjunction` method on the `CriteriaBuilder` interface may be used to incrementally build the compound predicate above:

```
CriteriaQuery<LineItem> cq = cb.createQuery(LineItem.class);
Root<Order> o = cq.from(Order.class);
ListJoin<Order, LineItem> i = o.join(Order_.lineItems);
cq.select(i);

Predicate condition = cb.conjunction();
condition = cb.and(condition, cb.gt(o.get(Order_.price), 2));
condition = cb.and(condition, cb.between(i.index(), 0, 1000));
cq.where(condition);
```

A similar method is `disjunction`. A conjunction with zero conjuncts is true, while a disjunction with zero disjuncts is false. These two methods are useful when building certain conditions incrementally based on, for example, a user's input from the browser.

Literal Expressions
The `CriteriaBuilder` interface has a `literal` method to create literal expressions, which may be used in certain cases where instances of the `Expression` interface are expected. The method `nullLiteral` creates a `NULL` literal expression. For example, the

method call `literal("Tony")` creates a literal expression which can be passed to the `isMember` method as in the following example:

```
SELECT c FROM Customer c WHERE 'Tony' MEMBER OF c.nickNames

CriteriaQuery<Customer> cq = cb.createQuery(Customer.class);
Root<Customer> c = cq.from(Customer.class);
cq.select(c);
cq.where(cb.isMember(cb.literal("Tony"), c.get(Customer_.nickNames)));
```

Input Parameters

Criteria queries support input parameters with the `ParameterExpression` interface. A parameter expression is created using one of the `parameter` methods on `CriteriaBuilder`. If a name is supplied when a `ParameterExpression` is created, the parameter may also be treated as a named parameter. Positional parameters are not supported by the Criteria API. One example is given in Section 7.3.3. Below is another example, but with two named parameters:

```
SELECT AVG(o.price) FROM Order o
WHERE o.status = :s OR o.status = :t

CriteriaQuery<Double> cq = cb.createQuery(Double.class);
Root<Order> order = cq.from(Order.class);
cq.select(cb.avg(order.get(Order_.price)));
ParameterExpression<OrderStatus> s1
  = cb.parameter(OrderStatus.class, "s");
ParameterExpression<OrderStatus> s2
  = cb.parameter(OrderStatus.class, "t");
Path<OrderStatus> status = order.get(Order_.status);
cq.where(cb.or(cb.equal(status, s1), cb.equal(status, s2)));

TypedQuery<Double> q = em.createQuery(cq);
q.setParameter("s", OrderStatus.BILLED);
q.setParameter("t", OrderStatus.NEW);
```

7.3.6 Expressions

An `Expression` or one of its subtypes can be used when creating the `SELECT` clause of a query or its `WHERE` or `HAVING` clauses. Instances of `Path`, `Predicate` and `ParameterExpression` are special expressions. See the class diagram in Figure 7-4.

Other expressions may be created by the `CriteriaBuilder` interface, which has methods corresponding to the built-in arithmetic, string, datetime, and case operators and

287

functions of JPQL. Table 7-2 gives these methods and their JPQL equivalents. Note that conditional methods are given in Table 7-1, the `index` method is defined on the `ListJoin` interface, and the `value`, `key`, `entry` methods are defined on `MapJoin`.

Table 7-2 Methods on the `CriteriaBuilder` interface and their corresponding JPQL equivalents. These methods include arithmetic, scalar and aggregate functions, and functions on string and datetime.

CriteriaBuilder method	JPQL Operator	CriteriaBuilder method	JPQL Operator
sum()	+	countDistinct()	COUNT DISTINCT
neg(), diff()	–	abs()	ABS
prod()	*	sqrt()	SQRT
quot()	/	mod()	MOD
all()	ALL	size()	SIZE
any()	ANY	length()	LENGTH
some()	SOME	locate()	LOCATE
nullif()	NULLIF	concat()	CONCAT
coalesce()	COALESCE	upper()	UPPER
selectCase()	CASE	lower()	LOWER
max(), greatest()	MAX	substring()	SUBSTRING
min(), least()	MIN	trim()	TRIM
avg()	AVG	currentDate()	CURRENT_DATE
sum(), sumAsLong(), sumAsDouble()	SUM	currentTime()	CURRENT_TIME
count()	COUNT	currentTimestamp()	CURRENT_TIMESTAMP

For example, the following query uses the `prod` and `sqrt` methods on the `CriteriaBuilder` interface:

```
SELECT VALUE(o).price*2.2, SQRT(i.quantity)
FROM Customer c JOIN c.orders o JOIN o.lineItems i
WHERE TYPE(c) <> GoldCustomer OR i.quantity < 22

CriteriaQuery<Tuple> cq = cb.createQuery(Tuple.class);
Root<Customer> c = cq.from(Customer.class);
MapJoin<Customer, Integer, Order> o = c.join(Customer_.orders);
Join<Order, LineItem> i = o.join(Order_.lineItems);
cq.multiselect(cb.prod(o.value().get(Order_.price), 2.2),
```

```
   cb.sqrt(i.get(LineItem_.quantity))));
cq.where(cb.or(cb.notEqual(c.type(), GoldCustomer.class),
   cb.lt(i.get(LineItem_.quantity), 22)));
```

In and Case Expressions

This query below uses the `type` method on `Path` and the `in` method on `CriteriaBuilder` to create expressions:

```
SELECT c FROM Customer c
WHERE TYPE(c) IN (Customer, GoldCustomer)

CriteriaQuery<Customer> cq = cb.createQuery(Customer.class);
Root<Customer> c = cq.from(Customer.class);
cq.select(c);
cq.where(cb.in(c.type()).value(Customer.class)
                        .value(GoldCustomer.class));
```

Notice that the `in` method returns an object of type `CriteriaBuilder.In`, and the `value` method can be used to add as many values as needed. Similar constructs are `CriteriaBuilder.Coalesce`   `CriteriaBuilder.Case`,   and `CriteriaBuilder.SimpleCase`. The query below uses the `selectCase` method that returns an object of type `CriteriaBuilder.Case`:

```
SELECT o.customer.name, i.book,
   CASE WHEN i.quantity > 10 THEN 'Large Order'
        WHEN i.quantity > 5  THEN 'Medium Order'
        ELSE 'Small or No Order'
   END
FROM Order o JOIN o.lineItems i

CriteriaQuery<Tuple> cq = cb.createQuery(Tuple.class);
Root<Order> o = cq.from(Order.class);
Join<Order, LineItem> i = o.join(Order_.lineItems);
cq.multiselect(o.get(Order_.customer).get(Customer_.name),
   i.get(LineItem_.book),
cb.selectCase()
   .when(cb.gt(i.get(LineItem_.quantity), 10), "Large Order")
   .when(cb.gt(i.get(LineItem_.quantity), 5), "Midium Order")
   .otherwise("Small or No Order"));
```

Result Types of Expressions

The `getJavaType` method, as defined in `TupleElement` and inherited by `Expression`, gives the runtime result type of the object on which it is invoked.

289

For the two-argument methods: `sum`, `prod`, `diff`, `quot`, `coalesce`, and `nullif`, and the `In`, `Case`, `SimpleCase`, `Coalesce` builder methods, the runtime result type will differ from the `Expression` type when the latter is `Number`. The following rules specify the results of numeric expressions involving these methods, which are consistent with JPQL.

- If there is an operand of type `Double`, the result of the operation is of type `Double`;
- Otherwise, if there is an operand of type `Float`, the result of the operation is of type `Float`;
- Otherwise, if there is an operand of type `BigDecimal`, the result of the operation is of type `BigDecimal`;
- Otherwise, if there is an operand of type `BigInteger`, the result of the operation is of type `BigInteger`, unless the method is `quot`;
- Otherwise, if there is an operand of type `Long`, the result of the operation is of type `Long`, unless the method is `quot`;
- Otherwise, if there is an operand of integral type, the result of the operation is of type `Integer`, unless the method is `quot`;

Below is an example that mixes `Double` and `Integer` expressions using the `sum` method:

```
CriteriaBuilder cb = em.getCriteriaBuilder();
Expression<Double> a = cb.literal(2.9);
Expression<Integer> b = cb.literal(5);
Expression<?> c = cb.sum(a, b);
Class type = c.getJavaType();   // it returns class: java.lang.Double
```

Function Expressions

The criteria API has an advanced feature that is not supported by JPQL due to the fixed grammar of JPQL. It is to create expressions for the execution of native database functions. The `function` method on `CriteriaBuilder` has the following signature:

```
<T> Expression<T> function(String fName, Class<T> type,
                           Expression<?>... args);
```

The first argument is the name of a database function, the second is the expected result type, and the rest are parameters to the database function. It returns the `Expression` created, which may be used in criteria queries.

For example, the Derby `CEILING` database function returns the ceiling of a number as a double precision value and it can be executed as:

```
CriteriaQuery<Object[]> cq = cb.createQuery(Object[].class);
Root<Order> o = cq.from(Order.class);
Join<Order, LineItem> i = o.join(Order_.lineItems);

Expression<Double> priceCeiling
  = cb.function("CEILING", Double.class, o.get(Order_.price));
cq.multiselect(priceCeiling,
  o.get(Order_.customer).get(Customer_.name),
  i.get(LineItem_.quantity));
```

There is no equivalent JPQL query to this criteria query, which generates a SQL statement at run-time like this:

```
SELECT CEILING(t0.PRICE), t1.NAME, t2.QUANTITY
FROM ORDERS t0, LINE_ITEM t2, CUSTOMER t1
WHERE ((t1.CUSTOMER_ID_PK = t0.CUSTOMER_ID_FK)
  AND (t2.ORDER_ID_FK = t0.ORDER_ID_PK))
```

However, it should be noted that the code developed this way may not be portable across databases, since a stored function in one database may not be supported by another database. Nevertheless, this is a nice way to integrate criteria queries with database stored functions. Without it, we would have to resort to native SQL queries.

7.3.7 Subqueries

The `AbstractQuery` interface, inherited by `CriteriaQuery`, provides the `subquery` method for creating instances of `Subquery`. A `Subquery` is an `AbstractQuery` and an `Expression`. See the class diagram in Figure 7-3. A `Subquery` instance may be passed as an argument to the `all`, `any`, or `some` methods of the `CriteriaBuilder` interface for use in conditional expressions, or to the `exists` method to create predicates. A subquery is called correlated if it references query objects of its parent query, such as a `Root`, `Path`, or `Join` of the parent query, and is called non-correlated otherwise.

For example, the following subquery is non-correlated since it does not reference query objects of its parent query:

```
SELECT richCustomer FROM Customer richCustomer
WHERE richCustomer.income*0.7 >
      (SELECT AVG(c.income) FROM Customer c)

CriteriaQuery<Customer> cq = cb.createQuery(Customer.class);
Root<Customer> richCustomer = cq.from(Customer.class);

// create subquery. The type parameter is the query result type
Subquery<Double> sq = cq.subquery(Double.class);
Root<Customer> c = sq.from(Customer.class);

cq.where(cb.gt(cb.prod(richCustomer.get(Customer_.income), 0.7),
  sq.select(cb.avg(c.get(Customer_.income)))));
cq.select(richCustomer);
```

Let us now explore correlated subqueries. Below is one and its equivalent JPQL for comparison. Notice that the subquery references a path expression from the parent query.

```
SELECT DISTINCT c FROM Category c
WHERE NOT EXISTS (
  SELECT parentCategory FROM Category parentCategory
  WHERE parentCategory = c.parentCategory )

CriteriaQuery<Category> cq = cb.createQuery(Category.class);
Root<Category> c = cq.from(Category.class);

// create subquery. The type parameter is the query result type
Subquery<Category> sq = cq.subquery(Category.class);
Root<Category> parentCategory = sq.from(Category.class);
sq.select(parentCategory);
sq.where(cb.equal(parentCategory, c.get(Category_.parentCategory)));

cq.select(c).distinct(true);
cq.where(cb.not(cb.exists(sq)));
```

When we need to base a subquery on a `Root` or `Join` object of the parent query, one of the `correlate` methods from the `Subquery` interface may be used. For example, the following subquery creates a `Root` object correlated to a `Root` object of the parent query:

```
SELECT c FROM Customer c
```

```
WHERE (
  SELECT COUNT(o) FROM c.orders o WHERE SIZE(o.lineItems) >= 2
  ) > :count

CriteriaQuery<Customer> cq = cb.createQuery(Customer.class);
Root<Customer> c = cq.from(Customer.class);

Subquery<Long> sq = cq.subquery(Long.class);
Root<Customer> customerSub = sq.correlate(c);
Join<Customer, Order> o = customerSub.join(Customer_.orders);
sq.where(cb.ge(cb.size(o.get(Order_.lineItems)), 2));

cq.select(c);
cq.where(cb.gt(sq.select(cb.count(o)),
               cb.parameter(Integer.class, "cnt")));

TypedQuery<Customer> q = em.createQuery(cq);
q.setParameter("cnt", 3);
List<Customer> resultList = q.getResultList();
```

The `correlate` methods have the following signatures. They are used to create a subquery `Root` or `Join` object correlated to a `Root` or `Join` object of the parent query.

```
<Y> Root<Y> correlate(Root<Y> parentRoot);
<X, Y> Join<X, Y> correlate(Join<X, Y> parentJoin);
<X, Y> CollectionJoin<X, Y> correlate(
     CollectionJoin<X, Y> parentColtn);
<X, Y> SetJoin<X, Y> correlate(SetJoin<X, Y> parentSet);
<X, Y> ListJoin<X, Y> correlate(ListJoin<X, Y> parentList);
<X, K, V> MapJoin<X, K, V> correlate(MapJoin<X, K, V> parentMap);
```

Finally, we show another subquery that uses the `correlate` method on a `Join` object:

```
SELECT c FROM Customer c JOIN c.orders o
WHERE :qt <=  ALL (
  SELECT i.quantity FROM o.lineItems i WHERE i.price > 5)

CriteriaQuery<Customer> cq = cb.createQuery(Customer.class);
Root<Customer> c = cq.from(Customer.class);
MapJoin<Customer, Integer, Order> o = c.join(Customer_.orders);

Subquery<Integer> sq = cq.subquery(Integer.class);
MapJoin<Customer, Integer, Order> orderSub = sq.correlate(o);
Join<Order, LineItem> i = orderSub.join(Order_.lineItems);
sq.where(cb.gt(i.get(LineItem_.price), 5));
```

```
cq.select(c);
cq.where(cb.ge(cb.all(sq.select(i.get(LineItem_.quantity))),
              cb.parameter(Integer.class, "qt"))));
```

7.3.8 GROUP BY and HAVING

The `groupBy` methods of the `CriteriaQuery` and `Subquery` interfaces are used to group the results of a query, while the `having` methods may be used to filter over the groups. The arguments to the `groupBy` methods are `Expression` objects, and the argument to the `having` methods is either `Expression<Boolean>` or `Predicate` objects.

When a `groupBy` method is used, each selection item must correspond to a path expression that is used for the grouping, or it must be the result of an aggregate method. This is the same rule as in the `GROUP BY` and `HAVING` clauses of JPQL queries.

Below is an example with a `groupBy` method and a `having` method, and its equivalent JPQL query, with two input parameters:

```
SELECT o.status, COUNT(c), AVG(o.price)
FROM Customer c JOIN c.orders o
WHERE o.price > 10
GROUP BY o.status
HAVING o.status IN (:s, :s2)

CriteriaQuery<Object[]> cq = cb.createQuery(Object[].class);
Root<Customer> c = cq.from(Customer.class);
Join<Customer, Order> o = c.join(Customer_.orders);
cq.multiselect(o.get(Order_.status), cb.count(c),
cb.avg(o.get(Order_.price)));
cq.where(cb.gt(o.get(Order_.price), 10));
cq.groupBy(o.get(Order_.status));
ParameterExpression<OrderStatus> os = cb.parameter(OrderStatus.class);
ParameterExpression<OrderStatus> os2
  = cb.parameter(OrderStatus.class);
cq.having(cb.in(o.get(Order_.status)).value(os).value(os2));

TypedQuery<Object[]> q = em.createQuery(cq);
q.setParameter(os, OrderStatus.BILLED);
q.setParameter(os2, OrderStatus.NEW);
```

7.3.9 ORDER BY Clause

The ordering of query results is defined by the `orderBy` method of the `CriteriaQuery` interface. The arguments to the method are instances of `javax.persistence.criteria.Order`. An `Order` instance is created by the `asc` or `desc` method of the `CriteriaBuilder` interface, for ascending or descending ordering respectively. If more than one `Order` instance is specified, the first item in the argument list has highest precedence. Null values, if existed in the result, appear together either before or after all non-null values, the same as in JPQL.

Below is a criteria query with an `orderBy` method, and its equivalent JPQL query:

```
SELECT o.price, i.price*2 AS itemPrice
FROM Customer c JOIN c.orders o JOIN o.lineItems i
WHERE c.name LIKE 'John%' AND o.price > 10
ORDER BY o.price, itemPrice DESC

CriteriaQuery<Object[]> cq = cb.createQuery(Object[].class);
Root<Customer> c = cq.from(Customer.class);
Join<Customer, Order> o = c.join(Customer_.orders);
Join<Order, LineItem> i = o.join(Order_.lineItems);

Expression<Double> orderExpr = o.get(Order_.price);
Expression<Double> itemExpr = i.get(LineItem_.price);
cq.multiselect(orderExpr, cb.prod(itemExpr, 2));
cq.where(cb.like(c.get(Customer_.name), "John%"),
        cb.gt(orderExpr,10));
cq.orderBy(cb.asc(orderExpr), cb.desc(cb.prod(itemExpr, 2)));
```

7.3.10   Criteria Queries Using Metamodel

In this subsection, we present another way of constructing strongly-typed criteria queries, using the `javax.persistence.metamodel` interfaces to access the metamodel objects of managed classes, instead of using generated static metamodel classes as in previous subsections.

The interfaces in package `javax.persistence.metamodel` are covered in Section 7.2. The `Metamodel` object of a persistence unit is obtained from an entity manger or the entity manager factory of the persistence unit. Then it can be used to access the metamodel objects for the managed classes referenced by a criteria query.

Below is an example to show how this is done. Its equivalent JPQL query is given in Section 7.3.8.

```
Metamodel mm = em.getMetamodel();
EntityType<Customer> customer_ = mm.entity(Customer.class);
EntityType<Order> order_ = mm.entity(Order.class);
CriteriaBuilder cb = em.getCriteriaBuilder();
CriteriaQuery<Object[]> cq = cb.createQuery(Object[].class);
Root<Customer> c = cq.from(Customer.class);
MapJoin<Customer, Integer, Order> o
  = c.join(customer_.getMap("orders", Integer.class, Order.class));

Expression<OrderStatus> status
  = o.get(order_.getSingularAttribute("status", OrderStatus.class));
Expression<Double> price
  = o.get(order_.getSingularAttribute("price", Double.class));

cq.multiselect(status, cb.count(c), cb.avg(price));
cq.where(cb.gt(price, 10));
cq.groupBy(status);
cq.having(cb.in(status).value(OrderStatus.BILLED)
                        .value(OrderStatus.NEW));
```

7.3.11   Weakly Typed Criteria Queries

This subsection presents a third way of constructing criteria queries by specifying attribute references in joins and expressions using attribute string names. We still use the various `join`, `fetch`, and `get` methods of the Criteria API, but it does not provide the same level of type safety as the other two.

For example, let o be an instance of `Join<Customer, Order>`. Both `o.get("price")` and `o.<Double> get("price")` return the expression of navigating to the `price` attribute using the string name `"price"`. Since the exact return type of the first expression `o.get("price")` cannot be known by the compiler, the second expression `o.<Double> get("price")` explicitly specifies the return type in angle brackets -- the so-called parameterized method invocation in Java generics.

Below is an example to show the details. Its equivalent JPQL query is given in Section 7.3.8.

```
CriteriaQuery<Object[]> cq = cb.createQuery(Object[].class);
Root<Customer> c = cq.from(Customer.class);
```

```
Join<Customer, Order> o = c.join("orders");

cq.multiselect(o.get("status"), cb.count(c),
                cb.avg(o.<Double> get("price")));
cq.where(cb.gt(o.<Double> get("price"), 10));
cq.groupBy(o.get("status"));
cq.having(cb.in(o.get("status")).value(OrderStatus.BILLED)
                                .value(OrderStatus.NEW));
```

7.3.12   Query Modification

A `CriteriaQuery` instance may be modified, either before or after `TypedQuery` objects have been created and executed. The selection items in the SELECT clause, predicates in the WHERE clause, and ordering items in the ORDER BY clause, can all be mutated. This feature enables a query to be refined in successive steps. For example,

```
CriteriaQuery<Customer> cq = cb.createQuery(Customer.class);
Root<Customer> c = cq.from(Customer.class);
Join<Customer, Address> a = c.join(Customer_.address);
cq.select(c);
cq.where(cb.like(c.get(Customer_.name), "John%"));
cq.orderBy(cb.asc(a.get(Address_.zip)));
TypedQuery<Customer> query = em.createQuery(cq);
List<Customer> resultList = query.getResultList();
```

Now we modify the query above by adding an ORDER BY item:

```
List<javax.persistence.criteria.Order> orders = cq.getOrderList();
List<javax.persistence.criteria.Order> orders2
  = new ArrayList<javax.persistence.criteria.Order>(orders);

// add ordering by state
orders2.add(cb.desc(a.get(Address_.state)));

cq.orderBy(orders2);                          // change to new ordering
TypedQuery<Customer> query2 = em.createQuery(cq);
List<Customer> resultList2 = query.getResultList();
```

Many interfaces in the Criteria API are immutable, in the sense that there are no setter methods to modify their values, once they are created. The methods such as `select`, `where`, `groupBy`, `having`, and `orderBy` on the `CriteriaQuery` and `SubQuery` interfaces enable the developer to modify a query as many times as needed. They erase the previous values and replace them by new values supplied. In particular, the example above gets the ordering expression from a query and replaces the ORDER BY clause by a completely new ordering. Note that the ordering list returned by the method cb.getOrderList is not live, in the sense that modifying this list will not affect the query itself.

7.3.13   Summary

There are three equivalent ways of writing criteria queries. The first way using generated static metamodel classes is typically preferred by many developers due to its relative terse syntax (compared to the approach using metamodel interfaces) and strong typing (compared to using strings to reference attribute names).

This concludes our coverage of criteria queries and you have seen their positive sides in action. You may be wondering what their drawbacks are. Well, it is clear that the drawbacks are that there is a learning curve and they are not as intuitive to write as JPQL queries. In addition, run-time errors from criteria queries are typically harder to debug than their JPQL counterparts. In terms of features, criteria queries and JPQL queries are almost equivalent, except that the former support the execution of stored database functions and the latter do not. In reality, many queries are easier to write, debug, and execute in JPQL, while others are easier in criteria queries. JPQL also has performance and maintenance advantages, as named queries may be stored in XML mapping files and pre-compiled.

An application team is advised to choose one way to do all or the majority of its queries, although JPQL queries and criteria queries can be mixed in an application. If the chosen way cannot handle certain queries due to technical difficulties or JPA implementation bugs, try the other way (even consider native SQL queries, if needed). This will most likely save development time and reduce maintenance cost.

8 Design Patterns and Performance

JPA can be used in standalone Java SE applications, and in the Web and EJB containers of Java EE application servers. Entity persistence may be application-managed or container-managed. Also, resource-local transactions or JTA transactions may be applied. Design patterns in these usage scenarios provide reusable, consistent, and maintainable approaches to applying JPA. Performance is a measure of application quality that must be considered up-front, which may be affected by the selection of design patterns.

The first section of this chapter discusses design patterns for these application scenarios, while the second section deals with JPA performance issues.

8.1 Design Patterns

Before ORM (object-relational mapping) frameworks such as TopLink and Hibernate, JDBC was the only popular way to write data access code in Java. The Data Access Object (DAO) design pattern is formulated in JDBC to decouple data access code from business logic, and the Data Transfer Object/Value Object pattern is used to transfer data between the persistence layer and business logic layer.

With JPA, the Entity Access Object (EAO) pattern may be used (see reference [PRL] in Section 9.2). It is pretty much the same pattern as the DAO pattern. However, it applies specifically to the context of JPA entities. Since JPA entities are POJOs, there is no need for separate Data Transfer Objects. Note that JPA manages a persistence context. Updates on managed entities in a persistence context may be saved to the database automatically, depending on the flush mode setting of the entity manager and the availability of an active transaction. A recommended approach is to detach a managed entity object before transferring it to a different layer for modification and then merge the modified object back into a persistence context before committing the change to the database. JPA also maintains a second-level cache, if enabled. Objects in this cache are shared by all users. If one user modifies the objects in this shared cache, other users would see the changes. Make sure to evict an entity object from this cache before modifying it.

The Entity Access Object (EAO) pattern decouples entity access code from business logic and improves maintainability and re-use in design and coding. It allows one to change the entity access logic without affecting the client calling code to the business logic. In terms of granularity, some people prefer to have an EAO class for every entity, while others prefer to have an EAO for a group of related entities.

For the domain objects in Figure 2-2 for our online book ordering system, let us create three EAOs as depicted in Figure 8-1. They are coarse-grained in the sense that one EAO is responsible for the persistence of several related entities. You may want to add a base EAO class for all common functionalities among all the EAO classes, but it is omitted in this picture for brevity. Also, some people prefer to define EAO interfaces and implementation classes, following the design-by-contract pattern.

In the following three subsections, we talk about sample implementations of these EAO classes in Java SE, the EJB container, and the Web container. Then in the next subsection, the facade pattern is briefly explained to possibly enhance the EAO pattern. Finally, in the last subsection, the thread-local design pattern is used to capture the user login and pass the user name to an auditing field listener.

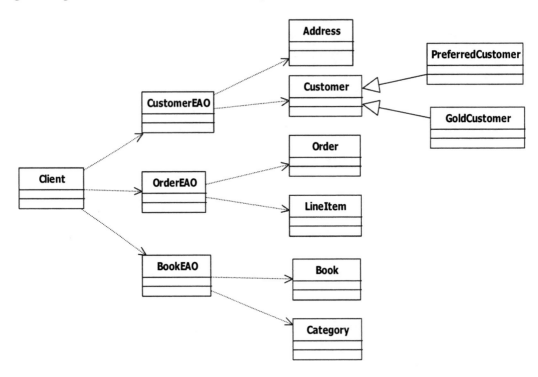

Figure 8-1 Entity Access Object (EAO) design pattern for our online book ordering system. An EAO is responsible for a group of related entities.

8.1.1 EAO in Java SE

In Java SE environments, only application-managed entity managers, resource-local transactions, and extended persistence contexts are available. Listing 8-1 gives a sample implementation of a base EAO and a derived order EAO to demonstrate the EAO pattern in such environments.

> Listing 8-1 BaseEAO.java and OrderEAO.java: A common Entity Access Object design pattern in Java SE environments.

```java
package jpatest.eao;

import javax.persistence.EntityManager;
import javax.persistence.EntityManagerFactory;
import javax.persistence.Persistence;

public class BaseEAO {
  static final EntityManagerFactory EMF =
    Persistence.createEntityManagerFactory("jpaTestPU");

  public static EntityManager createEntityManager() {
    return EMF.createEntityManager();
  }

  public static void closeEntityManager(EntityManager em) {
    if (em != null && em.isOpen()) {
      em.close();
    }
  }

  public static EntityManagerFactory getEntityManagerFactory() {
    return EMF;
  }
}

public class OrderEAO extends BaseEAO {

  public void createOrder(Order order) {
    EntityManager em = createEntityManager();
    try {
      em.getTransaction().begin();
      em.persist(order);          // cascade to associated line items
      em.getTransaction().commit();
    } catch (Throwable t) {
```

301

```
      t.printStackTrace();
      em.getTransaction().rollback();
    } finally {
      closeEntityManager(em);
    }
  }

  public void addLineItem(Order order, LineItem li) {
    EntityManager em = createEntityManager();
    try {
      em.getTransaction().begin();
      em.merge(order);
      order.getLineItems().add(li);
      li.setOrder(order);
      em.getTransaction().commit();
    } catch (Throwable t) {
      t.printStackTrace();
      em.getTransaction().rollback();
    } finally {
      closeEntityManager(em);
    }
  }

  public Order queryOrderWithMaxId() {
    Order order = null;
    EntityManager em = createEntityManager();

    try {
      Query query = em.createQuery(
        "SELECT o FROM Order o " +
        "WHERE o.orderId = (SELECT MAX(o2.orderId) FROM Order o2)");
      order = (Order) query.getSingleResult();
    } catch (Throwable t) {
      t.printStackTrace();
    } finally {
      closeEntityManager(em);
    }

    return order;
  }
}
```

Notice that an entity manager is created inside each method and closed before the method returns. When the entity manager is closed, the corresponding persistence context is cleared and all the managed entities become detached.

The code in Listing 8-1 is recommended in general. However, the code in Listing 8-2 has some problem. First, the entity manager instance *em* is shared by all methods and is not thread-safe. Second, managed entity objects (such as the object *order* below) may be accessed by different users and threads, since the persistence context has extended scope and managed entities remain managed even after the invoked method returns.

Listing 8-2 OrderEAO2.java: An Entity Access Object pattern that is not recommended in general since it is not thread-safe.

```java
public class OrderEAO2 {
  EntityManagerFactory emf = null;
  EntityManager em = null;

  public OrderEAO2() {
    emf = Persistence.createEntityManagerFactory("jpaTestPU");
    em = emf.createEntityManager();
  }

  public void createOrder(Order order) {
    try {
      em.getTransaction().begin();
      em.persist(order);
      em.getTransaction().commit();
    } catch (Throwable t) {
      t.printStackTrace();
      em.getTransaction().rollback();
    }
  }

  public void addLineItem(int orderId, int quantity, double price) {
    try {
      em.getTransaction().begin();
      Order order = em.find(Order.class, orderId);
      LineItem li = new LineItem();
      li.setQuantity(quantity);
      li.setPrice(price);
      li.setOrder(order);
      order.getLineItems().add(li);
      em.getTransaction().commit();
    } catch (Throwable t) {
      t.printStackTrace();
      em.getTransaction().rollback();
```

```
      }
  }

  public void release() {
    if (em != null && em.isOpen()) {
      em.close();
    }

    if (emf != null && emf.isOpen()) {
      emf.close();
    }
  }
}
```

8.1.2 EAO in Web Container

In this subsection, we give two examples for the Entity Access Object pattern in the Web container.

The first example is based on using a container-managed entity manager with JTA transaction and data source. The EAO code is shown in Listing 8-3 and the calling Servlet code is shown in Listing 8-5. A container-managed persistence context is defined using annotation in Listing 8-5, which may also be defined alternatively using XML inside `web.xml` as shown in Listing 8-6. This persistence context is looked up using JNDI in the `BaseEAO.java` class.

The second example is based on using an application-managed entity manager with resource-local transaction and data source. The EAO code is shown in Listing 8-4 and the calling Servlet code is shown in Listing 8-5. An application-managed entity manager factory is defined using annotation in Listing 8-5, which may also be defined alternatively using XML inside `web.xml` as shown in Listing 8-6. This entity manager factory is looked up using JNDI in the `BaseEAO2.java` class.

Listing 8-3 BaseEAO.java and OrderEAO.java: An EAO example with container-managed entity manager and JTA transaction in the Web container.

```
package jpatest.web.eao;

import javax.naming.InitialContext;
import javax.naming.NamingException;
import javax.persistence.EntityManager;
```

```java
import javax.transaction.UserTransaction;

// Base EAO for container-managed entity manager and JTA transaction
public class BaseEAO {
  public static EntityManager getEntityManager() {
    EntityManager em = null;
    try {
      InitialContext ctx = new InitialContext();

      // persistence context jpaTestJtaPC is defined in calling
      // Servlet or web.xml
      em = (EntityManager) ctx.lookup("java:comp/env/jpaTestJtaPC");
    } catch (NamingException e) {
      e.printStackTrace();
    }
    return em;
  }


  // Get the UserTransaction in the container managed JNDI tree.
  public static UserTransaction getUserTransaction() {
    UserTransaction ut = null;
    try {
      InitialContext context = new InitialContext();
      ut = (UserTransaction)
           context.lookup("java:comp/UserTransaction");
    } catch (NamingException e) {
      e.printStackTrace();
    }

    return ut;
  }
}


package jpatest.web.eao;

import javax.persistence.EntityManager;
import javax.persistence.Query;
import javax.transaction.UserTransaction;

import jpatest.entity.Order;

/**
 * Using container-managed transaction and entity manager in a Servlet
 * container. JTA data source is required for container-managed
 * transaction.
```

```
*/
public class OrderEAO extends BaseEAO {
  public void createOrder(Order order) {
    UserTransaction ut = getUserTransaction();
    try {
      ut.begin();
      EntityManager em = getEntityManager();
      em.joinTransaction();
      em.persist(order);          // cascade to associated line items
      ut.commit();
    } catch (Throwable e) {
      e.printStackTrace();
      try {
        ut.rollback();
      } catch (Throwable t) {
        t.printStackTrace();
      }
    }
  }

  public void deleteOrder(Order order) {
    UserTransaction ut = getUserTransaction();
    try {
      ut.begin();
      EntityManager em = getEntityManager();
      em.joinTransaction();
      em.remove(em.merge(order));  // cascade to associated line items
      ut.commit();
    } catch (Throwable e) {
      e.printStackTrace();
      try {
        ut.rollback();
      } catch (Throwable t) {
        t.printStackTrace();
      }
    }
  }

  public Order queryOrderWithMaxId() {
    Order order = null;
    EntityManager em = getEntityManager();

    Query query = em.createQuery("SELECT o FROM Order o "
      + "WHERE o.orderId = (SELECT MAX(o2.orderId) FROM Order o2)");
    order = (Order) query.getSingleResult();
```

```
    return order;
  }
}
```

Listing 8-4 BaseEAO2.java and OrderEAO2.java: An EAO example with application-managed entity manager and resource-local transaction in the Web container.

```java
package jpatest.web.eao;

import javax.naming.InitialContext;
import javax.naming.NamingException;
import javax.persistence.EntityManager;
import javax.persistence.EntityManagerFactory;

/**
 * Base EAO for application-managed entity manager and resource-local
 * transaction.
 */
public class BaseEAO2 {
  public static EntityManager createEntityManager() {
    InitialContext ctx = null;
    EntityManagerFactory emf = null;
    try {
      ctx = new InitialContext();

      // persistence unit jpaTestPUnit is defined in calling Servlet
      // or web.xml
      emf = (EntityManagerFactory)
          ctx.lookup("java:comp/env/jpaTestPUnit");
    } catch (NamingException e) {
      e.printStackTrace();
    }
    return emf.createEntityManager();
  }

  public static void closeEntityManager(EntityManager em) {
    if (em != null && em.isOpen()) {
      em.close();
    }
  }
}

package jpatest.web.eao;
```

```
import javax.persistence.EntityManager;
import javax.persistence.Query;

import jpatest.entity.Order;

/**
 * Using application-managed entity manager and resource-local
 * transaction in a Servlet container. Resource-local data source
 * is required in this case.
 */
public class OrderEAO2 extends BaseEAO2 {
  public void createOrder(Order order) {
    EntityManager em = createEntityManager();
    try {
      em.getTransaction().begin();
      em.persist(order);
      em.getTransaction().commit();
    } catch (Throwable t) {
      t.printStackTrace();
      em.getTransaction().rollback();
    } finally {
      closeEntityManager(em);
    }
  }

  public void deleteOrder(Order order) {
    EntityManager em = createEntityManager();
    try {
      em.getTransaction().begin();
      em.remove(em.merge(order));
      em.getTransaction().commit();
    } catch (Throwable t) {
      t.printStackTrace();
      em.getTransaction().rollback();
    } finally {
      closeEntityManager(em);
    }
  }

  public Order queryOrderWithMaxId() {
    Order order = null;
    EntityManager em = createEntityManager();
    try {
      Query query = em.createQuery("SELECT o FROM Order o "
        + "WHERE o.orderId = (SELECT MAX(o2.orderId) FROM Order o2)");
```

```
      order = (Order) query.getSingleResult();
    } catch (Throwable t) {
      t.printStackTrace();
    } finally {
      closeEntityManager(em);
    }

    return order;
  }
}
```

Listing 8-5 OrderServlet.java: An example Servlet to inject a container-managed persistence context and an application-managed entity manager factory, and call two different EAO classes. The injected persistence context and entity manager factory are used in the base EAO classes in Listing 8-3 and Listing 8-4.

```
package jpatest.web;

import java.io.IOException;
import java.sql.Timestamp;
import java.util.Date;
import java.util.HashSet;
import java.util.Set;

import javax.persistence.PersistenceContext;
import javax.persistence.PersistenceUnit;
import javax.servlet.ServletException;
import javax.servlet.http.HttpServlet;
import javax.servlet.http.HttpServletRequest;
import javax.servlet.http.HttpServletResponse;

import jpatest.entity.LineItem;
import jpatest.entity.Order;
import jpatest.web.eao.OrderEAO;
import jpatest.web.eao.OrderEAO2;

@PersistenceContext(name = "jpaTestJtaPC", unitName = "jpaTestJtaPU")
@PersistenceUnit(name = "jpaTestPUnit", unitName = "jpaTestPU")
public class OrderServlet extends HttpServlet {

  protected void doGet(HttpServletRequest req,
    HttpServletResponse resp) throws ServletException, IOException {
```

```java
      testOrderEAO();
      testOrderEAO2();
  }

  protected void testOrderEAO() {
    try {
      Order order = getOrderAndLineItems(1.5);
      OrderEAO orderEao = new OrderEAO();
      orderEao.createOrder(order);
      Order o = orderEao.queryOrderWithMaxId();
      orderEao.deleteOrder(order);
    } catch (Throwable t) {
      t.printStackTrace();
    }
  }

  protected void testOrderEAO2() {
    try {
      Order order = getOrderAndLineItems(2.5);
      OrderEAO2 orderEao = new OrderEAO2();
      orderEao.createOrder(order);
      Order o = orderEao.queryOrderWithMaxId();
      orderEao.deleteOrder(order);
    } catch (Throwable t) {
      t.printStackTrace();
    }
  }

  private Order getOrderAndLineItems(double price) {
    Order order = new Order();
    order.setOrderTime(new Timestamp(new Date().getTime()));
    order.setPrice(price);

    LineItem li = new LineItem();
    li.setPrice(10.00);
    li.setQuantity(10);
    li.setBook(null);
    li.setOrder(order);

    Set<LineItem> lineItems = new HashSet<LineItem>();
    lineItems.add(li);
    order.setLineItem(lineItems);

    return order;
  }
}
```

Listing 8-6 web.xml: A sample web configuration file showing the definition of a persistence context for container-managed entity managers and a persistence unit for an application-managed entity manager factory.

```xml
<?xml version="1.0" encoding="UTF-8"?>
<web-app xmlns:xsi="http://www.w3.org/2001/XMLSchema-instance"
  xmlns="http://java.sun.com/xml/ns/javaee"
  xmlns:web="http://java.sun.com/xml/ns/javaee/web-app_2_5.xsd"
  xsi:schemaLocation="http://java.sun.com/xml/ns/javaee
      http://java.sun.com/xml/ns/javaee/web-app_2_5.xsd"
  id="WebApp_ID" version="2.5">

  <display-name>jpatestWeb</display-name>
  <servlet>
    <servlet-name>Faces Servlet</servlet-name>
    <servlet-class>javax.faces.webapp.FacesServlet</servlet-class>
    <load-on-startup>1</load-on-startup>
  </servlet>
  <servlet-mapping>
    <servlet-name>Faces Servlet</servlet-name>
    <url-pattern>/faces/*</url-pattern>
  </servlet-mapping>

  <persistence-context-ref>
    <persistence-context-ref-name>jpaTestJtaPC
    </persistence-context-ref-name>
    <persistence-unit-name>jpaTestJtaPU</persistence-unit-name>
  </persistence-context-ref>

  <persistence-unit-ref>
    <persistence-unit-ref-name>jpaTestPUnit
    </persistence-unit-ref-name>
    <persistence-unit-name>jpaTestPU</persistence-unit-name>
  </persistence-unit-ref>
</web-app>
```

The advantage of XML descriptors is that the persistence context and persistence unit references defined this way are accessible any where inside the Servlet container using JNDI lookup. On the other hand, their corresponding annotations as in Listing 8-5 can only be injected on managed classes (such as Servlets and JSF managed beans), and do not apply to helper classes, for example.

8.1.3 EAO in EJB Container

In this subsection, we give two examples for the Entity Access Object pattern in the EJB container using stateless session beans, which will be invoked locally from the Web container. Thus only local interfaces are defined for these session beans.

The first example is based on using a container-managed entity manager and transaction with JTA data source. The EAO code is shown in Listing 8-7 and the calling JSF managed bean is shown in Listing 8-9.

The second example is based on using an application-managed entity manager with bean-managed and resource-local transaction. The EAO code is shown in Listing 8-8 and the calling JSF managed bean is shown in Listing 8-9.

Listing 8-7 OrderEAO.java and OrderEAOLocal.java: A sample stateless session bean as an EAO with container-managed entity manager and transaction, and JTA data source.

```java
package jpatest.ejb.eao;

import javax.ejb.Stateless;
import javax.ejb.TransactionAttribute;
import javax.ejb.TransactionAttributeType;
import javax.persistence.EntityManager;
import javax.persistence.PersistenceContext;
import javax.persistence.Query;

import jpatest.entity.Order;

@Stateless(mappedName = "OrderEAO")
public class OrderEAO implements OrderEAOLocal {
  @PersistenceContext(unitName = "jpaTestJtaPU")
  EntityManager em;

  public void createOrder(Order order) {
    em.persist(order);
  }

  public void deleteOrder(Order order) {
    em.remove(em.merge(order));
  }
```

```
@TransactionAttribute(TransactionAttributeType.SUPPORTS)
public Order queryOrderWithMaxId() {
  Query query = em.createQuery(
    "SELECT o FROM Order o " +
    "WHERE o.orderId = (SELECT MAX(o2.orderId) FROM Order o2)");
  Order order = (Order) query.getSingleResult();
  return order;
  }
}


package jpatest.ejb.eao;

import javax.ejb.Local;
import jpatest.entity.Order;

@Local
public interface OrderEAOLocal {
  public void createOrder(Order order);
  public void deleteOrder(Order order);
  public Order queryOrderWithMaxId();
}
```

Listing 8-8 OrderEAO2.java and OrderEAO2Local.java: A sample stateless session bean as an EAO with application-managed entity manager and bean-managed resource-local transaction.

```
package jpatest.ejb.eao;

import javax.ejb.Stateless;
import javax.ejb.TransactionManagement;
import javax.ejb.TransactionManagementType;
import javax.persistence.EntityManager;
import javax.persistence.EntityManagerFactory;
import javax.persistence.PersistenceUnit;
import javax.persistence.Query;

import jpatest.entity.Order;

@Stateless(mappedName = "OrderEAO2")
@TransactionManagement(TransactionManagementType.BEAN)
public class OrderEAO2 implements OrderEAO2Local {
  @PersistenceUnit(unitName = "jpaTestPU")
  private EntityManagerFactory emf;
```

313

```
  public void createOrder(Order order) {
    EntityManager em = emf.createEntityManager();
    try {
      em.getTransaction().begin();
      em.persist(order);
      em.getTransaction().commit();
    } catch (Throwable e) {
      e.printStackTrace();
      em.getTransaction().rollback();
    } finally {
      em.close();
    }
  }

  public void deleteOrder(Order order) {
    EntityManager em = emf.createEntityManager();
      try {
        em.getTransaction().begin();
        em.remove(em.merge(order));
        em.getTransaction().commit();
      } catch (Throwable e) {
        e.printStackTrace();
        em.getTransaction().rollback();
      } finally {
        em.close();
      }
  }

  public Order queryOrderWithMaxId() {

    Order order = null;
    EntityManager em = emf.createEntityManager();
    try {
      Query query = em.createQuery(
        "SELECT o FROM Order o " +
        "WHERE o.orderId = (SELECT MAX(o2.orderId) FROM Order o2)");
      order = (Order) query.getSingleResult();
    } finally {
      em.close();
    }
    return order;
  }
}

package jpatest.ejb.eao;
```

```
import javax.ejb.Local;
import jpatest.entity.Order;

@Local
public interface OrderEAO2Local {
  public void createOrder(Order order);
  public void deleteOrder(Order order);
  public Order queryOrderWithMaxId();
}
```

Listing 8-9 TestBean.java: A sample JSF managed bean to call EJBs as EAOs with container-managed and bean-managed transactions, respectively.

```
package jpatest.web;

public class TestBean {
  @EJB
  protected OrderEAOLocal orderEaoLocal;

  @EJB
  protected OrderEAO2Local orderEao2Local;

  protected void testOrderEJB_EAOs() {
    Order order = new Order();
    order.setOrderTime(new Timestamp( new Date().getTime()));

    LineItem li = new LineItem();
    li.setPrice(10.00);
    li.setQuantity(10);
    li.setOrder(order);

    Set<LineItem> lineItems = new HashSet<LineItem>();
    lineItems.add(li);
    order.setLineItem(lineItems);

    // call EAO with container-managed entity manager and
    // JTA transaction
    orderEaoLocal.createOrder(order);
    Order o = orderEaoLocal.queryOrderWithMaxId();
    orderEaoLocal.deleteOrder(order);
```

```
    // call EAO with application-managed entity manager and
    // bean-managed transaction
    orderEao2Local.createOrder(order);
    Order o2 = orderEao2Local.queryOrderWithMaxId();
    orderEao2Local.deleteOrder(order);
  }
}
```

The EJB container can do a lot of things for us, such as management of the entity-manager, transaction, security, and resource pooling. It is recommended to consider container-managed entity manager and transaction first. In case of two-phase commit, container-management is highly preferred. See Section 8.2.2 on performance comparisons for some tests using JTA transactions vs. resource-local transactions.

When concurrently updating a versioned entity, JPA would throw an `OptimisticLockException`. However, this exception will not propagate up to the caller if the EAO is implemented using an EJB, since the EJB container is required only to log this system exception and re-throw an `EJBException` instead. A *system exception* in the EJB world is any exception that inherits from `java.rmi.RemoteException` or `java.lang.RuntimeException`, and an *application exception* is any exception that is not a system exception. The original `OptimisticLockException` may or may not be wrapped in the new `EJBException`. What if the caller code in your use case expects to recover (eg, to re-try) when an `OptimisticLockException` is thrown?

The answer is to perform the `flush` operation programmatically inside the EJB at the end of the update method. If an `OptimisticLockException` has occurred, re-throw an application exception. The EJB container is supposed not to touch an application exception, but to throw it back to the calling client directly and unwrapped. EJB 3.0 has introduced the annotation `@ApplicationException` for use on checked and unchecked exceptions (see reference [PRL] in Section 9.2). When this annotation is applied, even unchecked exceptions will be thrown by the EJB container directly. We also have the option to mark the current transaction as rollback or not by specifying the `rollback` element to `true` or `false`. The code looks like this:

```
@Stateless(mappedName = "OrderEAO")
public class OrderEAO implements OrderEAOLocal {
  @PersistenceContext(unitName = "jpaTestJtaPU")
  EntityManager em;
```

```
public void discountOrder(int orderId, double percentage) {
    Order order = em.find(Order.class, orderId);
    double price = order.getPrice();
    price *= percentage;
    order.setPrice(price);

    try {
      em.flush();
    } catch(OptimisticLockException e) {
      throw new MyOptimisticLockException(e);
    }
  }
}

@javax.ejb.ApplicationException(rollback = true)
public class MyOptimisticLockException extends RuntimeException {

  public MyOptimisticLockException() {
    super();
  }

  public MyOptimisticLockException(String message) {
    super(message);
  }

  public MyOptimisticLockException(Throwable cause) {
    super(cause);
  }

  public MyOptimisticLockException(String message, Throwable cause) {
    super(message, cause);
  }
}
```

Then the calling code can try to catch MyOptimisticLockException and attempt to recover such as, to refresh the object and re-try the transaction.

The EAO pattern using stateful session beans may be created similarly, but is used less often. Extended persistence contexts may be used with stateful session beans; See Section 3.3.1 for details.

8.1.4 Façade Pattern

With the EAO pattern as depicted in Figure 8-1, the client code is tightly coupled with the EAO classes. When some of the EAO classes change, the client calling code needs to be changed as well. The façade pattern may be introduced to remediate this problem. Instead of calling the EAO classes directly, the client code will call the façade class, which in turn calls the EAO classes. The class diagram would look like the one in Figure 8-2.

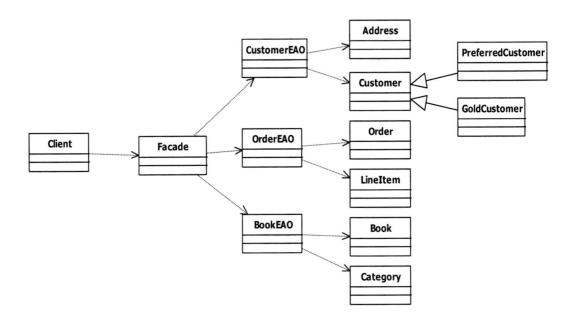

Figure 8-2 Façade pattern to access the EAO classes. Client calls the façade, which in turn calls the EAO classes to reduce tight-coupling.

Of course, an application may have many façade classes, each of which is responsible for a number of related EAO classes, depending on an application's usage pattern. In Java SE environments, a façade class is a POJO, while in Java EE, a façade may also be a stateless or stateful session bean. With the façade pattern, the client does not need to know the internal design of the EAO classes, and thus code maintainability is improved.

In both Java SE and Java EE environments, a façade class may help manage transactions. For example, if a customer has to be created along with some orders and line items in one transaction, the façade will start a transaction, call the customer EAO to persist the customer, then call the order EAO to persist the orders and the line items, and finally commit the transaction. The customer and order EAO classes will need to be refactored in this case. A two-phase commit may happen here when customers and orders are stored in two different databases.

A façade is typically called a session façade when it is implemented as a session bean. When EAO classes are implemented as session beans, a session façade could reduce the number of remote calls from the client to the business layer, and thus improve performance.

8.1.5 Thread Local Pattern

In Listing 3-10, a callback listener is given to automatically fill in auditing fields for entities upon pre-persist and pre-update events. However, the create user and update user names are hard-coded constants. The thread-local pattern may be used to capture the current user from the Web or EJB container and use it for the create user and update user. A thread-local variable differs from normal variables in that each thread that accesses it has its own, independently initialized copy of the variable. In contrast, normal static and instance variables of an object are shared by all threads in the same address space.

In the Web container, the current user login is stored inside the `HttpServletRequest` object. A Servlet filter may be used to retrieve the user from `HttpServletRequest` and then save it in a thread-local request context. The code for the thread-local request context is shown in Listing 8-10 and the Servlet filter in Listing 8-11.

Listing 8-10 RequestContext.java: A thread-local pattern for storing user name in a thread-local context.

```
package jpatest.util;

/**
 * This class stores some context information in the current request
 * thread. It may be initialized by a Servlet filter in the Web
 * container or an EJB interceptor in the EJB container. Make sure to
 * pass the user name to the initRequestContext() method.
 */
public class RequestContext {
  // Current user name associated with the current request.
  private String userName;

  // A Thread Local instance to store the request context
  private static ThreadLocalton localton = new ThreadLocalton();
```

```
  // Inner class storing thread local copy of request context.
  private static class ThreadLocalton extends ThreadLocal<Object> {
    protected synchronized Object initialValue() {
      RequestContext context = new RequestContext();
      return context;
    }
  }

  private RequestContext() {    // private constructor
  }

  /**
   * Returns the instance associated with the current thread.
   * The instance should have been initialized by calling
   * method initRequestContext().
   */
  public static RequestContext getLocalInstance() {
    RequestContext context = (RequestContext) localton.get();
    return context;
  }

  /**
   * Initialize the request context with user name. This method
   * may be called by a Servlet filter or an EJB interceptor.
   */
  public void initRequestContext(String userName) {
    this.userName = userName;
  }

  /**
   * Clears all request context info. Must be called at end of request
   * processing to guarantee information is not shared between
   * requests.
   */
  public void clearRequestContext() {
    this.userName = null;
  }

  public String getUserName() {
    return this.userName;
  }
}
```

Listing 8-11 RequestContextFilter.java: A Servlet filter for capturing user name and saving it in thread-local context.

```java
package jpatest.web.util;

import java.io.IOException;
import java.security.Principal;
import javax.servlet.Filter;
import javax.servlet.FilterChain;
import javax.servlet.FilterConfig;
import javax.servlet.ServletException;
import javax.servlet.ServletRequest;
import javax.servlet.ServletResponse;
import javax.servlet.http.HttpServletRequest;

import jpatest.util.RequestContext;

/**
 * This filer initializes the RequestContext with the calling user
 * name at the beginning of a request and clears the request context
 * and user name at the end of the request.
 */
public class RequestContextFilter implements Filter {

  public void init(FilterConfig config) throws ServletException {
  }

  /**
   * This method gets the RequestContext associated with the current
   * thread, initializes RequestContext with the user name prior to
   * servicing the request, and then clears the RequestContext
   * after servicing request.
   */
  public void doFilter(ServletRequest req, ServletResponse resp,
    FilterChain chain) throws IOException, ServletException {

    RequestContext requestContext = RequestContext.getLocalInstance();

    try {
      Principal p = ((HttpServletRequest) request).getUserPrincipal();
      String userName = "DefaultUser";
      if (p != null) {
        userName = p.getName();
      }
```

```
      requestContext.initRequestContext(userName);
      chain.doFilter(request, response);
    } finally {
      // clear context at the end of the request
      requestContext.clearRequestContext();
    }
  }

  public void destroy() {
  }
}
```

In the web configuration file `web.xml`, the Servlet filter has to be configured and the web pages have to be protected so that a user needs to log in. It is shown in Listing 8-12.

Listing 8-12 web.xml: Sample web XML elements for configuring a Servlet filter, filter mapping, and secure web resources with a security role.

```xml
<?xml version="1.0" encoding="UTF-8"?>
<web-app xmlns:xsi="http://www.w3.org/2001/XMLSchema-instance"
  xmlns="http://java.sun.com/xml/ns/javaee"
  xmlns:web="http://java.sun.com/xml/ns/javaee/web-app_2_5.xsd"
  xsi:schemaLocation="http://java.sun.com/xml/ns/javaee
      http://java.sun.com/xml/ns/javaee/web-app_2_5.xsd"
  id="WebApp_ID" version="2.5">

<filter>
  <filter-name>RequestContextFilter</filter-name>
  <filter-class>jpatest.web.util.RequestContextFilter</filter-class>
</filter>

<filter-mapping>
  <filter-name>RequestContextFilter</filter-name>
  <url-pattern>/*</url-pattern>
</filter-mapping>

<servlet>
  <servlet-name>Faces Servlet</servlet-name>
  <servlet-class>javax.faces.webapp.FacesServlet</servlet-class>
  <load-on-startup>1</load-on-startup>
</servlet>

<servlet-mapping>
```

```
      <servlet-name>Faces Servlet</servlet-name>
      <url-pattern>/faces/*</url-pattern>
   </servlet-mapping>

   <security-constraint>
     <web-resource-collection>
        <web-resource-name>AllPages</web-resource-name>
        <url-pattern>/*</url-pattern>
     </web-resource-collection>
     <auth-constraint>
        <role-name>admin</role-name>
     </auth-constraint>

     <user-data-constraint>
        <transport-guarantee>NONE</transport-guarantee>
     </user-data-constraint>
   </security-constraint>

   <login-config>
     <auth-method>BASIC</auth-method>
     <realm-name>web-console</realm-name>
   </login-config>

   <security-role>
     <role-name>admin</role-name>
   </security-role>
</web-app>
```

Notice the security realm `web-console`, role name `admin`, user name and password have to be defined in some way that is specific to the application server in use. For JBoss, see Section 9.6.2.

With this much preparation, our auditing field listener as shown in Listing 3-10 can now be defined as in Listing 8-13.

Listing 8-13 AuditingFieldListener.java: A sample listener for filling in auditing fields for entities. The create user and update user are captured from web login.

```
package jpatest.util;

import java.sql.Timestamp;
import java.util.Date;
import javax.persistence.PrePersist;
```

```java
import javax.persistence.PreUpdate;

import jpatest.entity.BaseEntity;

public class AuditingFieldListener {

  /**
   * Insert auditing fields: create user, create time, update user,
   * and update time
   */
  @PrePersist
  public void insertAuditingField(Object obj) {
    if (!(obj instanceof BaseEntity)) {
      return;
    }

    BaseEntity baseEntity = (BaseEntity) obj;
    Timestamp currentTime = new Timestamp(new Date().getTime());
    baseEntity.setCreateTime(currentTime);
    baseEntity.setUpdateTime(currentTime);

    String user = RequestContext.getLocalInstance().getUserName();
    if (user != null) {
      baseEntity.setCreateUser(user);
      baseEntity.setUpdateUser(user);
    } else {
      baseEntity.setCreateUser("jpaUser");
      baseEntity.setUpdateUser("jpaUser");
    }
  }

  /**
   * Update auditing fields: update user, and update time
   */
  @PreUpdate
  public void updateAuditingField(Object obj) {
    if (!(obj instanceof BaseEntity)) {
      return;
    }

    BaseEntity baseEntity = (BaseEntity) obj;
    Timestamp currentTime = new Timestamp(new Date().getTime());
    baseEntity.setUpdateTime(currentTime);

    String user = RequestContext.getLocalInstance().getUserName();
    if (user != null) {
```

```
      baseEntity.setUpdateUser(user);
   } else {
      baseEntity.setUpdateUser("jpaUser2");
   }
  }
}
```

The thread-local pattern together with a Servlet filter works well if the original request is from a Web login. The user login is captured in the Servlet filter and saved in a thread-local variable. The saved user login name can then be retrieved in the executing thread and used in the auditing field listener. This applies regardless whether we use a POJO as the EAO class in the Web tier or we use a session bean as the EAO class through a local interface.

However, EJBs may be remotely accessible without going through the Web container in the same Java EE application server. When an EJB is remotely accessed, the caller credential may be captured in an EJB interceptor, and saved in a thread-local variable. This is exactly analogous to the Servlet filter we just talked about in Listing 8-11. The code for such an EJB interceptor is shown in Listing 8-14. This interceptor may be configured in `ejb-jar.xml` as in Listing 8-15.

Listing 8-14 RequestContextInterceptor.java: A sample EJB interceptor to capture caller login when the caller accesses the EJB container remotely.

```
package jpatest.ejb.util;

import java.security.Principal;
import javax.annotation.Resource;
import javax.ejb.EJBContext;
import javax.interceptor.AroundInvoke;
import javax.interceptor.InvocationContext;

import jpatest.util.RequestContext;

public class RequestContextInterceptor {
  @Resource
  private EJBContext ctx;

  @AroundInvoke
  public Object initRequestContext(InvocationContext invCtx)
```

```java
    throws Exception {
    String userName = "DefaultUser";

    Principal p = ctx.getCallerPrincipal();
    if (p != null) {
      userName = p.getName();
    }

    RequestContext requestContext = RequestContext.getLocalInstance();
    requestContext.initRequestContext(userName);

    return invCtx.proceed();
  }
}
```

Listing 8-15 ejb-jar.xml: A sample EJB deployment descriptor file for configuring a default interceptor for all EJBs.

```xml
<?xml version="1.0" encoding="UTF-8"?>
<ejb-jar  version="3.0" xmlns="http://java.sun.com/xml/ns/javaee"
  xmlns:xsi="http://www.w3.org/2001/XMLSchema-instance"
  xsi:schemaLocation="http://java.sun.com/xml/ns/javaee
      http://java.sun.com/xml/ns/javaee/ejb-jar_3_0.xsd">

  <interceptors>
    <interceptor>
      <interceptor-class>jpatest.ejb.util.RequestContextInterceptor
      </interceptor-class>
    </interceptor>
  </interceptors>

  <assembly-descriptor>
    <interceptor-binding>
      <ejb-name>*</ejb-name>
      <interceptor-class>jpatest.ejb.util.RequestContextInterceptor
      </interceptor-class>
    </interceptor-binding>
  </assembly-descriptor>
</ejb-jar>
```

8.2 Performance

Performance is an important aspect of software quality. The persistence layer plays a critical role in overall performance of an application. JPA provides many features for data persistence. Proper use and understanding of these features often leads to improved performance. In this section, we talk about several techniques for fine tuning the JPA data access layer.

8.2.1 Database Design

In Section 2.1, we talked about domain modeling. From the domain model, a logic data model may be created. While a logic data model is not specific to a particular database (such as Oracle or MySQL), it may depend on the persistence technology in use (such as JPA or JDBC) and the usage pattern. When JPA is used, objects in the domain model are intimately connected to tables in the data model. Good design of both the domain model and the data model may dramatically improve the performance of an application. This subsection shows how to design the database for better performance. The domain model may need be adjusted based on the improved data model design.

Split a Table

When a table contains a column that stores large amount of binary or character data, it may make sense to split it into two, with a separate table storing the large column. This is especially true if the large column is not frequently used. For example, the domain object Customer is mapped to table CUSTOMER in Section 2.2 in the following fashion:

```
@Entity
@Table(name = "CUSTOMER")
public class Customer {

  @Id
  @GeneratedValue(
    strategy = GenerationType.TABLE, generator = "CUST_SEQ_GEN"
  )
  @Column(name = "CUSTOMER_ID_PK", updatable=false)
  protected int customerId;

  @Lob
  @Basic(fetch=FetchType.LAZY, optional=false)
  @Column(name="PICTURE", columnDefinition="BLOB NOT NULL")
  protected byte[] picture;
}
```

This kind of mapping could negatively impact performance, as the large customer picture column may significantly slow down queries using this table. These queries include hand-written native queries and SQL statements generated from JPQL queries or criteria queries.

Note that the lazy-loading fetch type specified for the picture LOB field is only a hint, as JPA does not mandate the support of lazy loading for entity fields. Your JPA persistence provider is permitted to eagerly fetch data for which the LAZY strategy hint has been specified. In particular, lazy fetching might only be available for @Basic mappings for which property-based access is used.

Thus we create a separate table named CUST_PICTURE for storing customer pictures (and possibly some other columns) and make the two tables share the same primary key. The domain model should be modified due to the data model change. We also specify a lazy-loading relationship from Customer to CustomerPicture, as shown below:

```
@Entity
@Table(name = "CUSTOMER")
public class Customer {

  @Id
  @GeneratedValue(
    strategy = GenerationType.TABLE, generator = "CUST_SEQ_GEN"
  )
  @Column(name = "CUSTOMER_ID_PK", updatable=false)
  protected int customerId;

  @OneToOne(mappedBy="customer", fetch=FetchType.LAZY,
    cascade={CascadeType.PERSIST,CascadeType.MERGE,CascadeType.REMOVE}
  )
  protected CustomerPicture custPicture;
}

@Entity
@Table(name="CUST_PICTURE")
public class CustomerPicture {
  @Id
  protected int customerId;

  @MapsId
  @OneToOne
  @JoinColumn(
    name = "CUSTOMER_ID_FPK", referencedColumnName="CUSTOMER_ID_PK"
```

```
  )
  protected Customer customer;

  @Lob
  @Column(name="PICTURE", columnDefinition="BLOB NOT NULL")
  protected byte[] picture;  protected int customerId;
}
```

The cascading policy from `Customer` to `CustomerPicture` also affects performance. For example, when a customer instance is refreshed, we do not want to refresh the corresponding customer picture, as such a refresh could take a long time. Since cascading policy can only be specified for a persistent relationship (not for a persistent field or property), using a separate table is a must in this respect.

Note that lazy fetching is a hint to the persistence provider and can be specified by means of the `@Basic`, `@OneToOne`, `@OneToMany`, `@ManyToOne`, `@ManyToMany`, `@ElementCollection` annotations and their equivalent XML descriptors. As mentioned in Section 2.2.5, lazy fetching requires one more trip to the database when the data is actually retrieved and the developer should fully understand the usage pattern when using it.

Merge Tables

It is sometimes more efficient when merging two small tables into one. Suppose we need to add country information to our `Address` entity. One way to do it is to create a table COUNTRY and an entity `Country` and model a one-to-one relationship from `Address` to Country:

```
@Entity
public class Address {
  @Id
  @GeneratedValue(
    strategy=GenerationType.TABLE, generator="ADDRESS_SEQ_GEN"
  )
  @Column(name = "ADDRESS_ID_PK", updatable=false)
  protected int addressId;

  @OneToOne
  @JoinColumn(
    name = "COUNTRY_ID_FK", referencedColumnName="COUNTRY_ID_PK"
  )
  protected Country country;
}
```

```
@Entity
public class Country {
  @Id
  @GeneratedValue(
    strategy=GenerationType.TABLE, generator="COUNTRY_SEQ_GEN"
  )
  @Column(name = "COUNTRY_ID_PK", updatable=false)
  protected int countryId;

  protected String countryName;
}
```

Since the country information is needed, every time we retrieve an `Address` object, we also retrieve the corresponding `Country` object. This will cause a `JOIN` to be performed between the `ADDRESS` and `COUNTRY` tables, and increase query time.

To improve performance, we may merge the two tables into one by storing country information into the `ADDRESS` table, and use an embeddable object for encapsulation:

```
@Entity
public class Address {
  @Id
  @GeneratedValue(
    strategy=GenerationType.TABLE, generator="ADDRESS_SEQ_GEN"
  )
  @Column(name = "ADDRESS_ID_PK", updatable=false)
  protected int addressId;

  @Embedded
  protected Country country;
}

@Embeddable
public class Country {
  @Column(name = "COUNTRY_CODE")
  protected int countryId;

  @Column(name = "COUNTRY_NAME")
  protected String countryName;
}
```

By doing this, `JOIN` statements can be avoided and performance may be boosted. The exact performance gain depends on the usage pattern and the number of records in the database. The downside is that this may increase maintenance work when a country changes its name.

Version Column

The version column is used for optimistic locking. Its data type can be numeric or timestamp. In terms of performance, a numeric value is more time and space efficient than timestamp. For example, when we insert a new entity into the database, a numeric version with typical value of 0 or 1 is inserted. However, with timestamp versioning, a function call is needed to get the current timestamp of the underlying operating system. Also, in the JVM a timestamp object takes much more memory than a `long` or `int`.

Sequence Generators

JPA has the ability to generate sequential numbers as IDs automatically when a new entity instance is inserted into the database. In Section 2.2.10, we presented three different ways of generating such sequences.

Sequencing using identity columns is not recommended in general, since the generated ID is not assigned by the database until the row is inserted and it does not support pre-allocation. When managing related objects, the generated ID may have to be retrieved by a select call to the database. It could have major performance problems.

Sequencing using database sequence objects has its own drawback, in that it is not portable across databases.

Table sequencing provides good performance because it allows for sequence pre-allocation, which is extremely important to insert performance. Its disadvantage is that the sequence table can become a concurrency and performance bottleneck (even causing deadlocks). If the sequence ID is allocated in the same transaction as the insert operation, this can cause poor performance, as the sequence row will be locked for the duration of the transaction and other transactions would have to wait to allocate sequence IDs.

If a large sequence pre-allocation size is used together with multiple sequence tables, performance can be dramatically improved. Some JPA providers even allow you to configure a non-JTA connection to allocate the sequence IDs when JTA data source is used for entity transactions.

Locking Types

JPA provides different locking options, including optimistic locking and pessimistic locking. When more than one user has to modify an entity at the same time, it is advised to consider some form of locking. The performance characteristics of different locking options are different. Generally speaking, optimistic locking should be considered first as it performs better in moderate contention scenarios and does not require long-term database locking. When optimistic locking is used, the entity must have a version attribute and the corresponding database table must contain a version column. What a developer needs to do is to map the version attribute to the version column.

When it is needed to lock an entity instance by calling one of the locking API methods to avoid dirty read and non-repeatable read, a READ lock is more efficient than a WRITE lock. Check your requirements and use an optimistic READ lock if it is sufficient. Refreshing an entity object before locking it can minimize the risk of locking failures. See Section 3.4 for more discussions.

Inheritance Strategy

JPA supports three types of inheritance mapping strategies. Each has its own advantages and disadvantages. In terms of performance, the single-table strategy is the best choice. The reason is that all entities in the inheritance hierarchy are stored in a single table and joins between tables are not needed. See Section 4.3 for details.

8.2.2 Entity Operations

The way that we are performing entity operations directly affects performance of an application. In the following, we talk about a few ways that a developer can do to boost run-time efficiency of entity operations.

Second-Level Cache

As noted in Section 3.7, managed entity instances are cached in the persistence context cache, which is not shared with other persistence contexts. The `find` operation returns an entity instance from this cache if it exists there, and updates to an entity instance are held in this cache until it is committed to the database. JPA 2.0 specifies a second-level cache, which caches entity objects within a persistence unit that are shared by different persistence contexts and users. Enabling of the second-level cache with proper configuration of the cache mode may improve performance, since JPA may retrieve the results of executing a query, or the result of the `find` method, from the cache directly, saving a round-trip to the database.

The advantages of the second-level cache are that it avoids database access for cached entity objects and it is suitable for objects that are read frequently but do not change often.

It has disadvantages as well. First, it may consume a lot of memory when a large number of objects are cached. Second, it could lead to stale data or inconsistent data when the data is modified in the database, especially by a different application or in a clustered environment. Third, it may not work well for frequently changed entities or concurrently updated entities.

Generally, the second-level cache performs well for entities that are read often, but updated infrequently, and that are not critical if they become stale.

Fetch Type

There are two fetch types: `EAGER` and `LAZY`. For a one-to-one or many-to-one relationship, and a basic persistent attribute, `EAGER` loading is the default behavior, while `LAZY` loading is the default for a one-to-many or many-to-many relationship, and for an element collection. With `LAZY` loading, persistent attributes or relationships are not retrieved from the database until when they are first accessed. However, it requires a separate trip to the database when a `LAZY` attribute or relationship is actually loaded. Proper setting of the fetch type may noticeably improve performance.

Lazy fetching may be specified by means of the `@Basic`, `@OneToOne`, `@OneToMany`, `@ManyToOne`, `@ManyToMany`, `@ElementCollection` annotations and their equivalent XML descriptors.

For efficiency reasons, there are also situations in which we may want to eagerly load relationships that are configured with `LAZY` loading. This may be achieved by the fetch join functionality, such as in the following example:

```
SELECT c FROM Customer c JOIN FETCH c.orders
WHERE c.customerType = ?1
```

This query will guarantee that the associated orders are retrieved from the database together with the customer objects, even if the one-to-many relationship from `Customer` to `Order` is configured with lazy loading.

Cascade Policy

There are different cascade types: PERSIST, MERGE, REMOVE, REFRESH, DETACH, and ALL. See Section 2.3.1. Each of them impacts how related entities are managed and causes performance consequences. For example, look at this one-to-many relationship and its cascade policy:

```
@Entity
@Table(name="ORDERS")
public class Order extends BaseEntity {
  @OneToMany(mappedBy="order", cascade={CascadeType.ALL})
  protected  Set<LineItem> lineItems;
}
```

With the cascade type CascadeType.ALL, whenever an order is merged, refreshed, or detached, its associated line items will be merged, refreshed, or detached as well. It could incur a lot of performance hit, especially when there are many line items associated with the order. Thus use cascade policy appropriately. In this case, it may just be sufficient to cascade the persist and remove operations as:

```
@Entity
@Table(name="ORDERS")
public class Order extends BaseEntity {
  @OneToMany(
    mappedBy="order",
    cascade={CascadeType.PERSIST, CascadeType.REMOVE}
  )
  protected  Set<LineItem> lineItems;
}
```

Note that many databases support enforcing a cascade delete constraint on database tables directly. For example in Derby, a cascade delete constraint on the LINE_ITEM table referencing to the ORDERS table may be created as:

```
CREATE TABLE LINE_ITEM (
  LINE_ITEM_ID_PK INTEGER PRIMARY KEY,
  QUANTITY INTEGER,
  ...
  ORDER_ID_FK INTEGER CONSTRAINT ORDERS_FK REFERENCES ORDERS
  ON DELETE CASCADE
);
```

That is, when a row in the ORDERS table is deleted, its associated rows in the LINE_ITEM table are deleted automatically by the database. This is obviously more efficient than performing a cascade remove on the JPA entities. However, caution must be taken if these deleted objects are present in the persistence context or second-level cache.

Flush Mode

The entity operations: `persist`, `merge`, and `remove` may not cause the affected data to be saved to the database immediately. Instead, they are deferred until flush or commit time. Performance may be improved if the database operations can be batched or optimized at flush or commit time. An entity manager has two flush modes: `COMMIT` and `AUTO`. The default is `AUTO`. This means that the entity manager performs a flush operation automatically as needed. If entities with pending changes are used in a query, JPA will flush the changes to the database so that the query will return the newly updated results.

The default behavior may be changed and a developer may programmatically call the flush operation:

```
// set flush mode to COMMIT
em.setFlushMode(FlushModeType.COMMIT);

// programmatically call flush
em.flush();
```

When the flush mode is set to `COMMIT` on an entity manager (all queries created by the entity manger will have the same flush mode by default), JPA will only write the changes to the database at transaction commit time, unless the developer invokes the `flush` operation programmatically. This may improve performance. However, care must be taken in that the developer may have to invoke the `flush` method call explicitly to synchronize entity state with the database before executing a query or before detaching an object. Otherwise, the query may return stale data or updates on the object prior to detachment may not be saved to the database.

Bulk Updates

When you need to update/delete many entity objects, one way to achieve it is to retrieve them in a query, iterate them through to update/delete each one at a time, as in the following code snippet:

```
em.getTransaction().begin();

Query query = em.createQuery(
```

```
  "SELECT o FROM Order o WHERE o.orderTime < ?1");
query.setParameter(1, new Date(), TemporalType.TIMESTAMP);
List<Order> resultList = query.getResultList();

for (Order result : resultList) {
    em.remove(result);
}

em.getTransaction().commit();
```

This would be very inefficient, since many database delete statements would be generated and executed from JPA. Instead, consider using the feature of bulk deletes as follows:

```
em.getTransaction().begin();

Query query = em.createQuery(
  "DELETE FROM Order o WHERE o.orderTime < ?1");
query.setParameter(1, new Date(), TemporalType.TIMESTAMP);
int deleted = query.executeUpdate();

em.getTransaction().commit();
```

Bulk update/delete queries are presented in Section 5.3.8.

JTA Transactions

When performing entity operations, using container-managed entity managers inside an EJB container makes coding much simpler. However, it requires JTA data sources. Generally speaking, JTA transactions are not as efficient as resource-local transactions. You need to make a decision on which one to use based on efficiency, ease-of-coding, and your application characteristics. For a typical web application, a slower transaction speed may be tolerated, since the user typically has to edit information and click a submit button to trigger a transaction, which is a slow process. If an application has millons of concurrent users, even a slightly slow transaction operation may noticeably affect the overall performance.

We now do some comparison on the efficiency between JTA transactions and resource-local transactions, using JBoss 5.0 and Derby 10.4.2 on a Windows XP computer with 2.20 GHz AMD Athlon 64 processor 3500+ and 2.5GB RAM.

Chapter 8   Design Patterns and Performance

First, we compare the `OrderEAO` class, defined in Listing 8-3, against the `OrderEAO2` class, defined in Listing 8-4, both of which are inside the Web container. The class `OrderEAO` uses container-managed entity manger with JTA transaction, while `OrderEAO2` uses application-managed entity manger with resource-local transaction. We iterate through many loops like this for both EAO classes:

```
Order order = getOrderAndLineItems(1.5);    // See Listing 8-5
OrderEAO orderEao = new OrderEAO();

int loops = 10000;
long time = System.currentTimeMillis();
for (int i = 0; i < loops; i++) {
  orderEao.createOrder(order);
  Order o = orderEao.queryOrderWithMaxId();
  orderEao.deleteOrder(order);
}
long time2 = System.currentTimeMillis();
long totalTime = (time2-time)/1000;
```

Inside each loop, we perform five operations: two inserts (for order and line item), one query execution, and two deletes (for order and line item). The running times are given in Table 8-1 for 100, 1000, and 10000 loops.

Table 8-1 Running times in seconds for entity operations in the Web container.

Number of loops	JTA Transaction	Non-JTA Transaction
100	1.5	0.9
1000	11.7	7
10000	119.6	69

Second, we compare the `OrderEAO` class, defined in Listing 8-7, against the `OrderEAO2` class, defined in Listing 8-8, both of which are inside the EJB container. The class `OrderEAO` uses EJB container-managed entity manger with JTA transaction, while `OrderEAO2` uses application-managed entity manger with bean-managed resource-local transaction. The running times are given in Table 8-2 for 100, 1000, and 10000 loops. These session bean EAOs are called from the `TestBean.java` class (Listing 8-9) in the Web container and thus the execution times are longer than the ones in Table 8-1.

Table 8-2 Running times in seconds for entity operations in the EJB container.

Number of loops	JTA Transaction	Non-JTA Transaction
100	1.8	1.0
1000	12.7	8.6
10000	132.5	85.0

In this test with a single user, JTA transactions run about 50% more slowly than resource-local transactions, and the EJB layer adds about 10% overhead.

8.2.3 Query Performance

Pretty much every application makes use of queries and query efficiency typically has a major impact on overall performance of an application. Query tuning is a big part of overall performance tuning. Many databases have tools that can analyze query performance bottlenecks. Based on such analysis, the DBA may create indexes on affected database tables and make other suggestions on improving the SQL queries. The developer can fine tune JPA queries to generate efficient SQL queries.

In this subsection, we discuss a few common scenarios that could help make your queries run faster.

Avoid Full-Table Scan

Full-table scans are typically expensive when there are a large number of records in the table. Avoid queries that perform full-table scans, if possible. For example, look at this JPQL query:

```
SELECT o FROM Order o
```

Your JPA provider typically translates this simple query into the following SQL query:

```
SELECT * FROM ORDERS
```

This would cause a full table scan in your database and slow down your query when there are a lot of data in the table. Also, your JPA will potentially bring in all the records in the table to the JVM as a collection of entity objects, which occupies a lot of memory and may cause OutOfMemoryError to be thrown.

This is not typically what you want. Instead, specify a search criteria to restrict the number of records in the query such as:

```
SELECT o FROM Order o WHERE o.orderTime < ?1
```

Such a query should typically run much faster.

Limit Query Results

Sometimes a query may return many records. Retrieving all of them at once not only costs performance, but also may not be necessary. In a typical web application, the user views the data one screen at a time. It may be more performant to retrieve a limited number of records at a time and retrieve more when needed. This can be done by setting the maximum results on a query as:

```
Query query = em.createQuery(
  "SELECT o.customer, o.price FROM Order o WHERE o.orderTime < ?1");
query.setParameter(1, new Date(), TemporalType.TIMESTAMP);

// retrieve the first 50 records, starting from 0th record
query.setMaxResults(50);
query.setFirstResult(0);
List<Object[]> resultList = query.getResultList();

for (Object[] result : resultList) {
  Customer customer = (Customer) result[0];
  Double price = (Double) result[1];

  // process the first 50 records
}

// retrieve the second 50 records, starting from 50th record
query.setMaxResults(50);
query.setFirstResult(50);
resultList = query.getResultList();
for (Object[] result : resultList) {
  // process the second 50 records
}
```

Set Fetch Size

There are times when you have to retrieve many records from the database to Java for processing. Setting an appropriate number for the query fetch size typically improves performance and can even avoid an `OutOfMemoryError`. This fetch size will translate to JDBC fetch size, which is the number of rows fetched with each database round trip for the query. The default fetch size in Oracle is 10.

Setting the fetch size too small will require many database round trips to fetch all the results, which can degrade performance. However, if the fetch size is too large, the fetched results may cause Java to run out of memory. The optimal fetch size depends on the JVM heap memory size and the size of each record row in the result set. If the result set contains a large image BLOB in each row, the fetch size should be adjusted small.

Unfortunately, JPA does not have a standard way to configure the fetch size. You have to check your persistence provider's documentation. In EclipseLink, we may configure the fetch size per query in annotation as:

```
@Entity
@Table(name="ORDERS")
@NamedQuery(name="selectCustomerAndPrice",
  Query =
    "SELECT o.customer, o.price FROM Order o WHERE o.orderTime < ?1",
  hints={@QueryHint(
          name="javax.persistence.query.timeout", value="1000"),
        @QueryHint(name="eclipselink.jdbc.fetch-size", value="256"),
        @QueryHint(name="eclipselink.read-only", value="TRUE") }
)
public class Order extends BaseEntity { ... }
```

Alternatively, we may do it programmatically:

```
query = em.createNamedQuery("selectCustomerAndPrice");
query.setHint("eclipselink.jdbc.fetch-size", "256");
query.setHint("eclipselink.read-only", "TRUE");
query.setHint("javax.persistence.query.timeout", "1000");
```

Set Query Timeout
Setting a query timeout also improves performance as long running queries will be terminated and appropriate actions may be taken accordingly. The standard query timeout property key is (in milliseconds):

```
javax.persistence.query.timeout
```

Named Queries
Named queries are prepared once and can be re-used in subsequent query executions. The generated SQL statements can also be cached. Some persistence providers have a query cache for caching query results based on query names and their parameters, which is

useful for queries that are run frequently with the same parameters on tables that do not change.

Named queries can be defined using annotations or in XML. See Section 5.2.1 for details.

Use Table Indexes

It is well known that indexes make queries run faster. Based on query usage patterns and data characteristics in the database, create enough indexes on the impacted tables. If a query includes the primary key, it always uses an indexed scan and no additional indexes are needed.

For example, suppose the following JPQL query causes performance problems:

```
SELECT c FROM Category c WHERE c.categoryName = ?1
```

By turning on logging when running JPA, the generated prepared SQL statement looks like:

```
SELECT * FROM CATEGORY WHERE CATEGORY_NAME = ?
```

If we create an index on the `CATEGORY_NAME` column in the `CATEGORY` table, the performance of the original JPQL should be improved.

Relationship Attributes

A one-to-one or one-to-many relationship is typically implemented in the database using a foreign key constraint. When such a relationship attribute is accessed, a join statement is generated between the related tables. Without an index created on the foreign key column, a full table scan would be executed and subsequently affect the performance. For example, look at the following `Order` to `LineItem` one-to-many relationship:

```
@Entity
@Table(name="ORDERS")
public class Order extends BaseEntity {
  @OneToMany(
    mappedBy="order",
    cascade={CascadeType.PERSIST, CascadeType.REMOVE}
  )
  protected  Set<LineItem> lineItems;
}
```

When the `lineItems` relationship field is accessed for a particular `Order` object, a SQL query such as the following may be generated:

```
SELECT LINE_ITEM_ID_PK, CREATE_TIME, CREATE_USER, PRICE, UPDATE_TIME,
   QUANTITY, VERSION, UPDATE_USER, ORDER_ID_FK, BOOK_ID_FK
FROM LINE_ITEM
WHERE ORDER_ID_FK = ?
```

If accessing this relationship attribute is slow, try to create an index on the `ORDER_ID_FK` column of the `LINE_ITEM` table.

Functions in WHERE Clauses

JPQL introduces functions that can be used in the `WHERE` clause of a query (see Section 5.3.4). For example, the following query uses the `SUBSTRING` function to search for all books whose first four characters of the book title is `'Java'`:

```
SELECT b FROM Book b
WHERE SUBSTRING (b.title, 1, 4) = 'Java'
```

JPA typically translates this into a SQL query utilizing the SQL substring function. The database typically will not use an indexed scan for this query, even if an index exists for the book title column.

The suggestion here is to try to avoid using functions in the `WHERE` clause of a query. This particular query above may be modified as follows:

```
SELECT b FROM Book b
WHERE b.title LIKE 'Java%'
```

Transaction Management

Queries are not required to be executed in a transaction. As transaction management is expensive in general, avoid using a transaction when executing a query if your requirements permit. Note that the default transaction attribute for a session bean method is `REQUIRED`. Change it to `NOT_SUPPORTED` or `SUPPORTS`, if you can.

8.2.4 Data Source Tuning

JPA connects to the database through the configuration of a data source. The data source characteristics, such as SQL statement caching and connection pooling, directly affects the performance of an application. This subsection addresses a few aspects of data source configuration to possibly improve performance.

SQL Statement Caching

When configuring a data source, we have the option to specify the size of a SQL statement cache. JPA translates queries into SQL statements, which may be cached in this cache. In many applications, the same SQL statement is executed many times. Caching such SQL statements will eliminate the overhead of parsing them each time they are used.

The configuration of the size of the SQL statement cache may depend on the Java EE application server and/or the JDBC driver in use. See Section 9.6.1 on how to configure it in JBoss. For Java EE 6.0 or later, see the end of the section for a sample standard configuration.

In order for an SQL statement to be cached, its corresponding JPA query must use parameter binding, instead of string concatenation. For example, the following query cannot be cached since it uses string concatenation:

```
Query query = em.createQuery(
  "SELECT o.customer, o.price FROM Order o WHERE o.orderTime < "
  + today);
```

Instead, rewrite it using parameter binding as:

```
Query query = em.createQuery(
  "SELECT o.customer, o.price FROM Order o WHERE o.orderTime < ?1");
query.setParameter(1, new Date(), TemporalType.TIMESTAMP);
```

This query will be a candidate for caching. It is even better if we define a named query for this as:

```
@Entity
@Table(name="ORDERS")
@NamedQuery(name="selectCustomerAndPrice",
  Query =
    "SELECT o.customer, o.price FROM Order o WHERE o.orderTime < ?1"
)
public class Order extends BaseEntity { ... }
```

And execute it as follows:

```
query = em.createNamedQuery("selectCustomerAndPrice");
query.setParameter(1, new Date(), TemporalType.TIMESTAMP);
List<Object[]> resultList = query.getResultList();
```

Named queries are typically more efficiently re-used than dynamic queries. Thus consider using a named query if it meets your need and performance is a major concern.

Connection Pooling

When configuring a data source, the connection pool characteristics can be adjusted as well. The configuration of the connection pool directly affects performance. For example, if there are more concurrent users than the number of connections available in the pool, some users have to wait until connections are available in order for them to access the database. Performance may be improved by appropriately adjusting the characteristics of the connection pool, including the minimum and maximum numbers of connections in the pool, and connection wait timeout.

The specific configuration may depend on the vendor in use. See Section 9.6.1 on how to configure it in JBoss. If you are using a Java EE 6.0 compliant application server, you may use the annotation `javax.annotation.sql.DataSourceDefinitions`, or insert the following XML fragment into your `web.xml`, `ejb-jar.xml` or `application.xml` file:

```
<data-source>
  <description>DataSource for Derby</description>
  <name>java:global/jpaTestDS</name>
  <class-name>org.apache.derby.jdbc.ClientDataSource</class-name>
  <server-name>localhost</server-name>
  <port-number>1527</port-number>
  <database-name>jpatest</database-name>
  <user>jpatest</user>
  <password>jpatest</password>
  <property>
    <name>create</name>
    <value>true</value>
  </property>

  <login-timeout>500</login-timeout>
  <transactional>false</transactional>
  <isolation-level>TRANSACTION_READ_COMMITTED</isolation-level>
  <initial-pool-size>2</initial-pool-size>
```

```
   <max-pool-size>5</max-pool-size>
   <min-pool-size>1</min-pool-size>
   <max-idle-time>500</max-idle-time>
   <max-statements>100</max-statements>
</data-source>
```

9 Resources

This chapter provides web resources, book references, and download, installation, and configuration information on various tools and libraries that are used throughout the book. These tools and libraries include EclipseLink, Hibernate, and OpenJPA implementations of the JPA specification, Apache Derby database, Java SE/EE development environment Eclipse, and Java application server JBoss.

9.1 Web Resources

This section lists web resources for Java specifications, Javadoc, XML schema definitions, and some other miscellaneous items.

Resources	URL
JPA 1.0 Specification	http://jcp.org/en/jsr/detail?id=220
JPA 2.0 Specification	http://jcp.org/en/jsr/detail?id=317
EJB 3.1 Specification	http://jcp.org/en/jsr/detail?id=318
Bean Validation 1.1 Specification	http://jcp.org/en/jsr/detail?id=303
Java SE 6 Javadoc	http://java.sun.com/javase/6/docs/api/
Java EE 6 Javadoc	http://java.sun.com/javaee/6/docs/api/
JPA 2.0 ORM Schema	http://java.sun.com/xml/ns/persistence/orm/orm_2_0.xsd
JPA 2.0 Persistence Schema	http://java.sun.com/xml/ns/persistence/persistence_2_0.xsd

9.2 Book References

[Lk] Kevin Loney, Oracle Database 11g The Complete Reference, McGraw Osborne, New York, 2008.

[PRL] Debu Panda, Reza Rahman, Derek Lane, EJB 3 In Action, Manning, Greenwich, 2007.

9.3 EclipseLink

The open source implementation of JPA from EclipseLink can be downloaded at

http://www.eclipse.org/eclipselink/

Uncompress the downloaded zip file. The jar file `eclipselink.jar` in the *jlib* folder contains the EclipseLink implementation of JPA and must be included on the class path. The standard JPA API jar file `javax.persistence.<version>.jar` in the *jlib/jpa* subfolder must be included in Java SE environments. It must also be included when running JPA 2.0 in Java EE 5.0 application servers. In addition, the jar file `eclipselink-jpa-modelgen_<version>.jar` must be put on the classpath when generating static metamodel classes. Here the versions of these files must be 2.0.0 or later.

The EclipseLink User Guide can be found at:

http://wiki.eclipse.org/EclipseLink/UserGuide

http://wiki.eclipse.org/EclipseLink/UserGuide/Developing_JPA_Projects_(ELUG)

http://wiki.eclipse.org/Using_EclipseLink_JPA_Extensions_(ELUG)

9.3.1 Metamodel Class Generation

At command line, the static metamodel classes (see Section 7.2) can be generated by specifying the standard `javac` option: `-processor` to be:

`org.eclipse.persistence.internal.jpa.modelgen.CanonicalModelProcessor`.

For example, the following DOS batch file will generate the static metamodel file `Vehicle_.java` corresponding to the entity class: `Vechicle.java`:

```
@Rem DOS file to generate static metamodel class for Vehicle.java

Set CLASSPATH=.;C:\eclipselink\jlib\eclipselink-jpamodelgen_2.0.jar
Set CLASSPATH=%CLASSPATH%;C:\eclipselink\jlib\javax.persistence_2.0.jar
set CLASSPATH=%CLASSPATH%;C:\eclipselink\jlib\eclipselink.jar

javac -processor org...CanonicalModelProcessor -proc:only Vehicle.java
```

348

Here you have to replace `org...CanonicalModelProcessor` by the fully qualified class name for the EclipseLink canonical model processor shown above. A sample generated canonical metamodel class is shown in Listing 7-1.

For the steps to configure the Eclipse Java IDE (Section 9.5) to generate the metamodel classes, see Section 9.5.1.

9.4 Derby Database

The Apache Derby open source database can be downloaded at the URL:

http://db.apache.org/derby

It is a small zip file. Just unzip it into a folder such as *C:\derby*, and you are done with installation. All the commands are in the *bin* subfolder. You may create a database instance called *jpatest* and table VEHICLE using the command *ij* (go to the *bin* subfolder first and then type *ij*):

```
C:\WINDOWS\system32\cmd.exe                          - □ ×

C:\>cd c:\derby\bin

C:\derby\bin>ij
ij version 10.4
ij> CONNECT 'jdbc:derby:jpatest;create=true;user=jpatest;password=jpatest';
ij> CREATE TABLE VEHICLE (VIN VARCHAR(17) PRIMARY KEY, MAKE VARCHAR(40),
>            MODEL VARCHAR(40), MODEL_YEAR INTEGER, VERSION INTEGER);
0 rows inserted/updated/deleted
ij> exit;
C:\derby\bin>
```

Here the `ij` command

```
CONNECT 'jdbc:derby:jpatest;create=true;user=jpatest;password=jpatest';
```

creates the *jpatest* database, and the next command creates a table named VEHICLE. If the table creation DDL is in a file called `jpatest_create.sql`, located in the *bin* subfolder, then the following command loads and executes the scripts inside the file:

```
ij> run 'jpatest_create.sql';
```

In this example, the `jpatest_create.sql` file just has the script to create the VEHICLE table, as shown in the DOS command screen capture above or in Section 1.1. To start the database server, go to folder *C:\derby\bin* and execute the command: *startNetworkServer.bat*. Then the table VEHICLE is accessible from Java programs using JDBC or JPA.

See the developer guide *getstartderby.pdf* in folder *C:\derby\docs\pdf\getstart* for more details. The JDBC driver `derbyclient.jar` is in folder *C:\derby\lib*. See Listing 1-2 on how to configure database access for JPA.

9.5 *Eclipse IDE*

The open source Eclipse IDE (Integrated Development Environment) can be downloaded at

http://www.eclipse.org/

Click on the *Downloads* tab and choose *Eclipse IDE for Java EE Developers*. Just unzip the downloaded file into a folder such as *C:\eclipse*. To start the IDE, type *C:\eclipse\eclipse.exe* at the command line or go to folder: *C:\eclipse* and double click on the *eclipse.exe* file. When the IDE starts up, it prompts you to enter a workspace to store Java project files. Just browse to a folder such as *C:\jpa\java*. See Section 1.2 on how to create a JPA project in Eclipse, and Section 9.7 on how to create an enterprise project.

9.5.1 Metamodel Class Generation

In this subsection, we show the steps on how to configure the Eclipse IDE for generating static metamodel classes (Section 7.2). For doing this using command line compiler options, see Section 9.3.1.

From the *Package Explorer* view of the *jpatest* project, right click on the project and select *Properties*. From the *Properties* dialog pane, select *Java Compiler* and ensure you choose JDK 1.6 (or higher). See Figure 9-1.

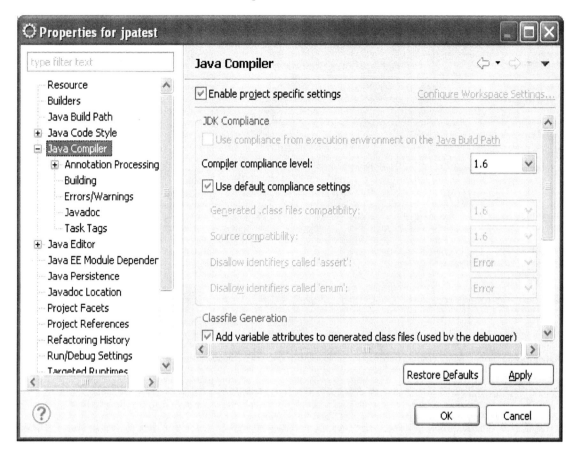

Figure 9-1 Configure Java compiler for metamodel generation in an Eclipse Java project.

Now expand the *Java Compiler* element and select *Annotation Processing*. Check the *Enable project specific settings* and *Enable annotation processing* options. In the *Generated source directory* field, enter the directory to store the generated metamodel classes, or keep the default: *.apt_generated*. See Figure 9-2.

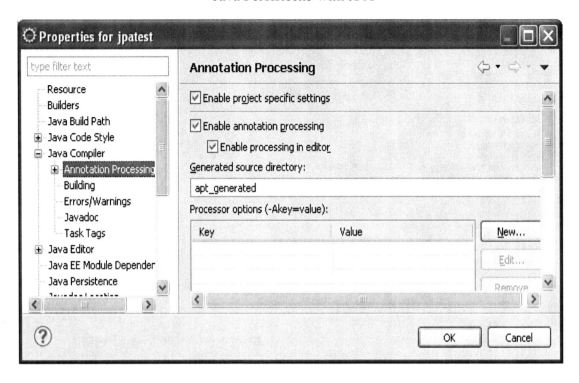

Figure 9-2 Configure Annotation Processing for metamodel class generation.

Expand the *Annotation Processing* element and select *Factory Path*. Check the *Enable project specific settings* and click on the *Add External JARs* button to add the files from EclipseLink download: `eclipselink.jar`, `javax.persistence_2.0.0.jar`, and `eclipselink-jpa-modelgen_2.0.0.jar`. The files with version 2.0.0 are shown here. Any version with 2.0.0 or higher will do. See Figure 9-3. If you are using another JPA persistence provider, add the corresponding jar files here.

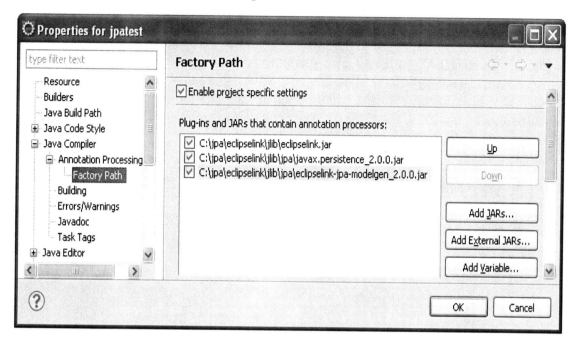

Figure 9-3 Add downloaded EclipseLink JPA implementation and annotation processing jar files.

9.6   JBoss

The open source Java EE application server JBoss can be downloaded at

http://www.jboss.org/jbossas/

To use EJB 3.0 and JSF 1.2 or later, download JBoss AS 5.0 or later. Just unzip the downloaded zip file into a folder such as *C:\jboss*. The default server folder is *C:\jboss\server\default*. JBoss includes the Hibernate JPA implementation as the default JPA provider and the related jar files are in folder *C:\jboss\common\lib*. The following link contains detailed installation and configuration information for the JBoss application server:

https://www.jboss.org/community/wiki/JBossApplicationServerOfficialDocumentationPage

9.6.1 Data Source Configuration

To configure data sources, first define a file with a name such as *derbydb-ds.xml* and the content as in Listing 9-1. Note that this is a JBoss-specific way for configuring data sources. If you are using a Java EE 6.0 compliant application server, you may use the standard annotation @DataSourceDefinition or its equivalent XML descriptor to configure a data source.

Listing 9-1 derbydb-ds.xml: Configuration of a Derby data source for JBoss AS

```xml
<?xml version="1.0" encoding="UTF-8"?>
<datasources>
  <xa-datasource>
    <jndi-name>jpaTestJtaDS</jndi-name>
    <use-java-context>true</use-java-context>
    <connection-url>jdbc:derby://localhost:1527/jpatest
    </connection-url>
    <xa-datasource-class>org.apache.derby.jdbc.ClientXADataSource
    </xa-datasource-class>
    <xa-datasource-property name="databaseName">jpatest
    </xa-datasource-property>
    <user-name>jpatest</user-name>
    <password>jpatest</password>

    <min-pool-size>5</min-pool-size>
    <max-pool-size>20</max-pool-size>
    <idle-timeout-minutes>0</idle-timeout-minutes>
    <prepared-statement-cache-size>32</prepared-statement-cache-size>
    <metadata>
      <type-mapping>Derby</type-mapping>
    </metadata>
  </xa-datasource>

  <local-tx-datasource>
    <jndi-name>jpaTestDS</jndi-name>
    <use-java-context>true</use-java-context>
    <connection-url>jdbc:derby://localhost:1527/jpatest
    </connection-url>
    <driver-class>org.apache.derby.jdbc.ClientDriver</driver-class>
    <user-name>jpatest</user-name>
    <password>jpatest</password>
    <transaction-isolation>TRANSACTION_SERIALIZABLE
```

```
    </transaction-isolation>
    <metadata>
      <type-mapping>Derby</type-mapping>
    </metadata>
  </local-tx-datasource>
</datasources>
```

This file defines a JTA data source and a resource-local data source for a Derby database instance. Then drop the *derbydb-ds.xml* file into folder *C:\jboss\server\default\deploy*. The Derby JDBC driver `derbyclient.jar` must be placed into a folder such as *C:\jboss\server\default\lib* in order for the data source configuration to work.

9.6.2 Security Realm and User

This subsection shows how to configure security realms and security roles and users in the JBoss application server.

Listing 9-2 defines the security realm: `web-console`, which is used in Listing 8-12. The `jboss-web.xml` file must be located in the same directory as `web.xml`. The JBoss specific file `login-config.xml`, in Listing 9-3, defines the security policy for the security realm `web-console` and point to the files `web-console-users.properties` and `web-console-roles.properties` for user and role definitions.

> Listing 9-2 jboss-web.xml: JBoss specific XML web descriptor file that contains a security domain realm `web-console`.

```
<!DOCTYPE jboss-web PUBLIC
    "-//JBoss//DTD Web Application 5.0//EN"
    "http://www.jboss.org/j2ee/dtd/jboss-web_5_0.dtd">

<jboss-web>
  <security-domain>java:/jaas/web-console</security-domain>
</jboss-web>
```

> Listing 9-3 login-config.xml: JBoss-specific login configuration file located in directory `C:\jboss\server\default\conf`. This listing has one application

policy configuration for the security realm: `web-console`.

```
<policy>
  <application-policy name="web-console">
    <authentication>
      <login-module
        code="org.jboss.security.auth.spi.UsersRolesLoginModule"
        flag="required">

        <module-option name="usersProperties">
           props/web-console-users.properties
        </module-option>
        <module-option name="rolesProperties">
           props/web-console-roles.properties
        </module-option>
      </login-module>
    </authentication>

  </application-policy>
</policy>
```

The login user names and roles may be configured in the following files respectively:

```
C:\jboss\server\default\conf\props\web-console-users.properties
C:\jboss\server\default\conf\props\web-console-roles.properties
```

They are shown in Listing 9-4 and Listing 9-5 respectively.

Listing 9-4 web-console-users.properties: User configuration property file for the `web-console` security realm. It only contains two users: `jpatest` and `jpa`.

```
# syntax: username=password
jpatest=jpatest
jpa=jpa
```

Listing 9-5 web-console-roles.properties: Security role configuration property file for the `web-console` security realm. It configures one security role with name `admin`, which contains users: `jpatest` and `jpa`.

```
# syntax username=rolename
jpatest=admin
jpa=admin
```

With the configurations in this subsection and in Listing 8-12, accessing any web page would prompt the user to input login name and password as in Figure 9-4.

Figure 9-4 User login screen to input login and password in order to access requested web pages.

Typing in `jpatest` as the login name and password will allow you to access the requested web page.

9.7   Configure an EJB example in Eclipse

In this section, we configure and run the EJB example, described in Section 1.3, in the Eclipse IDE with JBoss application server. It assumes that the Java project *jpatest* is already created and the OR mapping is done in the file `Vehicle.java` in the project (see Section 1.2). Follow the steps in the next subsections.

9.7.1 Create Enterprise Application

First start up the Eclipse IDE. We may create an enterprise application project by choosing menu *File → New → Other → Java EE → Enterprise Application Project*. Enter *jpatestEAR* for the project name and choose EAR version to be 5.0 (or later), and click on *Next*. Check *jpatest* under *Java EE Module Dependencies*, and click on *New Module*. Then choose only *EJB module* and *Web module* and change their names to *jpatestEJB* and *jpatestWeb,* as Figure 9-5 depicts.

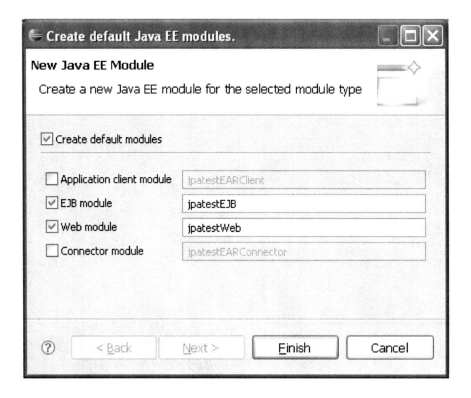

Figure 9-5 Add EJB and Web modules to EAR project

In this step, a Java enterprise project *jpatestEAR* has been created which contains the EJB module project *jpatestEJB* and Web module project *jpatestWeb*. The *jpatestEAR* project has been made dependent on the Java project *jpatest* as well. See Figure 9-7 for the three newly created projects and the JPA project *jpatest* created in Section 1.2.

Make sure that the file `persistence.xml` in project *jpatest* has the JTA data source configuration as defined in Listing 1-5. Also the same data source must be configured in JBoss as described in Section 9.6.

9.7.2 Configure Enterprise Project

In this subsection, we configure the newly created enterprise project *jpatestEAR*.

First, we add a required jar file to the *jpatestEAR* project. Right click on the *jpatestEAR* project and choose menu *Properties,* and then click on *Java EE Module Dependencies.* Add `eclipselink.jar` by clicking on *Add External JARs.* The other three jar files *jpatest.jar, jpatestEJB.jar and jpatestWeb.war* should have been checked. They are not real jar files that you can see physically in the file system, but represent the fact that *jpatestEAR* depends on the three projects*: jpatest, jpatestEJB, and jpatestWeb.* See Figure 9-6.

Note that the Derby JDBC driver jar file `derbyclient.jar` is not added here because it must have been put on the JBoss server class path in order for the data source configuration in `persistence.xml` to work (see JBoss in Section 9.6). Also, Hibernate JPA jar files come with the JBoss application server as the default JPA provider (in folder *C:\jboss\common\lib*). These files need to be replaced by the EclipseLink jar files, since we are using EclipseLink JPA for our examples.

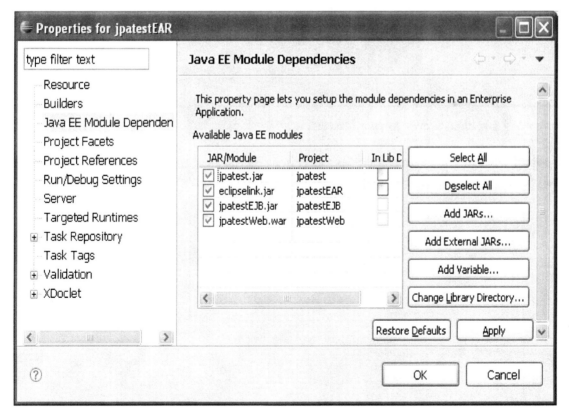

Figure 9-6 Add jar files to EAR project

Next, we configure a JBoss server in the Eclipse IDE to run our application. Open the server view by choosing the menu: *Window → Show View → Servers*. Under the *Servers* pane, right click on any blank open space and choose *New → Server*. *See* Figure 9-7.

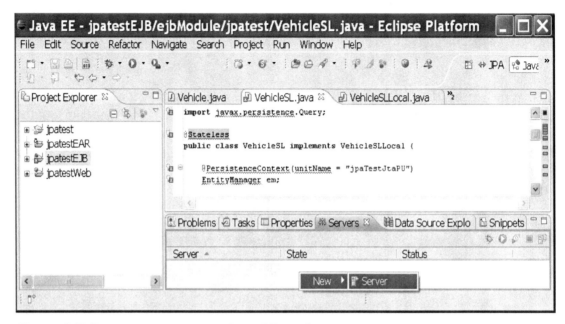

Figure 9-7 Create a server to run Java EE applications

A popup window opens up asking you to choose an application server type. Select JBoss and provide the JBoss home directory, as depicted in Figure 9-8.

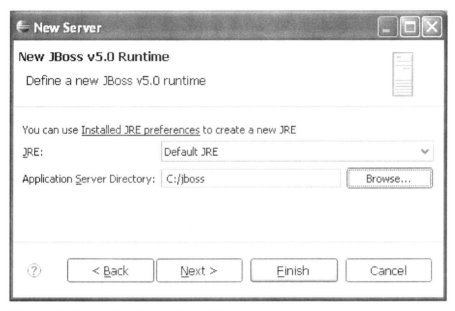

Figure 9-8 Install a JBoss Java EE runtime

Now configure the JBoss Java EE runtime for the *jpatestEAR* enterprise project. Right click on the *jpatestEAR* project and choose *Properties* → *Targeted Runtimes* and check *JBoss v5.0*. This means that the Java EE 5.0 runtime environment included in JBoss AS 5.0 will be provided for the *jpatestEAR* project, and standard Java EE classes such as in packages *javax.ejb* and *javax.persistence* will be available. See Figure 9-9.

Figure 9-9 Add JBoss Java EE runtime to enterprise project jpatestEAR

Finally add the *jpatestEAR* project to the newly configured JBoss server by right clicking on the server name (such as *JBoss v5.0 at localhost*) under the *Servers* pane and choose *Add and Remove Projects*.

9.7.3 Configure EJB Project

In this subsection, we create the session bean and configure the EJB project *jpatestEJB*.

To create a new EJB class, right click on the *jpatestEJB* project and then choose menu *New → Session Bean*. Enter *jpatest.ejb* for Java package and `VehicleSL` for Class name, `jpatest.ejb.VehicleSLLocal` for the local business interface name, and choose State type to be Stateless. Here we use the suffix *SL* for stateless session beans. See Figure 9-10. A remote business interface is not needed here since we will call the EJBs from the same JVM. Copy the contents in Listing 1-6 and Listing 1-7 to these two Java files `VehicleSLLocal.java` and `VehicleSL.java`, respectively.

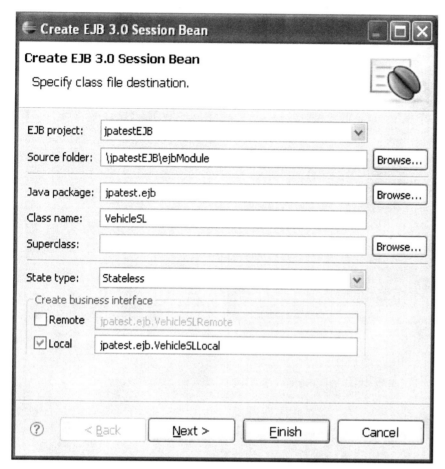

Figure 9-10 Create stateless session bean and its local interface

Now right click on project *jpatestEJB* and choose *Properties → Java EE Module Dependencies*. Check on *jpatest.jar* for the EJB project so that our EJBs can use the OR mapping class `Vehicle.java` in the *jpatest* project. See Figure 9-11. At this moment, the two Java files `VehicleSLLocal.java` and `VehicleSL.java` should compile without any errors.

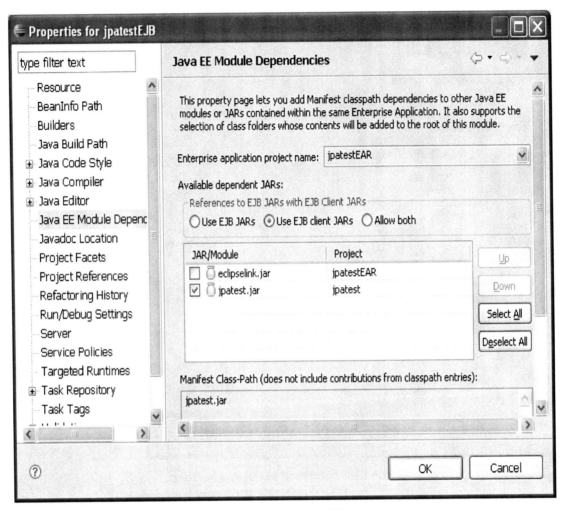

Figure 9-11 Add project jpatest as dependency for EJB project

9.7.4 Configure Web Project

To configure the *jpatestWeb* project, right click on the project name and choose *Properties → Project Facets*. Make sure the latest versions of *Dynamic Web Module* and *JavaServer Faces* are checked. See Figure 9-12. For JBoss application server 5.0, Dynamic Web Module version 2.5 and JavaServer Faces version 1.2 should be used. The generated web.xml is shown in Listing 9-6.

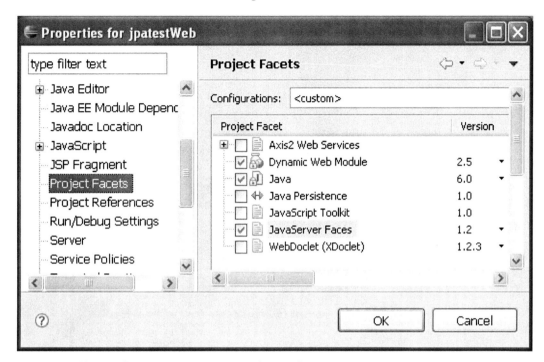

Figure 9-12 Configure Project Facets for Web project

Listing 9-6 web.xml: The generated web.xml file for this example with JSF
controller Servlet

```xml
<?xml version="1.0" encoding="UTF-8"?>
<web-app xmlns:xsi="http://www.w3.org/2001/XMLSchema-instance"
        xmlns="http://java.sun.com/xml/ns/javaee"
        xmlns:web="http://java.sun.com/xml/ns/javaee/web-app_2_5.xsd"
        xsi:schemaLocation="http://java.sun.com/xml/ns/javaee
            http://java.sun.com/xml/ns/javaee/web-app_2_5.xsd"
        id="WebApp_ID" version="2.5">
  <display-name>jpatestWeb</display-name>
  <servlet>
    <servlet-name>Faces Servlet</servlet-name>
    <servlet-class>javax.faces.webapp.FacesServlet</servlet-class>
    <load-on-startup>1</load-on-startup>
  </servlet>
  <servlet-mapping>
    <servlet-name>Faces Servlet</servlet-name>
```

```
    <url-pattern>/faces/*</url-pattern>
  </servlet-mapping>
```

</web-app>

Also, from *Properties*, choose *Java EE Module Dependencies*. Make sure *jpatest.jar* and *jpatestEJB.jar* are checked. See Figure 9-13. This means that the classes defined in projects *jpatest* and *jpatestEJB* such as `Vehicle.java` and `VehicleSLLocal.java` will be available in the web project.

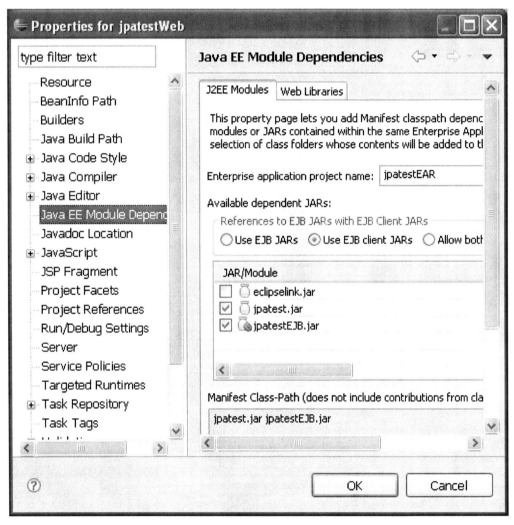

Figure 9-13 Configure Web project to depend on jpatest and jpatestEJB projects.

Now create the JSF managed bean class `TestBean.java` in *jpatestWeb* project by right clicking on *Java Resources:src* folder and choosing *New → Class*. Copy the content in Listing 1-8 to this class. A simple JSF page called `jpatest.jsp` in *WebContent* folder with the content in Listing 9-7 will bind a button click to the `doSubmit()` method on the *TestBean*.

Listing 9-7 jpatest.jsp: Sample JSF page to invoke EJB

```
<?xml version='1.0' encoding='UTF-8' ?>
<!DOCTYPE html PUBLIC "-//W3C//DTD XHTML 1.0 Transitional//EN"
          "http://www.w3.org/TR/xhtml1/DTD/xhtml1-transitional.dtd">

<html xmlns="http://www.w3.org/1999/xhtml"
      xmlns:f="http://java.sun.com/jsf/core"
      xmlns:h="http://java.sun.com/jsf/html" >

  <f:view>
    <body>
      <h:form>
        <h:outputText value="Click to call EJB"/>
        <br/>
        <h:commandButton
           value="Submit" action="#{testBean.doSubmit}"/>
      </h:form>
    </body>
  </f:view>
</html>
```

Of course, the managed bean must have been configured in *WEB-INF/faces-config.xml* as depicted in Listing 9-8.

Listing 9-8 faces-config.xml: Sample JSF configuration for managed bean

---

```
<faces-config
  xmlns="http://java.sun.com/xml/ns/javaee"
  xmlns:xsi="http://www.w3.org/2001/XMLSchema-instance"
  xsi:schemaLocation="http://java.sun.com/xml/ns/javaee
      http://java.sun.com/xml/ns/javaee/web-facesconfig_1_2.xsd"
```

```
version="1.2">

<managed-bean>
  <managed-bean-name>testBean</managed-bean-name>
  <managed-bean-class>jpatest.TestBean</managed-bean-class>
  <managed-bean-scope>session</managed-bean-scope>
</managed-bean>
</faces-config>
```

9.7.5 Run the Application

Finally, run the configured JBoss server by right clicking on it and choosing *Start* in the *Servers* pane. Check the *console* pane for server start and deployment messages. Now open a browser and point to the URL (default port is 8080):

http://localhost:8080/jpatestWeb/faces/jpatest.jsp

Clicking on the Submit button on the web page will invoke the `doSumit()` method on the managed bean, which in turn calls the EJB methods for performing CRUD operations on the `VEHICLE` table.

9.8 Hibernate

This section gives download information on the Hibernate JPA implementation and the Hibernate Validator library.

9.8.1 Hibernate JPA

Hibernate JPA implementation can be downloaded at

https://www.hibernate.org/344.html   ~downloads

https://www.hibernate.org/397.html   ~docs

The download comes with good documentation in PDF and HTML in different languages. Hibernate Core 3.5 or later is JPA 2.0 compliant.

9.8.2 Hibernate Validator

Hibernate Validator is a Bean Validation implementation, and can be used in Java SE 5.0 or later, and Java EE 5 environments. It can be downloaded at:

https://www.hibernate.org/412.html

Put the validator provider file `hibernate-validator-<version>.jar` , validator API file `validation-api-<version>.jar`, and a few ancillary files in your class path, and you are ready to use bean validation in your JPA applications. Java EE 6 already includes a bean validator, and does not need these library files.

9.9 OpenJPA

The open source JPA implementation from Apache OpenJPA can be downloaded at

http://openjpa.apache.org/

It has very good documentation in HTML and PDF at

http://openjpa.apache.org/documentation.html

The JPA implementation jar file is called `openjpa-2.0.0.jar`. The standard JPA API is in file `geronimo-jpa_2.0_spec.jar`. Make sure your downloaded versions are compatible with JPA 2.0.

Indexes

LaVergne, TN USA
09 February 2011

215836LV00005B/11/P